Yale French Studies

NUMBERS 131 & 132

Bande Dessinée: Thinking Outside the Boxes

SPECIAL EDITORS: LAURENCE GROVE AND MICHAEL SYROTINSKI

Yale French Studies

Laurence Grove and Michael Syrotinski,
  Special editors for this issue
Alyson Waters, *Managing editor*
Editorial board: Maurice Samuels (Chair),
  R. Howard Bloch, Morgane Cadieu, Jennifer Carr,
  Tom Connolly, Edwin Duval, Jill Jarvis, Laura B.
  Jensen, Alice Kaplan, Christopher L. Miller,
  Pierre Saint-Amand, Christopher Semk
Assistant editor: Laura B. Jensen
Editorial office: 82-90 Wall Street, Room 308
Mailing address: P.O. Box 208251, New Haven,
  Connecticut 06520-8251
Sales and subscription office:
Yale University Press, P.O. Box 209040
New Haven,Connecticut 06520-9040

Designed by James J. Johnson and set in Trump
  Medieval Roman by Newgen North America.
  Printed in the United States of America by Sheridan
  Books, Ann Arbor, Michigan.

ISSN 044-0078
ISBN for this issue 978-0-300-22598-3

**LAURENCE GROVE AND
MICHAEL SYROTINSKI**

Editors' Preface:
Thinking Outside the Boxes

Bande dessinée has undergone a quiet revolution since 1996 when, in the shadow of the centenary of cinema a year earlier, it struggled to promote its historical legitimacy by pitching Rodolphe Töpffer against Richard F. Outcault: Töpffer, the Genevan schoolteacher whose narrative images amused his pupils in the 1830s, was to bring Euro-kudos by predating the creator of America's 1896 *Yellow Kid*. Since then BD-specific conferences have come into being and proliferated, PhD theses and academic monographs increasingly have *bande dessinée* as their subject, and mainstream French-studies conferences have turned to comics for sessions and even plenaries. The visual form that French creators made into an art has been legitimized by English-language academia: *bande dessinée* studies might indeed now make a strong claim to rival cinema studies.

This volume of *Yale French Studies* devoted to the *bande dessinée* is the first sustained reflection on its newfound academic status, and goes beyond the simple question of its artistic legitimacy, now, we hope, settled beyond dispute, to think "outside the boxes," or *cases* themselves, and to explore the mutually enriching relationship between BD and the wider cultural and intellectual francophone world. Contributions thus intersect with art history, literary theory, cinema studies, postcolonialism, semiotics, and political sociology. Articles are by mainstream interdisciplinary scholars applying themselves to BD, BD artists, leading authorities on the *bande dessinée* itself, and key figures in contemporary French thought whose texts appear here in English for the first time.

The volume opens historically, with the central question of the definition itself of comics or *bande dessinée*. Thierry Groensteen takes as his point of departure Gérard Blanchard's seminal text, *La*

YFS 131/132, Bande Dessinée: *Thinking Outside the Boxes*, ed. Laurence Grove and Michael Syrotinski, © 2017 by Yale University.

bande dessinée: Histoire des histoires en images de la préhistoire à nos jours, which begins with the received view that BD was born in the nineteenth century sometime between Töpffer and Outcault's *Yellow Kid*. Once the historical context is stretched and expanded, however, the argument could be made that drawn literatures, or "literature in prints" as Töpffer termed them, are potentially assimilable even to the earliest of human artistic activity, as found on the walls of prehistoric caves. Groensteen thus weighs up what he terms its "Lascaux hypothesis," mindful of the risk such assimilation then poses to the specificity of *bande dessinée* as an autonomous art form. The question thus becomes of one determining when, and according to what criteria, *bande dessinée* broke free from a long history of picture-based stories of all kinds, a question that resonates throughout all the articles in some way or another. So Dominic Hardy, for example, looks at graphic political satires from the years of British colonial rule in Québec before 1830, and the evolving forms these took visually in a thriving turn-of-century comic culture, as one of the many fascinating discoveries of the *Caricature et satire graphique à Montréal* group, which has since 2009 been undertaking the first systematic survey of prints, drawings, letters, and journals from this period. Hardy indeed attests to an entire "industry of the image" in nineteenth-century francophone Canada, which in fact played a central role in the colony's visual culture. By the time of the 1837–1838 rebellions, this culture had shifted to the printed weekly journal, such as Quebec City's *Le Fantasque*, in which expatriate Swiss Protestant Napoléon Aubin supported the independence-seeking Patriotes with deft irony against British rule and the French Catholic Church. By the 1840s, the ascendant metropolis Montreal also boasted a series of ephemeral political caricature journals, francophone and anglophone, that both absorbed a mix of French and British models—culminating in the short-lived and incendiary *Punch in Canada* (1849–1850). His analysis centers on one of the early drawings from 1811, "En voilà encore De Bonnes!" and the findings of his painstaking archival detective work both surprise and delight. Laurence Grove's study of two previously unexplored Genevan manuscripts produces the startling revelation of Ferdinand de Saussure as an early BD artist, and details a surprising connection to Töpffer, as well as the latter's influence upon Saussure. This prompts an extended reflection upon the ways in which the core theoretical principles of structuralist linguistics might inform our understanding and interpretation of BD, but also in turn how BD might itself have inflected significantly the development of critical theory from the 1950s onwards.

From historical context, the issue then moves on to more specific considerations of form and genre in *bande dessinée*. As a way into this, Jan Baetens takes the example of the short-lived genre of the postwar *roman dessiné*, or drawn novel, precisely to point out how under-theorized the question of genre has been in BD studies. He begins by thinking about its origin and development in genealogical terms, situated historically as it is between the film novel and the photo novel. Once it becomes apparent that a genealogical analysis fails to do justice to the multi-dimensional complexity of the genre, he shifts to a more Foucauldian archeological approach, questioning a number of critical commonplaces about both medium and genre that are in fact challenged by the generic indeterminacy of the *roman dessiné*. Ultimately, as he argues, it becomes less a matter of the accuracy of any descriptive categorization, than of understanding the peformative nature of its impact within the cultural context in which it emerged, flourished briefly, and then died out. Catherine Labio's piece looks at the ways in which BD artists have always been keenly aware of the spatial nature of comic art, both in terms of the materiality of the object being read and of its reception by the reader, which accounts to an important degree for their growing interest in three-dimensional works. Indeed, experiments with three-dimensionality have been particularly numerous since the 1990s, a decade that saw the rise of several influential alternative presses. In particular, members of the collective FRMK (Frémok) have stepped outside the traditional boundaries of the book arts and created multi-panel books that merge the visual language of comics with engraving techniques. In their ongoing quest to test the limits of the comics genre, they have also collaborated with choreographers to create joint dance-and-book projects. At the same time, Tobias Schalken, the co-author of the Dutch avant-garde comics anthology *Eiland*, has also opened the comic book to other disciplines, including paintings and sculptural installations. Finally, this intense interest in cross-disciplinary exploration has led European as well as American comic book authors to move away from the codex and experiment with more sculptural and architectural three-dimensional formats, in a fascinating convergence between the comic book and artist's book traditions, to the point where it is not always possible to differentiate between the two. Keith Reader explores the interrelationship between *bande dessinée* and cinema, here via the work and context of Alain Resnais, one of France's foremost film directors, whose work has often borne traces of the *nouveau roman*, the theater, and political fiction. As Reader shows, *bande dessinée* has also been a major personal and intertextual influence. It is perhaps a little-known fact that Resnais was vice president of the *Centre d'étude des littératures d'expression graphique* (CELEG) and member of the editorial staff of *Giff-Wiff*, the first magazine in France dedicated to the history of comics. BD plays an important diegetic role in *I Want To Go Home* and has a major visual impact on the Ayckbourn adaptations *Smoking* and *No Smoking*.

A third section shifts the focus to BD and contemporary French culture and society. In her piece, Ann Miller considers the contribution made by the narrative and formal strategies of comic art to the analysis of *la politique politicienne*, or, in Rancière's term, *le politique*. The tradition of political caricature indeed has been revitalized in *bande dessinée* format, for example, by the gift that Nicolas Sarkozy's persona offers to artists. A further current, more akin to reportage, has chronicled internal struggles within the Socialist Party before the 2007 presidential election and the 2012 presidential campaign of François Hollande (Mathieu Sapin). Miller discusses specifically the work of Étienne Davodeau as an example of comic art, focusing on *Les mauvaises gens* (2005) as exemplifications of what Rancière has called the *distribution du sensible*, the relations between what is perceptible, thinkable, and doable at a given conjuncture. This section concludes with interviews with two well-known practicing BD artists: Nikola Witko, member of the iconoclastic Requins Marteaux group, who broaches the notion of how BD can express alternative anti-consumerist ideas and ideals; and Jean-Yves Ferri, scriptwriter of *Astérix chez les Pictes* (2013) and *Le papyrus de César* (2015) who presents his vision and understanding of *Astérix* and modern France, past, present, and future. In both interviews the artists present their background, past work, and current projects; they discuss the specific role of alternative BD in an increasingly hegemonic consumerist society (Witko), as well as the idea that France can often be most effectively depicted to the rest of the world via the best-selling book series, *Astérix le Gaul* (Ferri).

In the fourth section, three articles then explore BD in a more global, postcolonial context. Bill Marshall discusses a plethora of recent *bande dessinée* texts that point to a fascination with the first French Empire in the Americas. Embedded in a long history of the *ro-*

man populaire maritime, a sub-genre which since the late-eighteenth century has mapped French cultural figurations of oceanic and especially Atlantic space, these texts are characterized by continuing tensions between the French Atlantic as the nostalgic space of a national pastness *or* a convocation to identity debates of pre-republican difference. These tensions are played out in spatial terms—that is, in narrative structures, geographical itineraries, and the BD *case* itself—and, particularly in the representations of native and enslaved peoples, in terms of contested memory. Marshall looks to the specific examples of the work on the slave trade by the BD artist Serge Diantatu, but most acutely, that of the Québécois BD artist Jean-Sébastien Bérubé, whose series on the trapper and explorer, *Radisson*, began in 2009. Mark McKinney draws upon the postcolonial example of Cambodia's Killing Fields as portrayed in the work of Séra, which also raises the question of historical documentation and the role of photography in fiction. Three graphic novels or narratives by Séra—*Impasse et rouge* (1995, 2003), *L'eau et la terre: Cambodge 1975–1979* (2005) and *Lendemains de cendres: Cambodge, 1979–1993* (2007)—are fictional accounts of the conquest of Cambodia by the Khmer Rouge, and then of life and death under their rule. In Séra's Cambodian stories his references to photography clearly take on historical and (auto)biographical meanings that are less apparent in his other works. For McKinney, photographs serve in part as evidence of what has been destroyed and lost, and as they do in many comics, photographs provide a model for some of the book's imagery. However, Séra created several of his uncanny images in such a way that it is difficult to determine their precise nature or composition: are they touched-up photos, or instead are they paintings or drawings made to look like photos? Séra thereby imparts an eerie, spectral quality to his books about the Killing Fields and their aftermath. Finally Charles Forsdick looks at the case of Haiti. As he notes, although there has been increasing attention in scholarship to postcolonial approaches to the *bande dessinée*, as well as to BD produced in "postcolonial" contexts, the representation of Haiti in the genre has rarely been studied and Haitian comics similarly remain relatively neglected. Forsdick address this critical lacuna in scholarship by firstly exploring some of the key representations of Haiti in comic form in the USA and France, and showing how this is inseparably linked, both historically and artistically, to the BD in contemporary Haitian culture and society. The focal point of the first half of his article is Jacob Lawrence's 41-panel life of Toussaint

Louverture, produced in 1938 in the context of the Harlem Renaissance. This work has been compared to *bande dessinée*, and Lawrence's work is contrasted to subsequent representations, ranging from the Golden Legacy issue from 1966 on the "Saga of Toussaint L'Ouverture and the Birth of Haiti" and the recurrent Marvel character Brother Voodoo, to Pierre Briens and Nicolas Saint-Cyr's BD *Toussaint Louverture et la révolution de Saint-Domingue*, published in 1985 in the context of preparations for the bicentenary of the French Revolution. Contemporary examples of BD in Haiti, such as *Titouan en Haïti* (2003) and Nicole Augereau's *Tap Tap, récit d'un voyage en Haïti* (2004), are then read in relation to a rich and often distortive tradition of Western travel writing on the country. Subsequent representations, and most notably the sixth and seventh volumes of *Les passagers du vent* (2009, 2010), have presented the Haitian Revolution as an event of importance in its own right, but equally important is the emergence of BD art in contemporary Haiti itself.

The somewhat arbitrary thematic organization of the issue is, of course, more a matter of structural convenience than of distinct separation of genres, artistic styles, or approaches. There are many echoes and implicit dialogues between the different articles, whether historically (such that Baetens's careful teasing out of the generic indeterminacy of the *roman dessiné* could inform a renewed understanding of Québécois political caricature or Saussure's Töpffer-inspired drawings), formally (so the "exploded" diachronic-synchronic axes of the *Comic Invention* exhibition with which Grove ends in his article are of exactly the same nature as the artistic experimentation of FRMK which Labio discusses), or culturally (the clear thematic overlap between the various postcolonial contexts, which in turn inform political thinking in the metropolitan center). Indeed, what emerges is the sense that BD may be the most hybrid of all artistic media or genres, and that it is by its very nature destined to cross boundaries, and defy categorization.

It is perhaps fitting, then, that the volume closes with a section comprised of two case studies that mark the milestone of Tintin's entry into the Académie Française. Michel Serres's seminal and beautifully poetic tribute to Hergé and *Tintin*, "Light" ("Lumière"), and Jean-Luc Marion's bold phenomenological reading of Tintin, "Terrifying, Wondrous Tintin" ("Tintin le terrible"), are published here for the first time in English translation. In both cases, these texts demonstrate the extraordinary artistic genius and philosophical depth of Hergé, and of *bande dessinée* more generally; ironically, it is by drawing upon the work of two of the acclaimed contemporary French thinkers and pillars of France's most venerable academic establishment, that we are able most powerfully to "think outside the box."

I. History

THIERRY GROENSTEEN

Gérard Blanchard's
Lascaux Hypothesis

"We make no claim to erudition or fandom in relation to comics, and neither are we a collector of rare editions," wrote Gérard Blanchard in the introduction to his book about drawn literature.[1] In fact, comics were marginal to his academic interests, and the corpus of his output on the subject is limited to this one book and three articles.[2] He did not play a leading role in the "bédéphilia" of the 1960s and was not actively involved in the militant legitimizing project of the Centre d'étude des littératures d'expression graphique (CELEG) [Center for the study of literatures of graphic expression] nor of its successor, the Société civile d'études et de recherches des littératures dessinées [SOCERLID] [Civil society for the study of drawn literatures].

However, his book, *The History of Comics*, subtitled "The History of Picture Stories from Prehistory to Modern Times," was a landmark study. It appeared in 1969, the same year as the excellent textbook *How to Become a Comics Artist (Franquin and Gillain Answer Questions from Philippe Vandooren)*,[3] also published by Marabout, two years after the catalogue from the exhibition at the Musée des

---

1. Gérard Blanchard, *Histoire de la bande dessinée* (Verviers: Marabout Université, 1969), 7. All translations here, unless noted otherwise, are by the translator of this essay.
2. Blanchard, "Le véritable domaine de la bande dessinée," *Communication et langages* 3 (1969): 56–69; "Les bandes dessinées québécoises," *Communications et langages* 19 (1973): 47–62; "Lettrage en bande dessinée," *Communications et langages* 64 (1985): 65–73.
3. Philippe Vandooren, *Comment on devient créateur de bandes dessinées (Franquin et Gillain répondent aux questions de Philippe Vandooren)* (Verviers: Marabout, 1969).

YFS 131/132, Bande Dessinée: *Thinking Outside the Boxes*, ed. Laurence Grove and Michael Syrotinski, © 2017 by Yale University.

11

arts décoratifs in Paris, *Comics and Narrative Figuration* (1967),[4] but
two years before Francis Lacassin's manifesto in the form of the book
Toward a Ninth Art: Comics (1971).[5] These four works represent almost the entirety of French-language secondary literature on comics
during this pioneering period.[6]

Whereas the authors of *Comics and Narrative Figuration* devoted
chapters to "narrative technique" or "the readership of comics," and
Lacassin took a close look at certain recurring themes, as well as
discussing the relationship between comics and cinema, in his book
Blanchard was the only one to develop a strictly historical approach,
with no theoretical or aesthetic concerns. This perspective is both
the strength and weakness of the book, for the historical vision that
Blanchard's text shows cannot help but raise some important conceptual issues, although the text itself does not make clear whether the
author was consciously raising such questions.

The first page of the text (page 5) does not deliver on the promise of its title: "Definition of Comics." The author declares that he
has chosen to adopt a "wider perspective" than the usual one, which
situates the birth of comics "at the end of the last century, in newspapers from across the Atlantic." Indeed, the opposite page includes
an image that evokes the handprints that our distant ancestors left
on cave walls. The perspective that we are offered is, then, the wid-
est possible, since it presupposes that the origin of comics coincides
with. . . the beginning of human artistic activity. Blanchard implies
that this "wider perspective" corresponds, in reality, to "a more literal definition" of the subject. But no definition is forthcoming. And
even though the opening words of the book ("There are several possible definitions of comics") arouse expectations, the reader who
subsequently encounters the expressions "picture stories" and "narratives in pictures" can only conjecture—encouraged by the book's
subtitle—that the real subject of the study will not be comics as such
but "picture stories" in every sense of the term, and in every pos-

4. *Bande dessinée et narration figurative*, ed. Pierre Couperie et al. (Paris: Musée
des arts décoratifs/Musée du Louvre, 1967).

5. Francis Lacassin, *Pour un neuvième art: la bande dessinée* (Paris: 10/18, 1971).

6. Along with the very useful anthology *Les chefs-d'œuvre de la bande dessinée*,
ed. Jacques Sternberg, Michel Caen, and Jacques Lob (Paris: Planète, 1967) and the
more anecdotal essay by Jacques Marny, *Le monde étonnant des bandes dessinées*
(Paris: Le Centurion, 1968).

sible medium. This then raises the question, which will persist in the reader's mind for at least a hundred pages, as to whether everything that is shown and referred to in the book should be considered as part of the genealogy of modern comics.

Since the 1990s, debates over the origin of comics have mostly crystallized around two opposing theories. The first corresponds to the "usual one" described above (that is to say usual in the 1960s), and traces the inception of the medium back to *The Yellow Kid* by the American cartoonist Richard Outcault, and more specifically to an episode dated October 1896. The second considers the Genevan schoolmaster Rodolphe Töpffer (1799–1846) as the principal initiator of what would one day be called the "ninth art," which he himself baptized "literature in prints."

In the critical literature on comics that is contemporary with Blanchard's book, the question is addressed in different ways. The authors of *Comics and Figurative Narration* acknowledge a "filiation" between, on the one hand, the works of Töpffer and Wilhelm Busch and, on the other, the invention of "this new mode of artistic expression" constituted by the comic strip, an invention whose fine tuning reached completion in December 1897 with the beginning of Rudolph Dirks's *Katzenjammer Kids*, shortly after the *Yellow Kid*, which, already, "showed all the signs of being a precursor" of this "new formula."[7] Francis Lacassin prefers to set the starting point of comics in 1827, the year in which "the schoolmaster Töpffer circulated a pen-drawn album, *Les amours de M. Vieux Bois*,[8] that would not be published until ten years later." He covers the "prehistory" of comics in less than a page and a half, identifying the Egyptian *Book of the Dead* as "the most distant example of figurative stories whose successive scenes are organized into strips positioned one above each other." Lacassin takes the methodological precaution of beginning his study with a "dictionary definition," which reads as follows: "story in the press serialized in periodical booklets or albums sold in bookstores."[9] This succinct definition makes reference neither to sequentiality nor to the text-image relationship. It selects only two elements as essential: a narration in images and a print medium.

---

7. Couperie et al., *Bande dessinée et narration figurative*, 11–21.
8. Published in English, in 1842, as *The Adventures of Mr. Obadiah Oldbuck*.
9. Lacassin, *Pour un neuvième art*, 13.

The question of the origin of comics cannot be separated from that of its definition. We can take the example of Töpffer. As I have written elsewhere:

> [H]is albums, which have an oblong format, only have one strip per page, do not use speech balloons, and, when they first came out, had very limited print runs. This is why, depending on the definition of comics that is adopted, Töpffer can either be recognized as fully belonging to the medium, or, instead, relegated to its pre- or proto-history.[10]

We know that in America in particular, comics has often been perceived as a mass medium, which explains, even if it does not justify, the designation of the daily press as its birthplace.

Blanchard's chosen perspective may be criticized on two counts. First, it may not be regarded as strictly historical, because the author might appear to have a personal interest in promoting the medium. This reproach is most baldly set out by Alain Rey:

> For a cultural practice to be rehabilitated [. . .], it has to be provided with justifications that will guarantee its respectability. [. . .] The history of comics is therefore obliged to annex the Egyptian *Book of the Dead*, Mayan bas-reliefs, medieval illuminated manuscripts and the stained glass windows of Chartres Cathedral, the Bayeux Tapestry and 15th century woodcuts, Hogarth (the dictionary version), Rowlandson, Doré, Gavarni, Épinal prints and the entire illustrative and narrative graphic production of the 19th century. We can also throw in the Apocalypse Tapestry and the Unicorn Tapestries, 15th century altarpieces and thousands of Japanese handscrolls.[11]

However, in reality, there is no trace in Blanchard's text of any desire to rehabilitate or legitimize comics. The only place in the book where this intention is discernible is on the back cover, where we read: "In a challenge to received wisdom, Gérard Blanchard demonstrates that comics have a noble lineage, and that there is nothing incongruous about tracing the history of picture stories back to the distant past." But it is likely that this blurb is attributable not to the author but to his publisher.

---

10. Thierry Groensteen, *L'art de la bande dessinée* (Paris: Citadelles et Mazenod, 2012), 12. English translation of the chapter "Definitions" in *The French Comics Theory Reader*, ed. Ann Miller and Bart Beaty (Leuven: Leuven University Press, 2014), 93–114 (100).

11. Alain Rey, *Les spectres de la bande* (Paris: Minuit, 1978), 17.

The delving back into the "distant past" for antecedents assumed to bolster the cultural status of comics certainly became, for a while, a commonplace of secondary literature, as Harry Morgan and Manuel Hirtz have pointed out:

> This habit of going back to Egyptian frescos—or at least to the Bayeux Tapestry and medieval woodcuts—made a profound impression on subsequent comics scholars, who used it to legitimize the medium. The genealogy of the medium established by Gérard Blanchard was ritually recalled at the beginning of books over the next two decades, by authors who gained nothing and concluded nothing from it, in the absence of any real research.[12]

It would undoubtedly be worth posing the philosophical question as to why, when we are passionate about all that is new, we are still disposed to think that a cultural phenomenon is automatically ennobled and valorized if it can lay claim to ancient origins. In the particular case of comics, the answer is easily surmised. It is a medium that has no technologically added value. Video, digital media, and the internet derive their legitimacy from their aura of newness and the potentiality that they open up. Comics, a paper-based medium that consists of no more than a specific way of combining images with texts, does not give that same impression of being innovative.

The history of comics furnishes another explanation for its eternal quest for legitimacy: long confined within children's publishing, vilified by educationalists and lacking cultural recognition, comics have logically sought compensation by latching onto anything that could get them out of their rut.

If the first reproach to Blanchard was a matter of tactics and ideology, the second concerns heuristics and methodology. Such an all-encompassing point of view has the effect of dissolving the specificity of comics into a category so wide ("picture stories") that it is no longer clear where it begins or ends, which explains the temptation to opt for the simplest and most radical solution: it begins with the very origins of art. A modern medium is thereby absorbed into a tradition that goes back over several millennia. The entity that is comics becomes completely elusive.

12. Harry Morgan and Manuel Hirtz, *Le petit critique illustré* (Montrouge: PLG, 1997), 24–25.

In his article on "The real domain of comics," Blanchard was a little more explicit than in his book. We read in it that "comics are based on the principle of the picture story, although the synthesis of images and text lends them a particular character."[13] This is the closest that we get to a definition in Blanchard's writings. This "particular character" resides in the capacity of comics to "brutally emphasize the relationship between text and image because they are inserted one within the other, and so unify the reading space" that had remained divided in nineteenth-century books. It would seem that the distinguishing feature of comics is a never-before-attained degree of integration between image and text. Indeed, Blanchard continues:

> [I]t would be possible to show that a new kind of linguistic structure, engendered within the speech balloons, is both cause and effect of a different way of deploying images. It becomes increasingly the transcription of spoken language to the detriment of written language: there is a real attempt to convey sounds.[14]

This article is signed "Gérard Blanchard, graphic designer." In fact, it is above all as a typographer that Blanchard is so interested in the transcription of dialogue, which, in comics, takes the form of a "paratypography, or, better still, more often, a calligraphy." His intense fascination with the expressive potential of lettering and with onomatopoeia arises out of his expertise in the area.[15] It is therefore quite logical that the end of his article traces the genealogy of comics back to medieval manuscripts with their "speaking banners," which were already making speech visible.

The article appeared in the same year as his book, and thus cannot be regarded as a retraction or a correction. However, it must be acknowledged that Blanchard delimits his subject more in the article. And this time he identifies its distant origin no longer in the Magdalenian period but in the twelfth century.

Moreover, the attention paid to onomatopoeia is characteristic of the first generation of French-language critics. We can see this most notably in chapter 11 of Pierre Fresnault-Deruelle's essay *Narrative*

13. Blanchard, "Le véritable domaine," 59.
14. Ibid.
15. In 1980, Blanchard was awarded a doctorate by the Sorbonne for a dissertation entitled *Pour une sémiologie de la typographie*.

and Communication in Comic Strips,[16] devoted to the "visual rendition of sonic phenomena," and in the book by Robert Benayoun, *Vroom Tchac Zowie: The Speech Balloon in Comics.*[17] Onomatopoeias have long since ceased to be considered as a manifestation of the unique essence of comics, and they no longer arouse much interest. But Thierry Smolderen, a writer of considerable standing, concurs with Blanchard's analysis by noting that with the adoption of the speech balloon, a real "sound image," comics "tumbles into the audiovisual sphere."[18] The famous episode of *The Yellow Kid and His New Phonograph* created, he claims, "thirty years before talking cinema, [. . .] an audiovisual stage on paper."[19]

The theory according to which the origin of comics predates Töpffer and the *Kid* by several centuries is also propounded, as readers will know, by the British-born American historian David Kunzle. In his monumental *History of the Comic Strip*, Kunzle preferred to opt for Gutenberg as his hero, and the invention of printing as the starting point, one of his postulates being that comics are a medium "designed for reproduction."[20]

As I have demonstrated elsewhere, there is a close correlation between the question of the definition of comics and that of its origins.[21] If the subject of study is not defined, then no precise origin can be attributed to it. There are, logically, as many origins as there are definitions.

The merits of Blanchard's essay are justly highlighted by Morgan and Hirtz:

> The author should be given credit for emphasizing the technological evolutions and revolutions undergone by printing and publishing, and for stressing, as an attentive reader of McLuhan, the significance of the emergence of cinema and television.

16. Pierre Fresnault-Deruelle, *Récit et discours par la bande* (Paris: Hachette, 1977).

17. Robert Benayoun, *Vroom Tchac Zowie: Le ballon dans la bande dessinée* (Paris: Andre Balland, 1968).

18. Thierry Smolderen, *Naissances de la bande dessinée* (Brussels: Les Impressions nouvelles, 2009), 125. English translation, *The Origins of Comics*, trans. Bart Beaty and Nick Nguyen (Jackson, MS: University Press of Mississippi, 2014), 143.

19. Ibid., 127; 147.

20. David Kunzle, *The Early Comic Strip: Narrative Strips and Picture Stories in the European Broadsheet from c. 1450 to 1825* (Berkeley: University of California Press, 1973), 3.

21. Groensteen, "Definitions," 103–104.

They add further on:

> We should note that, even where the author draws on a limited range of sources, his judgment on the works is remarkably accurate. Moreover, he constantly urges readers to go back to the primary texts and to build up their own history of comics.[22]

The richness and variety of the illustrations are also worthy of note.

However, all these unquestionable qualities should not distract us from the main issue, which is the assertion, not theoretically justified, that since all picture stories are in a direct line of descent, we have to go back to the origins of art in order to grant comics their rightful place within that line—an assertion that, for the sake of brevity, I will call the "Lascaux hypothesis." In fact, when Blanchard refers to "picture stories," the more problematic of the two words is "stories." The pictures are not necessarily all narrative; an isolated image can suggest a situation but it cannot recount a story;[23] and multiple images placed end to end do not automatically constitute a story either (which enables us to contrast the notions of "string" and "series" to that of "sequence").[24] Alain Rey castigated Blanchard for the ragbag nature of his history, a catalogue of every occasion where "the history of art threw up a banal encounter between an image and a narrative intention."[25] Kunzle goes down the same track, doing his utmost to bring to light the "narrative character" of works by Callot, Rubens, Mitelli, Chodowiecki, Greuze, or Morland. Of course, picture stories have existed more or less throughout history, and Thierry Smolderen is undeniably correct to ask: "If the Bayeux Tapestry already corresponds to the definition of sequential art," surely we can no longer "consider Töpffer as its inventor?"[26]

The "Lascaux hypothesis" is reactivated from time to time by prehistorians themselves. One of them, Marc Azéma, curated an exhibition in 2008 at the Musée regional de préhistoire in Orgnac, in the Ardèche. The exhibition was accompanied by a richly-illustrated

22. Morgan and Hirtz, *Le petit critique*, 25.

23. See my book *Bande dessinée et narration* (Paris: PUF, 2011), 19–29. English translation, *Comics and Narration*, trans. Ann Miller (Jackson, MS: University of Mississippi Press, 2013), 21–29.

24. Ibid, 33–35 (in both versions).

25. Rey, *Les spectres*, 17.

26. Smolderen, "Histoire de la bande dessinée: Questions de méthodologie", in *La bande dessinée: une médiaculture*, ed. Éric Maigret and Matteo Stefanelli (Paris: Armand Colin, 2012), 71–90 (81–82).

catalogue, *The Prehistory of Comics*. In its preface, Jean Clottes notes that Azéma's great merit is to have "drawn attention to a still little-known aspect of the spectacular art to be found in caves." This aspect concerns the representation of movement, through its analytic decomposition. Some of the photographs reproduced in the catalogue are highly convincing in this respect.

I am much less convinced by the line of descent that Azéma attempts to establish from cave art to comics, on the basis that both involve narration. I cannot see in the catalogue a single painting or engraving in which something of the order of sequential narration occurs clearly and unequivocally. There are, of course, a few hunting scenes, and the famously enigmatic "well scene" at Lascaux (which represents, next to a gutted bison, a man with an erect penis and a birdlike head) whose "narrative potential" is undeniable. But there is nothing that amounts to a story that is coherent, intelligible, and sequenced.

As is far too often the case, Azéma uses words like "story," "spectacle," "sequence," or even "process of graphic narration" without ever giving a rigorous definition of them, and this semantic vagueness, along with the desire to prove his point, leads him to conclusions that are dubious, to say the least.

Anyone who wishes, in the wake of Blanchard, to insist on the continuity between all forms of "picture stories," and who considers that the same human gesture has been perpetuated for several millennia, in spite of changes in subject matter, materials, conventions, ways of arranging images, readerships, will still need to determine at what exact moment, and according to what criterion, comics broke away from this continuum and became a distinctive, autonomous artistic form.

Even if there were, on the wall of one cave or another, some drawings that really did resemble a comic in their arrangement, this similarity would not in fact be significant, given the huge distance that separates prehistoric aesthetic-magico-religious practices from the products of the modern entertainment industry. But what exactly is the defining feature of modern comics? Is it fictionality, a print medium, the text-image combination, the speech balloon, their institutionalization as "literature"? It seems that every specialist gives a different response according to his/her preferences, whims, or personal theoretical framework, and that it is impossible to reach a consensus. For example, Thierry Smolderen takes William Hogarth's cycles of engravings as a starting point, because they include two features that he regards as determining: a narrative sequence and what he calls "polygraphic language," that is to say a mixtures of disparate registers of images, some popular, others more high-cultural.

However fascinating they may be, these arguments are, in my view, futile. Éric Maigret formulates the key point: "'Comics are not historically invariant, they appear only when they are defined as such, that is to say *named*. . .'"[27]

In conclusion, I can only repeat what I have written elsewhere. It is thanks to Töpffer that:

> comics received for the first time a paternity claim, a name ("literature in prints"), and, therefore, social recognition, a cultural identity, self-awareness [. . .]. Töpffer established comics as a new form of literature, an instrument of fictional invention, and took them into bookshops. He set them up as an autonomous medium. These were decisive inaugural actions, which no one had performed before him.[28]

Töpffer's actions, by creating the *conditions* for comics, enable us to escape from the Lascaux hypothesis, and to register the origin of the ninth art in the "history of picture stories from prehistory to modern times."

—Translated from the French by Ann Miller

27. Éric Maigret, "Théorie des bandes débordées" in Maigret and Stefanelli, *La bande dessinée*, 50–70 (65). My italics.

28. See Groensteen, "De l'art séquentiel à l'art ludique," *Textimage* 3 (Winter 2013), www.revue-textimage.com/07_varia_3/groensteen1.html

DOMINIC HARDY

"En voilà encore De Bonnes!": Caricature and Graphic Satire in Quebec, 1792–1811

EN VOILÀ ENCORE DE BONNES! A CARICATURE OF PIERRE-AMABLE DE BONNE

The Musée national des beaux-arts du Québec (MNBAQ) has an exquisite collection of watercolor miniatures on vellum and ivory that survive from turn of the nineteenth-century Quebec. Among them is fine pendant pairing, true to so much portraiture of the colonial era through which itinerant artists gained their living by going from town to town, staying at hamlets or residences of the bourgeoisie or the wealthy along the way: these are the miniature portraits of the judge, politician, and *seigneur* Pierre-Amable De Bonne (1758–1816) and his second wife Louise-Élisabeth Marcoux (c.1782–1848) (Figs. 1 and 2). These watercolor miniatures were made by the émigré German painter William Berczy (1744–1813) at De Bonne's country residence in the early autumn of 1808. They were commissioned as complements to two portraits in oil which he made at the same time (Figs. 3 and 4).

Berczy had travelled to the De Bonne residence with his son William Bent Berczy from Montreal, where the Berczy family had established a home in 1805: William and his wife, the painter Jeanne-Charlotte Allamand (1760–1839), became tenants of their friend, the painter Louis Dulongpré (1759–1843, active in Canada from 1785).[1] William and Charlotte had worked as professional artists in Vienna,

1. Jules Bazin, "Dulongpré, Louis," in Dictionary of Canadian Biography, vol. 7 (Toronto: University of Toronto/Université Laval, 2003), http://www.biographi.ca/en/bio/dulongpre_louis_7E.html; Pierre Tousignant and Jean-Pierre Wallot, "De Bonne, Pierre-Amable," in Dictionary of Canadian Biography, vol. 5, http://www.biographi.ca/en/bio/de_bonne_pierre_amable_5E.html; and Ronald J. Stagg, "Berczy, William,"

YFS 131/132, Bande Dessinée: *Thinking Outside the Boxes*, ed. Laurence Grove and Michael Syrotinski, © 2017 by Yale University.

Fig. 1. William Berczy (1744–1813), *Portrait of Pierre-Amable De Bonne*, 1808, watercolor on ivory, 6.3 × 5 cm. Collection of the Musée national des beaux-arts du Québec, purchase (1991.103.01) Photo: MNBAQ, Patrick Altman.

Fig. 2. William Berczy (1744–1813), *Portrait of Madame Pierre-Amable De Bonne, née Louise-Élizabeth Marcoux*, 1808, watercolor on ivory, 6.5 × 5.2 cm. Collection of the Musée national des beaux-arts du Québec, purchase (1991.104.01) Photo: MNBAQ, Patrick Altman.

Fig. 3. William Berczy (1744–1813), *Portrait of Pierre-Amable De Bonne*, 1808, oil on canvas, 81.2 × 66 cm. Collection of the Musée national des beaux-arts du Québec, purchase (1991.113) Photo: MNBAQ, Patrick Altman.

Lausanne, Florence, and London before agreeing to lead a group of German settlers to the Genessee region of upstate New York in 1792.[2] The Berczy family had known difficult years as the settlement project faltered repeatedly, first in New York and then in Upper Canada. Despite these travails, Berczy's career as a painter brought significant contributions to early Canadian art. In 1808, Willian Berczy began a two-year stay in the Quebec City area in order to carry out a series of portrait commissions, with William Bent in tow as his assistant.

in *Dictionary of Canadian Biography*, vol. 5, http://www.biographi.ca/en/bio/berczy_william_5E.html. For the fullest account of the careers of William Berczy, Charlotte Allamand, and their children, see Mary Macauley Allodi, *Berczy* (Ottawa: National Gallery of Canada, 1991).

   2. Allodi, *Berczy*, 55–59.

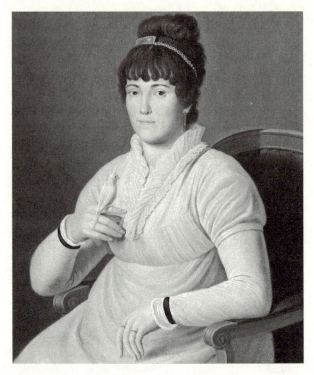

Fig. 4. William Berczy (1744–1813), *Portrait of Mrs Pierre-Amable De Bonne,
née Louise-Élizabeth Marcou*, 1808, oil on canvas, 81 × 65.8 cm. Collection
of the Musée national des beaux-arts du Québec, purchase (1996.97) Photo:
MNBAQ, Patrick Altman.

The miniature portrait of Pierre-Amable De Bonne is still in its
original casing, described in the 1991 catalogue of the exhibition organized by Mary Allodi and devoted to the career of William Berczy
as a "medallion of gilt copper; on the reverse of which is a wheat
sheaf motif made up of strands of hair of two different colors, braided
hair flowers embellished with pearls on a background of opalescent
glass."[3] Without doubt, here is a present that is intended to bear
witness to precious affection, quite in keeping with the tradition of
portrait miniatures that had become *de rigueur* commodities of sen-
timental or matrimonial exchange and representation in European
visual culture for over half a century.

3. Ibid., 215.

William and Charlotte were devoted to one another and kept up an important correspondence throughout William's frequent absences. He updated her on the progress of work *chez* the De Bonne couple:

> As Mr. Debonne had to go into town today for the Criminal Court I began with Madame in his absence, which succeeded no less well than that of her husband.... I amuse myself a lot very well with the master of the house who is a very well educated man and who likes to talk—As to the rest, as I have no pretense of making a friend of him. I take advantage of what is good in him without worrying about what may be justly alleged against him...[4]

We know that the couple's marriage agreement called for the separation of goods, with a guarantee of three thousand pounds for the wife at the death of the husband. But when Pierre-Amable died in 1816, it was found that a distant cousin was designated as sole heir. Dispossessed, Louise-Élisabeth Marcoux eventually ended her days in a mental asylum. The touching emotions signaled by both the large portraits and the charming miniatures had apparently not survived.

This fascinating turn of events might be explained by an unsigned and undated drawing that is part of the small Fonds Louis-Dulongpré held at the Centre Vieux-Montréal of the Bibliothèque et archives nationales du Québec. This is one of the earliest caricatures to have survived from colonial era Quebec (or, as it was known from 1791 to 1840, Lower Canada).[5] Bearing the penciled inscription "En voilà encore De Bonnes!/Finis Coronat Opus," the drawing, in sepia ink, presents a scowling bust-length male figure in an oval medallion format, his countenance strikingly similar to that of the Berczy portraits—so much so that one might well suppose that the drawing is also from the same hand (Fig. 5). Adorned in a judge's robe, this De Bonne turns, like his miniature counterpart, slightly to his left, peering intently downwards, perhaps in judgment, perhaps in shame.

The many registers of De Bonne's notoriety would have been available to any well-informed observer. De Bonne had been active in politics and in the legal profession since the early 1780s. He built

4. Ibid., 212–13. Translations are my own throughout this article.
5. Bibliothèque et archives nationales du Québec, Centre d'archives de Vieux-Montréal, Fonds Louis-Dulongpré (MSS 147).

Fig. 5. Unidentified artist, caricature of Pierre-Amable De Bonne (1758–1816), *En voilà encore De Bonnes!/Finis coronat opus*, sepia ink on laid paper, 17 × 13.5 cm, n.d. BAnQ Vieux-Montréal, Fonds Louis-Dulongpré (MSS147).

a fortune through the acquisition of property in line with the *ancien régime* seigneurial system that was among the key institutions protected by Britain when it established the Province of Quebec in 1763; and he keenly defended the privileges, both material and symbolic, that were afforded by this system at every turn.[6]

De Bonne was also a member of a section of the francophone cultural political élite in 1780s Montreal that promoted what might be called a *Lumières* ideal for *canadien* (that is, francophone) society. Beginning in his twenties, De Bonne had built an imposing library that showed his acquaintance with all the leading ideas of the Enlightenment: he was a reader of Voltaire, d'Alembert, Diderot, and the abbé Raynal; in William Berczy's 1808 oil portrait, he poses with a volume of Montesquieu's *L'esprit des lois* on his lap, opened by his right hand.

6. In 1799, he commissioned a "portrait" of an ancestor from François Baillargé (1759–1830), *François De Bonne, Duc de Lesdiguères (1543–1626), Connétable de France* (oil on canvas, 200.5 x 147.5 cm, now in the Château de Ramezay, Montreal).

In 1789, along with Louis Dulongpré, Joseph Quesnel, Joseph-François Perrault, Jacques-Clément Herse, and Jean-Guillaume De Lisle, he founded Montreal's Théâtre de Société—an initiative well-suited to earn the disapproval of the highly conservative Catholic clergy that was also intent on asserting its control over *canadien* society.[7]

Throughout this period, De Bonne was also vehemently opposed to the projects for reform, formulated by both British merchants and some of the *Canadiens*, who were eventually successful in leading the British government to reorganize the colony's political structure in 1791. Calling for the division of the Province of Quebec into Lower and Upper Canada and for the creation of elected legislative assemblies, this new constitution was also intended to shift the burden of raising and administering colonial finances to the citizens of the newly created provinces, who were given power to make laws under the control of a Governor-General, Lieutenants-Governor, and Legislative Councils appointed by London. The first elections to the Legislative Assemblies of the newly constituted provinces were duly organized to take place in the summer of 1792. These elections were also the occasion for the emergence of the earliest graphic satires known to have been designed and printed in Quebec. Oddly enough, as we shall see, the figure of Pierre-Amable De Bonne hovered in their vicinity as well.

ELECTORAL PRINTS IN LOWER CANADA, 1792–1811

Only one of a handful of these graphic satires, each one printed in hundreds of copies in the two months of the campaign, is known to us. This is the large etched broadsheet *À tous les électeurs: Messieurs, et concitoyens de la ville de Québec*, held in the Lawrence Lande Canadiana collection of McGill University in Montreal. Long heralded as a significant event in the history of printmaking in Canada, this print also provides a relatively early example of sequential narrative and speech balloons in Canadian visual culture (Fig. 6).[8] Published in June 1792, the plate contrasts the virtues of the (unnamed) Merchant

7. Having forbidden theater since 1711, the clergy evenually succeeded in shutting down the Théâtre de Société, but could do nothing about the theatrical entertainments—both French and English—put on by the British Governor-General in his own precincts for the benefit of friends and associates from both linguistic communities.

8. Mary Allodi, *Printmaking in Canada: The Earliest Views and Portraits/Les débuts de l'estampe imprimée au Canada: Vues et portraits* (Toronto: Royal Ontario

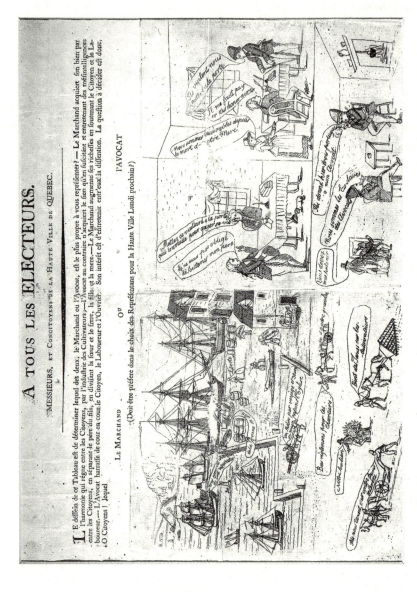

Fig. 6. Unidentified artist, *À tous les électeurs: Messieurs, et concitoyens de la Haute Ville de Québec,* 1792, etching, 24 × 35 cm, mounted on mat 28 × 46 cm. Lawrence Lande Canadiana Collection, department of rare books and special collections, McGill University.

candidate with the evils of the (equally unnamed) Lawyer candidate, both contesting the riding (district) of the "Haute-Ville" (Upper Town) of Quebec City. Although the representational codes are fairly schematic, the print presents a formal organization, bearing a headline and a typeset text above a left-to-right sequence of discrete scenes, set alternatively in the open public spaces of the Quebec port area and the more intimate spaces of domestic and professional quarters, each presenting narrative content through action and speech bubbles.[9]

The didactic tenor of the typeset text is unmistakable.

> TO ALL THE ELECTORS. | GENTLEMEN, AND FELLOW CITI-ZENS OF THE UPPER TOWN OF QUEBEC/THE purpose of this tableau is to determine which of the two, the Merchant or the Lawyer, is best suited to represent you? —The Merchant acquires his goods through the harmony that obtains between citizens, by the industry of the farmers; —the Lawyer, on the contrary, only acquires his by inciting and maintaining misunderstanding between citizens, separating the father from the son, dividing sister and brother, daughter and mother. —The Merchant increases his wealth by supporting the Citizen and the Labourer.—the Lawyer harasses the Citizen, the Labourer and the Worker in court. His interest lies in maintaining dissent between them. The question to decide is therefore, O Citizens! Which of THE MERCHANT or the LAWYER (Should be preferred in the choice of representatives for the Upper Town next Monday?)

Below this text, men and women give their views on the contrasting impacts of a concentration on trade or an *engouement* for familial strife. On the side of the Merchant, a set of farmworkers has wandered into the port area to declare: "If they tax us, it's against their interests"; "No taxes on farmers"; "Our support." Further in the distance, a drayman extols the good regulations for his work that the Merchant will doubtless legislate; a driver evokes the fee of a shilling per journey, with an added 30 *sous* if it takes the passenger past a church; while in the distance different figures extoll *Liberté* and the new products, from wheat to *graine de lin*, that will help expand commerce. On the side of the Lawyer, all is connivance: an ungrateful son

---

Museum, 1980); Nicole Allard in *Jean-Baptiste Côté caricaturiste et sculpteur*, ed. Mario Béland (Quebec: Musée du Québec, 1996), 35–59.

9. Even if this is not yet *bande dessinée*, the choice of this formal organization for one of the first graphic satires to be published in Quebec raises questions to which I return at the close of this article.

claims "I'm not obliged to support my father," to which his lawyer answers "Throw the old man out the door so that he'll work to earn his living"; a *canadien* couple, anxious at being evicted following the death of their mother, are told first of all that the lawyer's *honoraires* must be paid; a lawyer stands by two *habitants*, reminding them that "you must support us"; and two *habitants* reflect, smoking their pipes, that "we are the Lawyer's slaves."[10] One *habitant* has just the previous day given his lawyer "trois portugaises." Of such projected tensions were Quebec's first graphic satires constituted.

This plate was one of a number of "caricatures" recorded by the firm of Samuel Neilson that printed them in the hundreds. Sandra Alston and Patricia Lockhart Fleming listed it in their 1999 supplement to Marie Tremaine's foundational study of 1952, *A Bibliography of Canadian Imprints, 1751–1800*. According to Neilson's registers, it was paid for on 17 June 1792 by Quebec City British merchants Mathew and John Macnider, who ordered five other printings of "caricatures" in all in May and June of that year. Since *À tous les électeurs: Messieurs, et concitoyens de la ville de Québec* favored the man who eventually won the riding of Upper Town, the Scots-born merchant William Grant (1744–1805),[11] it may be wondered to what extent he planned the broadsheet's design himself. The visual treatment of figures, spaces, and architectural elements (notably of the ships seen in the port area) can be likened to some of the work produced by German émigré printer J. G. Hochstetter for Neilson's short-lived illustrated *Quebec Magazine*; it would not be unusual for an artist like Hochstetter to follow instructions given to him by an image's designer. Grant, president of the Constitutional Club founded in January 1792 to promote the new constitution for the colony adopted by the British parliament in December 1791, was supported by his friend and fellow *seigneur* (and Club vice-president) Charles-Louis Tarieu de Lanaudière (1743–1811).[12] The latter was also recorded by Neilson, who noted in his journal the production

10. This was not just a figure of speech; slave ownership was still prevalent in Lower Canada at this time. David Gilles, "La norme esclavagiste, entre pratique coutumière et norme étatique: Les ésclaves panis et leur statut juridique au Canada (XVIIe–XVIIIe s)," *Ottawa Law Review* 40/1 (2008–2009): 73–116.

11. David Roberts, "Grant, William (1744–1805)," *Dictionary of Canadian Biography*, vol. 5, http://www.biographi.ca/en/bio/grant_william_1744_1805_5E.html

12. Marie Tremaine, *A Bibliography of Canadian Imprints, 1751–1800* (Toronto: University of Toronto Press, 1999 [1952]), 361.

of "500 copies in English and French editions of 'Lanaudière's Song with an engraved caricature.'"[13]

Through the participation of its members in the election, it is likely that the Constitutional Club was the incubator for some of Quebec's first graphic satires—devised for publication in both French and English. Grant's biographer helps us to piece together the story:

> [. . .] the Constitutional Club [was] reputedly composed of those 165 citizens of Quebec who had gathered at Franks' Tavern on 16 December 1791 to celebrate the Constitutional Act. A debating society that met fortnightly, the club sought to promote knowledge of the British constitution and "diffuse [. . .] a spirit of Commercial and Agricultural industry." Recognizing the improving grasp by Canadians of British parliamentary authority, Grant carefully scheduled a discussion on "the rights of Canadian citizens" under the Quebec and Constitutional acts [. . .] Although Grant had taken an active interest in obtaining the new constitution, he was not reappointed to the Legislative Council. Determined to remain a political leader, however, in June 1792 he sought election in Upper Town Quebec to the first House of Assembly. With the energetic support of Charles-Louis Tarieu de Lanaudière, a long-time friend and vice-president of the Constitutional Club, and the merchants Mathew and John Macnider, he was elected with Jean-Antoine Panet, largely on the support of artisans, eligible labourers, and Canadian and British businessmen.[14]

The supporters of their opponents in the election were also active in the printing of broadsides, even if they are not recorded as having included "caricature" in their productions. The "Avocat" candidate was Michel-Amable Berthelot Dartigny (1738–1815). Dartigny was supported, along with Gabriel-Elzear Taschereau (1749–1809), by his colleague, Pierre-Amable De Bonne, who owned *seigneurie* property in Quebec City as well as in nearby rural domains; although himself a candidate in a riding just west of Montreal, De Bonne entered the fray by campaigning for candidates in the three ridings of Quebec.[15] De Bonne announced his support for his Upper Town choices by advertising the publication of his *Avis aux canadiens* in Neilson's

13. Ibid., 259.
14. Roberts, "Grant, William."
15. John Hare, *Aux origines du parlementarisme québécois 1791–1793* (Sillery: Septentrion, 1993), 155.

Quebec Gazette on May 17, 1792. Four days later, Grant's camp replied with *Aux electeurs du Bas Canada,/Et à ceux du comté et des villes de Quebec en particulier: Signe, Probus, Quebec, 21 mai, 1792,* which was a "categorical refutation of *Avis aux Canadiens* [...]. It shows the English merchant to be the benefactor and ally of the French Canadian—providing work for wages, stimulating agriculture, increasing property values, and circulating wealth. It depicts the *seigneur* as ever the despot over his compatriots."[16]

Notwithstanding this retort, De Bonne replied with a new broadside, *Aux canadiens,* each of these blasts and counterblasts being printed by Samuel Neilson—such was the printer's monopoly on public discourse in 1792. De Bonne declared "The intention and opinions of the author of the Notice to Canadians are too well known for him to pay any attention to a document signed 'Probus' which is no more than a tissue of insults and sophisms [etc.]" and followed by a "Song, on Probus's Profession of Faith, to the tune of 'Barbari My Friend.'"

Pierre-Amable De Bonne thus emerged simultaneously as both keen participant and favored target in electoral politics. He was rewarded for his steadfast support of the Governor's party in the new Assembly in 1794 when he was made judge of the court of the King's Bench for the District of Quebec and appointed to the Legislative Council. His biographers describe his talents and contributions to the newly organized political life of Lower Canada well:

> De Bonne may be considered the first professional political schemer in Lower Canada. His rapid advancement in public office, his ostentatious loyalism, his steady support for government measures in the house, his unquestionable influence on voters and on some Canadian "placemen" in the assembly, the apparent abandonment of his nationalism of the 1780s and 90s, earned him the resentment and then the ferocious hostility of those in the Canadian party. He returned their feelings.[17]

Throughout his public career, De Bonne had also earned a reputation as a dedicated libertine. His first marriage, in 1781, was annulled in the following year, both parties having taken their vows none too seriously; a later liaison with a married society woman was settled through a "gentleman's agreement" before the chief prosecutor of the

16. Tremaine, *A Bibliography of Canadian Imprints,* 362.
17. Tousignant and Wallot, "De Bonne, Pierre-Amable."

colony. In Louise-Élisabeth Marcoux he was marrying the 23-year-old daughter of a family of farmers resident in his constituency. The marriage was widely held to have been meant to give him a false respectability at a time when he hoped to win favor in what had become, by 1805, an increasingly conservative and nationalist francophone community—after a life valiantly spent affirming his independence from the precepts of the Catholic Church. It is rather ironic that De Bonne had been "appointed a commissioner with authority to build and repair churches in 1799 and 1805."[18]

In the Fonds Louis-Dulongpré, *En voilà encore De Bonnes!* rests alongside a second image, this one an etching, unsigned and undated like the drawing, which presents juxtaposed scenes in two staggered horizontal registers that invite the reader to reflect on the worth of "D.B." (Fig. 7). This print is closer in structure to *À tous les électeurs: Messieurs, et concitoyens de la ville de Québec* of 1792 than to the elegant draughtsmanship of *En voilà encore De Bonnes!*; it also bears some kinship to the earlier print in terms of the schematic quality of its figurative and spatial representation. If it seems as though De Bonne is the subject, the position of this graphic satire (for or against him?) is at first sight unclear. It is worth considering the representation of the church in the upper vignette. While not an exact rendering, it resembles Quebec City's Anglican church, which was completed and opened for worship in 1804. On our right we see a group of men standing, discoursing on the topic of "D.B.," most of them turning away while the first, on our left, gazes toward the church, holding his hand to his heart: "My God, a deaf man couldn't do more" he says, while the others expand: "D.B. a man of the people" says a man in the background; at the center, an *habitant* with characteristic *tuque* reaches to tap the back of a man in front of him, "Listen cousin, an ignoramus will never do anything for us in the chamber." "He'll protect our rights," intervenes a second background figure; finally, the cousin avers, "so let's go vote for D ... a man of experience." Facing the group, another man offers a conclusion to this sequence: "Hon D.B. forever."

In the lower register, two vignettes encompass situations at school and at work. In the first, an apparently fully grown "member seen at school," who does not know his ABCs, is corrected by his teacher;

18. Ibid.

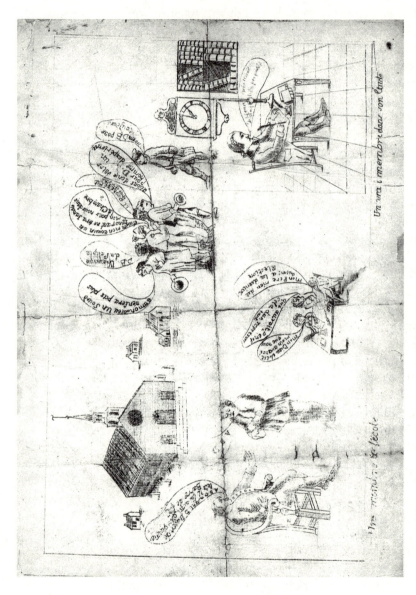

Fig. 7. Unidentified artist, electoral broadsheet, etching, 31.5 × 23.5 cm, c 1811. BAnQ Vieux-Montréal, Fonds Louis-Dulongpré, MSS147.

three other students comment "My God, he's less advanced than us"; "who'd have thought that of a representative"; "my father told me as much at the last election." To the right, a "real member in his study" is working into the late hours: "2 hours after midnight and five bills ready."

This print, if its reference to "D.B" can be taken to confirm Pierre-Amable De Bonne as its subject, appears to favor him. Perhaps it is intended to show him as a studious, responsible legislator looking after the spiritual well-being of his community. On the other hand, if the church building is indeed the one built for Quebec's English-speaking Anglicans, it may also be that this print is an exercise in dry irony, the visual identification of the church providing a foil to the propaganda discourse embodied in the group of onlookers and in the *école* and *étude* vignettes. If this is the case, it might be necessary to assign authorship of this image to De Bonne's opponents.[19]

In either reading, the insistence on education may well be an allusion to De Bonne's self-interest: for the nationalist *canadien* party, it was a matter of principle that judges, in order to remain impartial, should not be allowed to participate in elections. Against this, De Bonne argued that it was necessary to ensure that members of the judiciary, who were almost by definition among the best educated members of the Assembly, be enabled to take part in the drafting and presentation of the province's legislation. The challenges to De Bonne's position were but one aspect of the wider contestation of the British administration's manipulations of its legal, political, and social privileges in the decade 1800–1810. Against the increasingly xenophobic climate fostered among the British merchants, exemplified by their newspaper the *Quebec Mercury*, leaders of the *canadien* party founded their own newspaper, *Le Canadien*, in November 1806. Their contestation found a potent target in De Bonne, one of the leaders of the government's party in the Assembly. After the accession of Sir James Craig as Governor-General in 1807, the insistence of the *canadien* party on the matter of the ineligibility of judges became one of the principal irritants in the Assembly's relations with the colonial government. Craig treated the matter as one of the impertinent challenges to Britain's authority in ruling its colony. Against the increasing tensions between Britain and the United States in this period, with

19. Philippe Reid, "L'émergence du nationalisme canadien-français: L'idéologie du Canadien (1806–1842)," *Recherches sociographiques* 21(1980): 11–51.

Craig and his administration nervous about any movement that might be considered seditious, and fearing more precisely a *rapprochement* between the *canadiens* and Britain's enemy Napoleon, the political situation in Lower Canada reached crisis points repeatedly in these years, culminating in Craig's dissolution of the Assembly in March 1810 after its members declared vacant the seat of Pierre-Amable De Bonne. In short order, Craig also ordered *Le Canadien* to be closed down, sequestering its equipment and imprisoning its editors.

By 1810, then, De Bonne was a deposed leader, a victim without doubt of the increasingly violent polemics that marked early Canadian journalism, who was indeed regularly demonized in the contemporary press, as he would be later in the first efforts at writing a nationalist history of Canada. In *En voilà encore De Bonnes!*, this demonization was made explicit by the set of devil's horns that arose from his forehead—and which, of course, would bear for any beholder a secondary signification: that of the cuckolded husband. The fusion of a political and an erotic reading may well be justified. Just before his expulsion from the Legislative Assembly, rumors held that accusations of his disdain for fellow *canadien* citizens were being circulated—by his former mistresses. So much for the veil of respectability afforded by the marriage to Louise-Élisabeth Marcoux—or by overseeing the building of any number of churches. In the Assembly itself, De Bonne had been taken to task for intimidating his constituents by menacing them with lawsuits if they would not pledge him their votes. Expelled from the legislative chamber, expelled from the nuptial chamber?

We have no idea whether or not *En voilà encore De Bonnes!* was ever made into a print. In the Fonds Louis Dulongpré, this drawing and the *Un membre à l'école/un vrai membre dans son étude* etching are accompanied by three letters addressed by Dulongpré to John Neilson (1776–1848). John Neilson had taken over his brother Samuel's printing firm at the latter's death in January 1793. From 1799, he entered into a silent partnership with the official printer of the provincial statutes, Pierre-Édouard Desbarats.[20] In 1811, at 35 years

---

20. Sonia Chassé, Rita Girard-Wallot, and Jean-Pierre Wallot, "Neilson, John," in *Dictionary of Canadian Biography*, vol. 7, http://www.biographi.ca/en/bio/neilson_john_7E.html . Jean-Marie Lebel in collaboration with Aileen Desbarats, "Desbarats, Pierre-Édouard," in *Dictionary of Canadian Biography*, vol. 6, http://www.biographi.ca/en/bio/desbarats_pierre_edouard_6E.html

of age, he was the most important printer and bookseller in the country as well as the publisher of the *Gazette de Québec*. The letters addressed to Neilson by Dulongpré concern the production of over one hundred caricatures and their circulation between Montreal and Quebec in the winter of 1811–1812. Nothing in the letters links this huge offering overtly to the two "De Bonne" images, but they provide more tantalizing evidence of the existence of personal and political caricature in early nineteenth-century Lower Canada.

LOUIS DULONGPRÉ'S LETTERS TO JOHN NEILSON, 1811

Born in 1759 in Paris, Louis Dulongpré arrived in Montreal in 1785 after service in the French Navy's Atlantic campaigns, both in support of the United States toward the close of the Revolutionary War and in subsequent action in the Caribbean. Within two years he married a Canadian woman, Marguerite Campeau, with whom he established first a "dancing school for boys and girls" and then a "boarding school for young ladies" in which the teaching of useful arts and skills was to be given—including drawing. As we have seen, he was involved in the foundation of the short-lived Théâtre de Société with De Bonne and others in 1789. Deciding in 1793 to add painting to his professional skills, Dulongpré sought a training that was not available in Montreal at the time. He traveled to the US to take lessons, chiefly studying with artists in Baltimore. By taking advantage of resources offered by the Franco-American network established throughout the main cities of the northeastern US, Dulongpré gives us an early indication of the importance of the North American context for the development of visual arts in Quebec. He returned to Montreal in March 1794 to advertise himself as a master of portraits in "miniature, crayons, and pastels."

Thus was launched a career that by one posthumous account saw the creation of some three thousand portraits. Although Dulongpré would also be much in demand as a copyist of religious paintings for the Catholic parishes that proliferated throughout Lower Canada during this period, he shared the market in Lower Canada with local painters such as François Malépart de Beaucourt and François Baillargé, and émigrés John Ramage, William Berczy, and Gerritt Schipper. But Dulongpré clearly did much to develop this market himself through his extensive social and political connections. Dulongpré must have been a veritable entrepreneur, as was necessary for what we might call the industry of the image in early nineteenth-century Lower Canada. Artists like his friend François Baillargé, chiefly occupied with sculptural commissions in the Quebec City area, or Louis Quévillon, whose workshop came close to cornering the market in church decorations in the Montreal environs after 1810, responded to challenging local conditions—the lack of academic training and the absence of a strong culture of private patronage—by reorganizing methods of production and distribution in ways that help us to understand how the roles and the status of the artist actually function in a given colonial society such as Lower Canada. For Louis Dulongpré (or, later, William Berczy), it became important to have what we might call "diversification strategies": their work as painters has to be understood as part of a range of activities. For Dulongpré, portraits and religious commissions were part of a wider set of practices that included not only teaching but also real estate speculation, the manufacture of painted carpets and eventually (and disastrously) financial investments. According to the letters from his hand that survive in the Dulongpré *fonds*, he was also an entrepreneur in graphic satires, a fitting role for an artist who was above all an image merchant.

The first of Dulongpré's letters to John Neilson was dated 5 December 1811. This was also the date of a by-election won by a certain James Stuart, former leading light of the British colonial administration who, stripped of his functions in 1809 by the feared Governor-General Sir James Craig, had aligned himself with the nationalist *Parti canadien*. Following the election, Stuart would lead this party in the Assembly at Quebec. This was a vivid political moment and Louis Dulongpré sought to profit from it.

> Sir: circumstances give me the occasion to present you my humble respects, the election of our county has given subjects for caricature, I send you twenty-eight today. The time being too short to print more I will send you a 150 more by the next mail. As I think they will give pleasure to many of your citizens, the thing being so extraordinary, I do not doubt that you will have the detail by other means having only the time to sign myself as your humble servant L. Dulongpré. The price is two shillings without being illuminated. Do me the pleasure of announcing them; if you need a greater quantity let me know forgive me I am very rushed for the mail.

On the reverse side of this letter, Dulongpré enumerated some of the characters who were presumably the topics of the caricatures: *habitant* figures; "Capitaine monarque"; a spear-carrier; Denis Viger; a Valois; a King, a Papineau, perhaps Joseph Papineau (1752–1841), whom Dulongpré would portray in 1825.

Four days later, Dulongpré renewed his appeal to Nelson:

> Sir, trusting that you have received my most recent letter, and 28 caricatures; of the Royal election. Imagining well that that you don't have enough I send you 76 to add to the 28. Fix the price as you see fit if you think that you will need more send word by this mail I will have the quantity that would please you printed up. I do not relate the election to you [because] your Gazette gives you a fairly precise detail of it. Please receive, sir, the respectful salutations of one who has the honour to be your humble servant, Ls Dulongpré—I'll expect a few words from you today of the present.

A second hand has inscribed a note on this document: "Dulongpré Caricatures/Answ. d next post/only 1 [illeg.]." Nevertheless, the impatient Dulongpré took up his pen once again on 16 December:

> I see my dear Mr Nelson that you have forgotten me I do not know if you have received my two letters and the hundred-odd caricatures that I have sent you through the mails. Not doubting that you have received them. If you have disposed of them withhold your commission and send the rest of the sums by one of the mails they do not belong to me, I am obliged to account for them. I hope of you and have no doubt that you will be so polite as to answer this third letter knowing that you will oblige your humble servant, Ls Dulongpré.

All of this activity on the part of Dulongpré is indeed promising, but the trail goes cold almost immediately. The last trace we have of these hundred-odd images is a receipt dated 18 February 1812: "Recd of J. Neilson one hundred caricatures belonging to Mr Dulongpré of Montreal."[21]

21. Bibliothèque et archives nationales du Québec, Centre d'archives de Vieux-Montréal, Fonds Louis-Dulongpré (MSS 147). For an account of these letters in their original (and idiosyncratic) French versions, see Dominic Hardy, "Les collections d'imprimés et les fonds d'archives de BAnQ: Des ressources importantes pour l'histoire de la caricature et de la satire graphique québécoises avant 1960," *Revue de Bibliothèque et archives nationales du Québec* 4 (2012): 96–109.

Taken together, these documents allow us to affirm several things. First of all, neither of the two satirical images found in the Fonds Dulongpré have anything to do with the artist's letters, nor can we say that they are part of the 104 caricatures he has offered to Neilson. Still, the friendly tone of the letters can lead us to suppose that other groups of such images had been offered to Neilson in the past. The letters give us a solid indication that some kind of market for caricature existed, or at least that it did at the time of by-elections. The versions that are *enluminé*, that is, colored by hand (and this, likely by women painters) are more costly. Finally, Dulongpré tells us clearly that he is not the author of the caricatures he is hoping to sell: "they do not belong to me." He is beholden to others to make payment. He is an agent—just like Neilson and the signatory of the receipt who may, we can suppose, have been in a position to ensure the images' circulation, which might be more private, or even clandestine. For if more than one hand at work in Montreal is responsible for these images, we can imagine that either the city of Quebec had no working caricaturist among its workforce, or that this production was socially and politically inadmissible in a capital under military surveillance. As we have seen, this was a period of grave political tension and censorship. The British metropolis, in a state of constant hostility with Napoleon's France, feared the presence of French agents in Lower Canada; Craig had stifled the opposition newspaper and dissolved the Assembly on its expulsion of one of his favorites, Pierre-Amable De Bonne. By December 1811, the British colony was on the eve of the War of 1812. Perhaps Dulongpré's 104 caricatures were indeed circulated in Quebec, perhaps not. If we can suppose that they were just as likely to have been scrapped by a printing firm that maintained close ties to the administration, we have to remember that John Neilson's own political position drew him into close friendships with members of the *Canadien* party, among whose ranks he would eventually join the Assembly in 1818.

Further research in newspapers and private archives of artists, politicians, printers, writers—among the informal and formal literary productions of men and women of the time—will be needed before we can recover what are, for now, lost treasures. There is every indication that the political life of early Canadian society was indeed marked by the production and circulation of graphic political satire. The traditional questions of art-historical investigation will perhaps eventually be answered. Who made these images, where, with what resources? What accounts for their stylistic appearance, the material choices made? Who were the readers, how were the images made part of the social fabric of Canadian life? How were they shared in public and enjoyed in private?

FINIS CORONAT OPUS

More immediately, who drew *En voilà encore De Bonnes*? By opening this article with a comparison between the drawing and the portraits carried out by William Berczy in 1808, I set out a likely attribution. Indeed, the 1991 retrospective exhibition devoted to Berczy's career made the point that informal caricature drawing is to be found in his sketchbooks and letters (Fig. 8). But other possibilities should be

Fig. 8. William Berczy (1744–1813), Two profiles and a box, c. 1797, sepia ink on laid paper, Library and Archives Canada. Reproduced in Mary Allodi, *Berczy*, 1991.

considered. William Bent Berczy assisted his father with the prepara-
tion of miniatures and cannot be ruled out as the person responsible
for this caricature. This is also true of Charlotte Allamand Berczy
who taught drawing in quarters rented from Louis Dulongpré, as did
Dulongpré's wife Marguerite Campeau. The Berczys' future daughter-
in-law, Louise-Amélie Panet, attended Charlotte's school; we know
her to have been an artist in drawing and watercolor. The cover of
one of her notebooks, part of the Fonds Baby in the special collections
of the Université de Montréal, is adorned with humorous renditions
of women sporting straw bonnets (Fig. 9). At the very least, it seems
reasonable to affirm that Louis Dulongpré was acting on behalf of a
veritable *fabrique* of caricatures, likely established on his own prem-
ises and sustained by the members of the Berczy and Dulongpré fami-
lies, both constantly preoccupied with making the best possible use
of the art market according to the vagaries of circumstances in Lower
Canada's visual culture.

The similarities and contrasts between 1792 and 1811 are compelling. In both cases, a concise social structure was responsible for
the production and circulation of graphic satire. On the first occa-

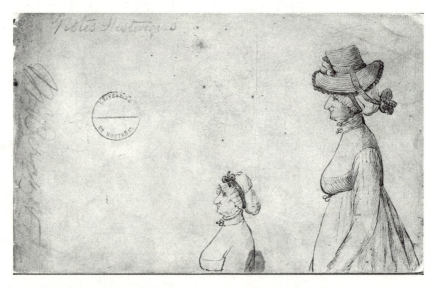

Fig. 9. Louise-Amélie Panet Berczy (1789–1862), Notebook cover, sepia ink
on laid paper, n.d. Division des Archives de l'Université de Montréal, A2/56,
box 11347.

sion, the intended audience was the electorate: authorship was vested with the powerful and wealthy members of a short-lived Constitutional Club who caused "caricatures" to be created, printed, and distributed. These few "agents" were themselves the "market," producing commodities for almost immediate dispersal with no corresponding immediate return to offset the cost of production. There was almost no formal artistic involvement in an academic sense, although the resources available through Samuel Nelson's firm enabled some creation of schematic imagery. It is remarkable that both printed electoral images use a sequential structure that, although a common but by no means omnipresent strategy in much English, French, and American satirical print material of this period, seems in Lower Canada to be the "first port of call" for the conception of graphic satire.

Nineteen years later, the milieu of artistic production had changed considerably in Lower Canada. While there was still no academic training available to artists within the Province, imported resources (the presence of immigrant practitioners such as Dulongpré and Berczy) helped to structure the marketplace for visual images that increasingly acquired status as commodities within the Lower Canada social economy. The portable image (the portrait, the miniature, and from time to time the caricature) helped give cohesion to the colony's visual culture, strengthening its bonds to that of Europe's (increasingly transatlantic) cultural territories. In this context, Montreal developed—at least for a time—a small-scale speculative manufacture of satirical images. Here, there was a place for physiognomic satire: for caricature in the strictest sense of the term, not in the sense used by Samuel Neilson in 1792 when he designated the electoral satires as "caricatures." This suggests that in the bilingual context of Quebec, the term already enjoyed the semantic instability it has retained in francophone usages from the nineteenth century onward.

It is within this instability that we can finally consider the enigmatic pen and graphite drawing of Pierre-Amable De Bonne nestled in the Fonds Louis Dulongpré. The full image is really powerfully emblematic. *En voilà encore DE BONNEs!* De Bonne is the name inscribed on the drawing, but it's also *De Bonnes...* these good ones, these horns protruding from the forehead, and also the *bonnes histoires qu'on se raconte, des mensonges*; as we say in English, that's a good one (perhaps that's a tall tale). *En voilà*: monstrative words that point us toward what we must see. *En voilà encore*: here again are—or, *en/corps,* here is, embodied: De Bonne, and thus here are horns in the body of De Bonne (*voilà des cornes dans le corps de De Bonne*).

And then there is the subtitle: "Finis Coronat Opus." The work completed is crowned. *Coronat* also extends the sounds of the written word *encore,* and the evoked word *cornes. La fin couronne l'œuvre:* the proverb was well known and used repeatedly in polemical writings of the period. In the context of an amorous dimension (if cuckoldry is at stake), the recourse to such a subtitle calls to mind the tradition of early-modern emblem books and folios of engravings festooned with cherubim in seventeenth-century Holland. Constructed around just such proverbs, with the aim of instructing a couple through allegories on the realities and pathways of Love, these manuals were well known in the eighteenth century and have their descendants in the literary traditions of the end of the *ancien régime.*

Should the misbegotten marriage entered into by De Bonne be seen as the allegory of his "marriage," in the workings of the Legislative Assembly, to the British—or indeed of that of the British subjects with the *anciens canadiens* who are the newer subjects of the King? All the negotiations in this mined territory that De Bonne had undertaken since 1792 only led to his downfall. The drawing's configuration as an oval, the very identifier of the miniature format, is surely no accident. In somewhat grotesque fashion, the oval still structures the love of the De Bonne-Marcoux represented in the watercolor miniatures that we may even today examine at the Musée national des beaux-arts du Québec. Perhaps the satirical pen drawing shows us just how grotesque De Bonne's marital union was seen to be by his enemies; it certainly reminds us how ubiquitous was this art form among Lower Canada's middle class and nobility as the bread-and-butter production of artists such as Dulongpré, Berczy, and Schipper. Perhaps too there is a comment on the popularity of such art forms in a social system dominated by the British to whom De Bonne is being held to have assimilated—assimilation of the *canadiens* having proven to be one of the key goals of British merchant policies in these years as would be the case later on, after the failed rebellions of 1837–1838.

This sense of imitation evokes the mirror, but also the sense of absorption that situates this representation at the level of the wider cultural territory, both field of exchange and market for images that build a structure in Lower Canada for the signs, the ideas, the ideologies and, finally, the whole scopic regime of British influence. Within this regime, the treatment of De Bonne as cuckolded devil, bereft of the mirror that would be provided by the necessary, now-missing pendant, the paired representation of his beloved, starts fatally to inverse the whole structure of this kind of representation, taking in its collapse its cultural value as fetishized representation of the British culture defended by De Bonne. Finally, the caricatural turn introduced into Lower Canada by this image—quite distinct in this physiognomic function from that of the electoral images we have considered here—comes to make an ironic, self-reflexive comment on all these quite specific formats of the manufactured image that were made according to the social and economic conditions of any artist who is of necessity given to an intimate relationship with his or her subject. This relationship may yield private knowledge, precious to another form of circulation whose rewards are not monetary. It is tempting to consider *En voilà encore De Bonnes!* as a meta-representation: the aggrieved expression of Pierre-Amable De Bonne quietly bearing witness to those things that he knows the beholder to know about him; a coruscating intelligence which, accumulated in the spirit of the informed observer, casts De Bonne among the living damned, damned in the very act of seeing; caught in the mirror of a caricature.

LAURENCE GROVE

Ferdinand de Saussure's Unknown *Bandes Dessinées*

SAUSSURE AND TÖPFFER

From 1938 onwards, the Bibliothèque de Genève (BGE) has received various gifts or deposits relating to the Saussure family, including one gift resulting from the discovery in 1996 of a major collection in the conservatory of the family home on the banks of Lake Geneva. Among the papers found in the upmarket greenhouse was a hitherto unexplored comic strip created by the young Ferdinand at the age of 17, or maybe 16, *M. Sibidi*, now BGE arch. Saussure 371/11. *M. Sibidi* has no individual online catalogue entry, has not of yet, to the best of my knowledge, been analyzed or even commented, and is not mentioned in John Joseph's monumental biography of 2012.[1] A further 1875 manuscript strip by the linguist-to-be is also in the library's possession, *Les aventures de Polytychus*, now BGE ms. fr. 3974a.

As we shall see, both manuscripts elicit comparisons between the Father of Linguistics, as Ferdinand de Saussure (1857–1913) is often labeled, and the Father of the Comic Strip (to quote David Kunzle's epithet for Saussure's fellow Genevan), Rodolphe Töpffer (1799–1846).[2] Initially, the Genevan manuscripts inspire us to consider what Saussure might tell us about the history, or at least the reception history, of comics. More broadly and for many more importantly, the connections between the two men allow us to look back to Töpffer's influence upon the young Ferdinand, and ask how BD might have marked the progress of linguistics and associated critical theory: indeed if

---

1. John E. Joseph, *Saussure* (Oxford: Oxford University Press, 2012).
2. David Kunzle, *Father of the Comic Strip: Rodolphe Töpffer* (Jackson, MS: University Press of Mississippi, 2007).

YFS 131/132, Bande Dessinée: *Thinking Outside the Boxes*, ed. Laurence Grove and Michael Syrotinski, © 2017 by Yale University.

it can be argued that structuralist linguistics transformed the *sciences humaines* in France, then by extension BD has a rightful place among the influences on contemporary thought. Key terms, as we shall see, are *langage* and *parole*, the difference underlined by Saussure between the individual utterance (*parole*) and the system as a whole (*langage*), and the implications for a more general relationship between component parts and overall creation. Within this system Saussure contrasts the *signifiant* or signifier, the arbitrary sign used to express meaning, and the *signifié* or signified, the object that system is to represent, however approximately. It is the pathways and interactions between the *significant* and the *signifié* that will make for our comparison with the workings of the *bande dessinée*.

According to John Joseph,[3] the teacher who had the greatest influence on Ferdinand was Antoine Verchère, who in turn had been taught by, and continued to disseminate the ideas of, Adolphe Pictet, but also Rodolphe Töpffer. It is also to be noted that the Saussure-Töpffer link goes in both directions, in that one of the key influences on Töpffer's best known work (at least at the time), his *Voyages en zigzag*,[4] was Horace-Bénédicte de Saussure (1740–1799), Ferdinand's great grandfather, the celebrated Alpinist. Indeed Sainte-Beuve was to note in his "Notice sur Töpffer" for the *Nouveaux voyages en zigzag* that,

> These mountainous regions were to some extent discovered and conquered by Saussure, the illustrious physicist [. . .]
> Saussure was thus discovering the Alps and calmly spreading the word as to their innate poetry around the same time that Bernadin de Saint-Pierre was waxing lyrical about the newly discovered treasures of the tropical peaks of Mauritius, and just before Chateaubriand would have discovered the American savanna.[5]

With respect to Nicolas-Théodore de Saussure (1767–1845), Ferdinand's grandfather, the chemist and entomologist, according to David

3. Joseph, *Saussure*, 143–45.
4. Rodolphe Töpffer, *Voyages en zigzag* (Paris: Garnier, 1844) and *Nouveaux voyages en zigzag* (Paris: Garnier, 1854). The editions consulted are those of 1860 (*Voyages en zigzag*; Glasgow University Library Ba 4-a. 4) and 1858 (*Nouveaux voyages en zigzag*; Glasgow University Library Ba 4-a. 5).
5. Charles-Augustin Sainte-Beuve, "Notice sur Töpffer," in Töpffer, *Nouveaux voyages en zigzag* (Paris: Garnier, 1858), i–xvii (vi). The *notice* was first published in 1853. The translation is my own, with much appreciated input (here and elsewhere) from Michael Syrotinski.

Kunzle the effects in Töpffer's *M. Pencil* of an "underground wind" (*vent souterrain*) were a direct reference to Nicolas-Théodore's experiments on carbonic gases, for which he was known.[6] In addition it is not hard to imagine Töpffer's *M. Cryptogame*—whose name means hidden union, but is also a sort of fungus—as a reference to the entomologist (the eponymous hero is frequently chasing butterflies), one picked up later by Saussure's Polytychus via the name's proximity to Polyptychus, a type of African moth.

THE GENEVA MANUSCRIPTS: PRESENTATION

Moving from the general context to the specific object, from *langage* to *parole*, let us consider the details of BGE arch. Saussure 371/11 and BGE ms. fr. 3974a. The two date from 1874 and 1875 respectively, with the latter, *Les aventures de Polytychus*, described in a handwritten note added to the library's catalogues:

> Ms. fr. 3974a Books of notes and drawings probably written by F. de S. in 1875 (at the age of 17). 1 book written recto verso and containing:
> —"The Adventures of Polytychus" (in the style of Töpffer) 26 folios
> —collections of Homeric epithets 17 ff.[7]

The note is cited by Sémir Badir in his presentation and edition of the manuscript,[8] however Badir does not analyze the work in his introduction of less than two pages. The strip in question tells the story of Polytychus of Athens and his servant Hypurge, both characters, so it would seem, of Saussure's creation. The Greek subject matter reflects the young Ferdinand's interests—two years previously in 1873 he had translated 40 pages-worth of the fourteenth book of the *Odyssey*[9]—but we can also see again the potential influence of Töpffer, who had given one of his key characters, M. Cryptogame, a Greek name.

The main character of Töpffer's *L'héritage*, one of the *Nouvelles genevoises* and also published within *La bibliothèque de*

---

6. Kunzle, *Father of the Comic Strip*, 44.
7. My translation.
8. Sémir Badir, "Les aventures de Polytychus: Présentation et édition par Sémir Badir," in *Ferdinand de Saussure: Cahier de l'Herne*, ed. Simon Bouquet (Paris: L'Herne, 2003), 473–500 (473).
9. Joseph, *Saussure*, 137.

À Athènes je m'ennuyais énormément.

Fig. 1. Ferdinand de Saussure, *Les aventures de Polytychus*, 1875, folio 3r. Bibliothèque de Genève ms. fr. 3974a.

mon oncle,[10] is plagued with boredom, as emphasized by the story's opening:

> Boredom is my curse, dear reader. I live boredom everywhere, be it at home or outside; whilst eating, as soon as I am no longer hungry; at the ball; as soon as I leave the ballroom. There is nothing that takes hold of my spirit, of my heart, of my fancies, and nothing seems as long as each day that passes.[11]

This *ennui* prefigures that of Polytychus, who likewise first appears with the words "In Athens I was enormously bored" (*À Athènes je m'ennuyais énormément*) (Fig. 1).

The 1874 manuscript is unpublished. It is a 27-page *cahier*, of which 18 give the story of M. Sibidi: how he discovers a new star, his travels in a hot air balloon to the land of cannibals, and to a sea

10. *L'héritage* dates from 1834. The copy consulted is Töpffer, *La bibliothèque de mon oncle* (Paris: Nilsson, [1920]).
11. My translation.

monster's innards, his battles, the lectures he gives, and more battles, dropping off at the end thus leading to suppose that the story is
unfinished.

Here, as for *Polytychus*, the format is that of Töpffer's picture stories, and often the content is so similar that the influence, be it direct
or subconscious, is undeniable.[12] In *M. Pencil* (first published in 1840),
the telescope scene mirrors that of the opening of *M. Sibidi* (Figs. 2
and 3), but the theme also appears in *Dr. Festus* (first published 1846).
The depiction of air travel in *M. Sibidi* also echoes scenes in *M. Pencil*; the abrupt landing into the sea that Sibidi endures reminds us
of a similar episode in *Dr. Festus*; and the ensuing battle with a sea
monster could well be directly inspired by that in *Cryptogame* (1845).
M. Sibidi's lecture scene has a similar layout, podium, and character
stance as that of *Dr. Festus*. Also like *Dr. Festus*, *M. Sibidi* has a king's
giant telescope episode. Finally *M. Sibidi*'s battle scenes, with their
scattered throngs, remind us again of those of *Dr. Festus*, as well as of
Vieux Bois (first published 1837). Overall it would be hard to imagine
that the young Ferdinand de Saussure did not have copies of Töpffer's
strips available to him when composing his own pictorial adventures.

THE GENEVA MANUSCRIPTS: SIGNIFICANCE

Both manuscripts are interesting and amusing *per se*, as well as point-
ing to the influence of Töpffer on Saussure exactly at the time when,
according to John Joseph,[13] the young Ferdinand was beginning to
take an interest in linguistics as a result of the teachings of Adolphe
Pictet. But if these manuscripts are the *signifiant*, what is the *signifié*:

---

12. On the cultural context of Töpffer with specific reference to his picture stories,
see David Kunzle, *The Early Comic Strip: The Nineteenth Century: History of the
Comic Strip Volume 2* (Berkeley: University of California Press, 1990). Most accessible
of the French editions of the *histoires en images* is the 1996 three-volume collection
produced by Thierry Groensteen for Seuil of Paris: *Monsieur Jabot: Monsieur Vieux
Bois: Deux histoires d'amour* (vol. 1); *Monsieur Crépin: Monsieur Pencil: Deux égarements de la science* (vol. 2); *Le Docteur Festus: Histoire de monsieur Cryptogame:
Deux odyssées* (vol. 3). An annotated English translation of the *histoires en images* has
been produced and edited by David Kunzle: *Rodolphe Töpffer: The Complete Comic
Strips* (Jackson, MS: University Press of Mississippi, 2007). This volume is the com-
panion to Kunzle's *Father of the Comic Strip: Rodolphe Töpffer*, which includes a full
secondary bibliography. The editions used for this study are those of Groensteen, while
also consulting the originals (Kunzle Collection copies) of *Histoire de Mr. Jabot* (Geneva: Freydig, [1835]) and *Les amours de Mr. Vieux Bois* (Geneva: Freydig, 1837).
13. Joseph, *Saussure*, 147–58.

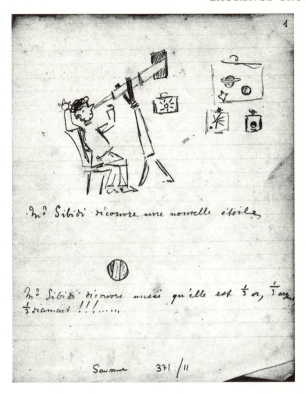

Fig. 2. Ferdinand de Saussure, *M. Sibidi*, 1874, folio 1r. Bibliothèque de Genève arch. Saussure 371/11.

what do they mean, and what do they show us? Here Ferdinand's father could help us, via a remark in an unpublished diary entry of 1872, cited by Sémir Badir:

> Ferdinand has always been a little prodigy. [. . .] At the age of 4 his drawings were extremely fine. He has that inborn talent for putting his thoughts into drawings. At the age of ten he would create caricature stories in the style of Töpffer, but in that regard he has not lived up to his promise. He finds it hard to copy directly. When he was little he would constantly come into my office to examine the engraving of the Swiss landing at Coligny, then he would rush off into the lounge and reproduce what he had seen from memory. But if you gave him a model to copy, he just couldn't do it.[14]

14. Unpublished diary entry by Henri de Saussure, 27 January 1872. Quoted by Badir, "Les aventures de Polytychus," 404. The translation is my own.

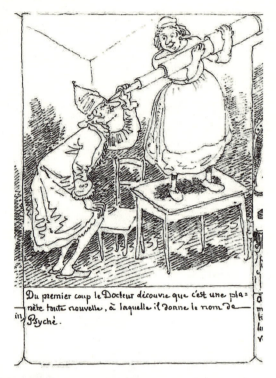

Du premier coup le Docteur découvre que c'est une pla=
nète toute nouvelle, à laquelle il donne le nom de
in Psyché.

Fig. 3. Rodolphe Töpffer, *M. Pencil*, 1840, p. 9 (detail). In Rodolphe Töpffer, *Monsieur Crépin: Monsieur Pencil: Deux égarements de la science*, ed. Thierry Groensteen (Paris: Seuil, 1996 [vol. 2]).

As Badir goes on to point out, Saussure's works are marked not only by graphic expressions of his thoughts directly in the comic strip manuscripts, but also by little drawings to be found throughout his archives, or through the figures that underline his best known writings, such as the tree and horse/*arbor et equos* diagram in the opening section of the *Cours de linguistique générale*. It is a mind-set that is also discernible in Saussure's widespread use of metaphorical images, whether it be the planets in the solar system, the painting of the Alps, or his famous game of chess. In this latter example Saussure likens words to chess pieces, whereby a knight, for example, can be switched for another symbol without effect, but if the rules for the knight's movement are changed then the system is altered. A quick aside here can serve as a reminder that chess in particular has long been a favored motif in text/image forms; one example is Gilles Cor-

rozet's chess emblem from 1540, here to say that death is a great lev-
eler, with kings and pawns ending up in the same bag at the end of
the game.[15]

Above all, once we know that the mind-set of the young Ferdinand
was influenced by the type of creative expression that today we label
as *bande dessinée*, we can understand much better certain key elements of his thought and theory. In order to explore such connections
let us return to one of Töpffer's most often quoted theory statements
on his understanding of the form that was to become known as BD.
In the "Annonce de l'histoire de M. Jabot" that appeared in Töpffer's
Mélanges as a form of post-preface,[16] the author describes *Jabot* as
follows:

> This little book is of a mixed nature. It is composed of a series of au-
> tographed line drawings [*dessins autographiés au trait*]. Each of the
> drawings is accompanied by one or two lines of text. Without the text
> the meaning of the drawings would be obscure. Without the drawings
> the text would be meaningless.[17]

The key point is that *Jabot*, and indeed comics in general, are mixed,
a hybrid form that is marked and defined by duality.

The essence of Saussure's work is likewise marked by duality
and opposition: diachronic/synchronic; *langage/parole*; *signifiant/
signifié*; *arbitraire/motivé*; *immutabilité/mutabilité*. But as with
comics, each opposition, each duality, requires a form of coming-
together, an amalgamation, in order to create the final effect. It is
through diachronic evolution that the synchronic exists. It is language that is "purely social and independent of the individual and
exclusively psychological," however *langue*, the overall spoken
language, must nonetheless go hand-in-hand with *parole*, the individual utterance or speech, in order to make *langage* (language), the
full communication network including written language. Furthermore, it is the link that brings together the *signifiant*, or signifier,
and the *signifié*, or signified, the creates the overall *signe* (sign). (In an

15. Gilles Corrozet, *Hecatomgraphie* (Paris: Denis Janot, 1540). The chess emblem
is on folios D4v–D5r.

16. The edition consulted is Töpffer, "Annonce de l'histoire de M. Jabot," in *Mélanges* (Paris: Joël Cherbuliez, 1852), 161–73 (167). The "Annonce" was first published
in 1837.

17. The translation is my own. "Autographiés" refers to the system of reproduction, one similar to lithography.

additional aside, the above quotation on language as psychological, from the McGraw-Hill translated edition of the *Course in General Linguistics*,[18] is of added interest in that it drew the particular attention of psychoanalyst R. D. Laing, who commented in a handwritten note, "how fundamental that proposition is! That which is purely social, *independent of the individual*, is psychological!")

It is by allowing us to grasp the mind-set of the young Ferdinand through these manuscripts that we can understand a mind-set that will be marked by text/image duality and by metaphorical imagery, methods of expression that are in fact homologous to, and influenced profoundly, the linguistic models that Saussure was to develop. In addition such image-based expression was to provide a vehicle for Saussure to explore concepts such as the nature of knowledge, the attraction of the exotic, and the notion of value. Thus it is through these manuscripts that we start to get a feel for the breadth of Saussure's genius.

SAUSSURE AND HOW TO READ COMICS

A shift of viewpoint will allow us to look at the text/image duality in the opposite but complementary sense: how can Saussure help us to understand comics? First of all in their historical context—thus from a diachronic viewpoint—our manuscripts can bring something to the Töpffer debate and that of the birth of comics. From about 1996, at the very time when *M. Sibidi* was discovered, Töpffer was being proclaimed as inventor of the comic strip,[19] backed up by research in Geneva and elsewhere.

However the retrospective nature of that label is problematic as Töpffer himself referred to his picture stories as no more than a pas-

18. Ferdinand de Saussure, *Course in General Linguistics*, ed. Charles Bally, Albert Sechehaye and Albert Riedlinger, trans. Wade Baskin (New York: McGraw-Hill, 1966), 18. The copy consulted is that previously belonging to and annotated by R. D. Laing (Glasgow University Library Laing 1519).

19. See, for example, Groensteen and Benoît Peeters, *Töpffer: L'invention de la bande dessinée* (Paris: Hermann, 1994). See also *Les origines de la bande dessinée, Collectionneur de bandes dessinées*, ed. Groensteen, hors série 79 (Spring 1996). I discuss the 1996 debate, with specific reference to Yves Fremion's (playfully) anti-American and pro-Töpffer opening speech that is reproduced in *Les origines de la bande dessinée*, in my *Comics in French: The European Bande Dessinée in Context* (Oxford: Berghahn, 2010 and 2013), and in my "*État présent: Bande dessinée* Studies," *French Studies* 68/1 (2014): 78–87. See also Laurence Grove and Peter Black, *Comic Invention* (Glasgow: BHP Comics, 2016).

time to amuse his pupils, a statement underlined by Pierre-Maxime Relave in one of the first monographs dedicated to Töpffer:

> These series of engravings are nonetheless relatively secondary amongst the work of Töpffer; he himself called them "follies, mixed with a pinch of seriousness," and we should not look for anything more than that in them.[20]

In his lifetime Töpffer was above all known for his *Voyages en zigzag*. In what seems to be the earliest article on Töpffer in English, "Rodolphe Töpffer: Draftsman, Humorist and Schoolmaster" in *The Monthly Review* of 1901 (when Ferdinand was at the University of Geneva just a few years prior to his course on General Linguistics) the author, J. A. Fuller Maitland, feels the need to describe the "tales in which the vehicle of caricature was used" in opposition to what he calls his "literary work." Nonetheless Fuller Maitland underlines the popular success of these "caricature-stories" (again, Fuller Maitland's term):

> In the sentimental "thirties" there cannot have been many people, among the admirers of a certain Genevan school-master, who foresaw that his fame would be carried down, not by the handful of short stories of a sentimentality quite in keeping with the taste of the time, but by half a dozen oblong volumes of tales in which the vehicle of caricature was used with all the felicity of a genuine impromptu. M. Vieuxbois, M. Crépin, and the rest, seem to have been created before the eyes of their author's pupils to beguile the long winter evenings, and their adventures to have been literally invented on the spur of the moment. [. . .]
>
> If M. Jabot, "qui se remet en position" [*who takes up the position once again*], has given one phrase to the French language, M. Vieuxbois, "qui change de linge" [*changes underwear*] continually, has provided another allusion which even now is not uncommonly met with.[21]

Of particular interest is the fact that our Saussure manuscripts suggest that over a quarter of a century before Fuller Maitland was writing on Töpffer, the caricature tales in question were already common currency not only for the readers of the popular illustrated journals, but also in the Genevan teaching circles of the bourgeoisie and of the

20. Abbé Pierre-Maxime Relave, *Rodolphe Töpffer* (Lyon: Librairie générale catholique et classique, 1899), 35. The translation is my own.

21. J. A. Fuller Maitland, "Rodolphe Töpffer: Draftsman, Humorist and Schoolmaster," *The Monthly Review* (1901–1902): 112–22 (112 and 117). The translations (my own) are additional.

intellectual elite. Our manuscripts can perhaps allow us therefore to return to the question of the reception and influence of Töpffer and of the status of the *"bande dessinée"* in the nineteenth century.

As far as the comic strips of today are concerned, we might consider this popular text/image form as a bridge between written and spoken cultures, and accordingly the most direct access to one of Saussure's preoccupations: how language can evolve via phonetic analogy as a result of everyday usage. It is a concept that can be hard to document given that everyday phonetic usage, historically at least, tends to be spoken and unrecorded. Functioning however as a mimetic popular cultural form, *bande dessinée* can break with such traditions. Remaining in Geneva with Swiss artist Zep, we can see this in the eponymous star of the *Titeuf* series, whose pronouncements such as "c'est pô juste" (*it ain't right*), "c moi ki l'ai fait" (*it was me what dunnit*), or "t'es qu'un pourri du slip" (*you're just pants*) not only reflect playground French as it is spoken, but have gone on to mold developing usage.

A further example for reflection might be the overlap between BD and Roland Barthes's system of connotations, one that is based upon Saussurean linguistics but then applied to modern social narratives. Barthes takes the *signe* formed by *signifiant* and *signifié* from the Saussurean linguistic level of expression, and uses this as the *signifiant* in the evolved social schema of *mythologies*, whereby a connotative *signifié* then produces the overall *signe* on this level of *mythe*. So for example the word "car"—Saussaurean *signifiant*—would indicate a four-wheeled motor vehicle—Saussurean *signifié*—with the two elements together forming the *signe*. But for Barthes this is then the *signifiant* whose connotative value in the case of the Citroën DS is that of power, aesthetic beauty, and sexual prowess, the image—mental or literal, imagined, photographed or drawn—of such attributes providing the *signifié* and creating the overall *signe*.

Barthes was fascinated by press cartoons, and the take on popular culture that he was to provide in *Mythologies*—although perhaps surprisingly no *bandes dessinées* were to figure among the final subjects—was later to be reflected in an icon of such popular culture, the *Astérix* series. In *Astérix et les Normands*, Goudurix, the young tearaway visiting family in the Gauls' village, drives a curvy souped-up chariot whose attributes remind us of Barthes's DS. *Astérix gladiateur* mocks the omnipresence of advertising with a break in the gladiatorial show to parade walk-on amphorae telling us "To forget

the worries of life in Antiquity. . . always drink. . . wine of authenticity" (*Pour oublier les soucis de la vie antique. . . buvez toujours. . . du
vin authentique*). Prior to the show, a salesman for "Super-Persique"
bawls "wash your togas with Super-Persique! Super-Persique washes
purpler than purple" (*laver vos toges avec Super-Persique! Super-
Persique lave encore plus pourpre*), a direct reference to the analysis
of connotative popular language in Barthes's "Soap-powders and De-
tergents" (*Saponides et détergents*).[22]

Above all, the process of reading that is inherent to comics is by
its very nature Saussurean. To understand Saussure—specifically to
understand that Saussure in his formative years was influenced by the
cultural assimilations we now associate with *bande dessinée*—is also
to understand comics themselves. At the base of the *Cours de linguistique générale*, from the third chapter on General Principles, Saussure
lays out the opposition between diachronic and synchronic studies,
but also the entwining of the two, represented in his famous schema
of two intersecting lines, the horizontal "axis of simultaneities" (*axe
des simultanéités*) from A to B, and the vertical "axis of successions"
(*axe des successivités*) from C to D. The latter diachronic approach
tells us the story of language in terms of how Latin became French in
its evolution from C to D, with movement being indicated in the diagram by arrowheads, whereas the synchronic approach, the flat line
covering A to B, gives a single viewpoint. Saussure explains as follows:

> Certainly all sciences would profit by indicating more precisely
> the co-ordinates along which their subject matter is aligned. Every-
> where distinctions should be made, according to the following illus-
> tration, between (1) *the axis of simultaneities* (AB), which stands for
> the relations of coexisting things and from which the intervention of
> time is excluded; and (2) *the axis of successions* (CD), on which only
> one thing can be considered at a time but upon which are located all
> the things on the first axis together with their changes. [. . .]
>
> The first thing that strikes us when we study the facts of lan-
> guage is that their succession in time does not exist insofar as the
> speaker is concerned. He is confronted with a state. That is why the
> linguist who wishes to understand a state must discard all knowledge

22. René Goscinny and Albert Uderzo, *Astérix et les Normands* (Paris: Dargaud,
1966) and *Astérix gladiateur* (Paris: Dargaud, 1964); Roland Barthes, *Mythologies* (Paris:
Pierres Vives, 1957). For further exploration of this topic see Laurence Grove, "*Bande
dessinée*: The Missing *Mythologie*," *Mythologies at 50: Barthes and Popular Culture*,
ed. Douglas Smith, *Nottingham French Studies* Special Number 47/2 (2008): 29–40.

of everything that produced it and ignore diachrony. He can enter the mind of speakers only by completely suppressing the past. The intervention of history can only falsify his judgment. It would be absurd to attempt to sketch a panorama of the Alps by viewing them simultaneously from several peaks of the Jura; a panorama must be made from a single vantage point. The same applies to language; the linguist can neither describe it not draw up standards of usage except by concentrating on one state. When he follows the evolution of the language, he resembles the moving observer who goes from one peak of the Jura to another in order to record the shifts in perspective.[23]

Similarly, the reading of a comic strip is diachronic, as one flips through an album from opening page to final banquet (in the case of *Astérix*), with evolution from page to page, but also from frame to frame. But comics are also synchronic, in that key scenes can be visibly static providing pleasure in the contemplation of a single image, as in the anachronistic view of Geneva in *Astérix chez les Helvètes* (Fig. 4).[24] Nonetheless, such an image is dependent on the narrative and its evolution—here the arrival of the Gauls after their journey—while being independent of it.

The overlap between a diachronic and a synchronic reading of comics and their cultural context is at the heart of the 2016 *Comic Invention* exhibition at the Hunterian Art Gallery in Glasgow (Fig. 5).[25] In it we present the misleading question of the world's first comic, showcasing the *Glasgow Looking Glass* of 1825 as victorious, juxtaposed with Töpffer's *Mr. Jabot* (1835) and its original manuscript (1833). But a timeline allows us to present graphic narrative chronologically from the Ancient Egyptians onwards, while contrasting themes in each object with original artwork by Frank Quitely (b. 1968), the Glasgow-based panjandrum of DC Comics, responsible for the current artwork, *inter alia*, of *X-Men*, *Batman* and *Superman*. The synchronic viewpoint is that the text/image mind-set of comics

23. Saussure, *Course in General Linguistics*, 79–80 and 81–82. The edition consulted for the original French version is Ferdinand de Saussure, *Cours de linguistique générale*, ed. Charles Bally, Albert Sechehaye, and Albert Riedlinger (Paris: Payot, 1968 [1916]). These passages appear on pages 115 and 117.

24. Goscinny and Uderzo, *Astérix chez les Helvètes* (Paris: Dargaud, 1970). The anachronistic image of Geneva is on page 24.

25. *Comic Invention*, Hunterian Art Gallery, Glasgow, 18 March to 17 July 2016. The accompanying box set is a collection of five publications with no set reading order, thereby avoiding the diachronic beginning and end of a conventional book: Laurence Grove and Peter Black, *Comic Invention*.

Fig. 4. René Goscinny and Albert Uderzo, *Astérix chez les Helvètes* (Paris: Dargaud, 1970), 24.

Fig. 5. Sha Nazir, *Two Hipsters in the Car*, 2016. Poster for *Comic Invention* exhibition, The Hunterian, Glasgow, 2016.

is all around us, as we display works by Picasso and Rembrandt next to, and on an equal footing with, others by Warhol and Lichtenstein, alongside Disney and further pieces by Frank Quitely.

Comic Invention provides a provocative out-of-the-box view on the culture of comics, spanning off from the *bandes dessinées* of Töpffer, and thriving on the diachronic/synchronic overlap that was the vision of the young Ferdinand de Saussure. And as we have seen, Saussure imitated his fellow Genevan in creating his own strips, which until now have gone almost entirely unnoticed.

What is the potential legacy of these strips? First of all, their discovery makes explicit the connection between Ferdinand de Saussure and the world of *bande dessinée*. Once the link is made, Saussurean linguistics take on new light both in terms of the text/image influences that led to their exposition, and the range of their contemporary impact.

Initially, the playful Töpfferian nature of the young Ferdinand's strips tells us that the influence of the nascent BD form was, whatever Töpffer himself might have imagined, well beyond anti-intellectual fantasy narratives for the amusement of children or possibly the vulgar masses. In Geneva at least, what we now see as the culture of the comic infiltrated the education and resulting mind-set of the elite from as far back as the mid-nineteenth century.

In turn, and perhaps most significantly, we might consider how modern critical theory can play on the inherent oppositions and interplays between the static and the linear, between what we see and how we receive what we see. Saussure was writing at the age of the rise of the image in a textual context. He plays on oppositions, often on what is implied rather than what is stated directly, on visual evocations that interact with word-based statements. His early comic strips bear the seeds of such thought (albeit perhaps unconsciously), and as such they now allow the reader-viewer of the twenty-first century to be more aware of the visual connections that are intrinsic to the foundations of some of our current critical givens.

II. Form and Genre

JAN BAETENS

The *Roman Dessiné*:
A Little-Known Genre

What might be the "box" outside of which it is now urgent to think comics? There are two good reasons to believe that comics is a "genre": first because genre is everywhere in comics, both production- and reception-wise, second because its presence is hardly noticed in comics theory, as demonstrated by the near-invisibility of the notion in the indices of major comics studies.[1]

In literary theory, genre is a classic, long-standing issue, and one that is here to stay. Whatever approach to a definition one adopts, there will probably never be a final answer to the many questions raised by genre theory. At the same time, the fundamental openness of genre debates is never a pretext simply to drop a notion whose inevitable usefulness is recognized by all those involved in writing and reading. Whatever the status of this notion and the difficulty of matching satisfactorily the unequal domain of genre (as a taxonomic category) and works (as concrete items), we simply need genres when making or reading creative pieces.

Although hardly debated in comics theory, genre is, in practice, a tool that is present in most discussions in the field. Centering on a very specific genre or subgenre, the *drawn novel*—distinct from the broader *bande dessinée* and once very popular, but now virtually unknown—the present essay aims not only to fill a gap in comics

1. Good examples of this are the two landmark theoretical publications by Thierry Groensteen, currently the best-known and most-quoted scholar in the field: *The System of Comics* (Jackson: University Press of Mississippi, 2007 [1999]) refers only twice, and in extremely general terms, to "genre," whereas *Comics and Narration* (Jackson: University Press of Mississippi, 2013 [2011]) does not list it in the index. Genre issues are however discussed with great acumen by Groensteen in these and other publications. Genre is there, but symptomatically below the radar, so to speak.

YFS 131/132, Bande Dessinée: *Thinking Outside the Boxes*, ed. Laurence Grove and Michael Syrotinski, © 2017 by Yale University.

studies in particular, but also to make a contribution to genre theory in graphic storytelling in general.

GENEALOGY OF A GENRE:
FORM, FUNCTION, FORMAT

The short-lived *roman dessiné* or *drawn novel* (the terminology varies from one source to another) is a lesser known chapter of the history of comics. It was extremely popular in the postwar era (its heyday was, roughly speaking, during the period 1946 to 1950), but at the end of the next decade it had virtually disappeared, with its last examples published in 1963. This particular genre is considered nowadays to be the missing link between the classic forms of the *film novel*—whose first forms appeared in the 1910s and 20s—and the *photo novel*, which was launched almost overnight in 1947, and most studies on the *drawn novel* will be found in the context of photo narrative rather than that of comics, as will be detailed below.[2]

From a genre theoretical point of view, the *roman dessiné* seems to be an easy option: there is a clear match between the name of the genre (never a detail!) and the corpus that illustrates it, while the limits that separate the *drawn novel* from other genres look quite clear: it is not possible, for instance, to confuse the *roman dessiné*, the *film novel*, and the *photo novel*. Yet things become more complicated once the genre is framed in the larger story and context of comics.[3] Here, all the traditional problems associated with genre studies arise immediately. What is the *drawn novel*, and even more importantly: what is it not? Where and when does it begin and where does it end? Is there something like a set of specific features and how necessary are they to the genre? How might we link genre and medium? What about hybrid or transmedial forms, if there are any? And how might

2. For more general information on the relationship between the *drawn novel* and the *photo novel*, see Sylvette Giet, *Nous deux 1947–1997: Apprendre la langue du coeur* (Leuven and Paris: Peeters and Vrin, 1998); Jan Baetens, *Pour le roman-photo* (Brussels: Les impressions nouvelles, 2010) and Marion Minuit, Dominique Faber, and Bruno Takodjerad, *Nous deux: La saga du roman-photo* (Paris: J.C. Gawsewitch, 2012). The use throughout of italics for *drawn novel*, *film novel* and *photo novel* is to emphasize their status in this context as a single semantic unit.

3. To use the notion of "graphic novel" would be an anachronism, and for this reason it will not appear in this study.

we envisage its relationships with non-visual counterparts, such as the literary material it allegedly adapts?

When a new genre appears (or a new medium—and this distinction is much more than just a semantic one), the classic way of reading is *genealogical.* One tries to construct or reconstruct where the genre *comes from* and how it *evolves,* even within cultural practices such as film that do not rely for their genre classification upon classic, Aristotelian categories and subcategories.[4] But how does such a genealogical approach work in practice?

Since absolute novelty is always an illusion, genealogists will analyze first which transformations of existing forms and practices have eventually produced the genre in question. Given our strong disbelief in any essential forms or formats, we easily accept nowadays that such a genre is to a certain extent always a hybrid (some would even say "impure") construction or even reconstruction. "Remediation" theory by Jay David Bolter and Richard Grusin is one of the conceptual frameworks that is often used nowadays to help understand medium and genre innovation in terms of adaptation,[5] merger, repurposing, and conflict, but there are of course many others.[6]

Secondly, a genealogical analysis aims also at understanding how the genre is institutionalized, and it is now commonly agreed that such institutionalization may be a long and complex process. In this respect, one should bring to the fore the idea of "second birth," a notion coined by André Gaudreault and Philippe Marion in their attempt to rethink genre and medium history.[7] The "second birth" theory stresses the distance between the emergence of a new form

4. Rick Altman, *Film/Genre* (London: BFI, 1999), is the best exemplification of this stance. In francophone scholarship, one should add here the book by Raphaëlle Moine, *Les genres du cinéma* (Paris: Colin, 2005), whose position is quite close to that of Altman.

5. Jay David Bolter and Richard Grusin, *Remediation: Understanding New Media* (Cambridge, Mass.: MIT Press, 1999).

6. Among many other examples, one might quote here: *Adaptations* (New York: Routledge, 2000), ed. Deborah Cartmell and Lisa Wehelan; Dominique Kalifa, *La culture de masse en France: Tome 1, 1860–1930* (Paris: La Découverte, 2001); Michael Punt, "Image, Light and the Passage to the Semi-Material Object," in *Light, Image, Imagination,* ed. Martha Blassnigg (Amsterdam: Amsterdam University Press, 2013), 193–214.

7. See their seminal article "Un média naît toujours deux fois . . . ," *Société & Représentations* 9 (2000): 21–36, and their subsequent book publication *The Kinematic Turn: Film in the Digital Era and its Ten Problems* (Montreal: Kino-Agora, 2012).

and its eventual integration and institutionalization within a given yet always changing mediascape. The notion of "second birth" refers thus to the fact that a genre or medium, or form or format, can only succeed *eventually*, after finding a place in a larger cultural, social, and economic context. This larger context may be that, for instance, of the medium's "expanded field," to use the term suggested by Rosalind Krauss in her study of sculpture between landscape and architecture.[8] No genre or medium stands on its own and its institutionalization is always the result of an interaction with its environment.

Third and finally, a genealogical analysis will often make certain claims on the contribution of the new form or genre to the possibilities, challenges, limits, or constraints of the medium that helps outline and materialize the genre. Innovations shape and reshape what is easy or difficult, possible or impossible, interesting or not within a certain practice. Here one meets inevitably the age-old debate on medium-specificity, a position both contested and maintained in contemporary debates on media.[9] Genealogy is never just a matter of history; it always entails an aesthetic and therefore philosophical dimension.

A good example of such a genealogy is the traditional vision of cinema as *narrative cinema*. It takes at its starting point the appearance of a new technology that gradually discloses and strengthens its most appropriated functions and format, which have to do with storytelling, while marginalizing at the same time, and for the same reason, other possibilities, until the moment when it is fully, and apparently definitively, institutionalized as *narrative cinema*. The adjective "narrative" is then a quasi-pleonastic accompaniment to the noun "cinema"—and vice versa: filmic or visual narrative is then seen as "automatically" more efficient than verbal narrative.

It seems logical at first sight to make a genealogical analysis of the *drawn novel*, of which we are reproducing two examples here: the first pages of the work that launched the genre, *Âmes ensorcelées*,[10]

---

8. Rosalind Krauss, "Sculpture in the Expanded Field," *October* 8 (Spring 1979): 30–44.

9. See Noel Carroll, *Theorizing the Moving Image* (New York: Oxford University Press, 1994) and Lev Manovich , *The Language of New Media* (Cambridge, Mass.: MIT Press, 2000) for examples of differing positions, with Carroll critical of medium-specificity, but Manovich in favor of it.

10. *Âmes ensorcelées* is the French translation of *Anime incatenate*, serialized in the Italian magazine *Grand Hôtel* in 1946. There are three French editions: the serial

Fig. 1. M. Dukey and J. W. Symes, "Âmes ensorcelées," *Nous deux* 1 (1947), 1.

Fig. 2. Christian Gérard, *3 belles et un garçon* (Paris: Éditions de la Flamme d'Or, 1953).

and the opening pages of *3 belles et un garcon*[11] (Figs. 1 and 2), which illustrate the more "exploitative" side of the genre. A typical example of mass-media genre and media hybridization, as indeed were the "instanagazines" that first specialized in the genre, these were an instant hit. The *drawn novel* catered to a new public—female adults, a hitherto less targeted audience in comics—and it did so in a new publication format, that of the "true confessions" magazines, copied from American models of the 1920s and '30s.

Since the 1920s, various forms of "genre fiction" in comics—the adventure comic à la *Terry and the Pirates*, the science fiction comic à la *Flash Gordon*, the jungle comic à la *Tarzan*, for instance—had been aimed at special niche audiences, but none of these was specifically aimed at a female audience, the rise of romance comics being subsequent to that of the *drawn novel*, with the eponymous flagship series by Joe Simon and Jack Kirby only starting in 1947.[12] In addition, the novelty of the publication format was equally important, since the comics found in the "true confessions" women's *magazines*, already present in Europe in the late 1930s, broke away from those found in the comic *strips* in dailies and weeklies, as well as those of the comic *books* specializing in superhero stories, crime fiction, and horror tales. From the very beginning, the *drawn novel* genre was recognized as something radically new, as can be inferred from its marked success in leading magazines such as *Grand Hôtel* in Italy and *Nous deux* in France.[13] In other words, it was the encounter between a certain type of storytelling, a certain type of publishing, and a certain type of public, that made possible the almost instantaneous yet, as we will see, less than robust institutionalization of the genre. Very soon, the *drawn novel* section of the true confessions women's magazines was to condemn other sections—short stories, true stories, serialized novels, letters to the editors, reportages—to a more peripheral position. However, if the drawn novel could kill off such rivals for page space, it proved to be a very short-lived killer.

---

published by the magazine *Nous deux* in 1947; the reissue as a separate volume by *Nous deux Éditions* (Paris) in 1948 (this is the edition that is quoted here); and, still by *Nous deux Éditions*, a colorized version in 2010.

11. Published in 1953 by Éditions de la Flamme d'Or (Paris).

12. Charles Hatfield, *Hand of Fire: The Comics Art of Jack Kirby* (Jackson: University Press of Mississippi, 2012).

13. In its first years *Nous deux* contained mainly French translations of Italian originals, but very soon the journal would launch its own series and artwork.

As is the case for many genres in the field of popular culture, there is little explicit contemporaneous critical discussion, but later analyses were to put strong emphasis on how the *drawn novel* made an innovative contribution to aspects of page composition, rhythm, point of view, and general storytelling in the field of comics.[14] The *drawn novel* appeared thus as a comic story with a (big) difference, one that highlighted by contrast the relative poverty of mainstream comic publishing of the period. It stretched the limits of comics, thematically as well as formally, while opening out to new niche audiences.

If one defines a medium not just in terms of channel and transmission technology but as the complex interaction of 1) a certain type of sign, 2) content and subject matter, and 3) a certain support or host medium,[15] then it is possible to circumscribe the *drawn novel* accordingly.

As far as the *sign structure* is concerned, the major changes are at least threefold. Firstly, the drawings claim implicitly to adapt a photographical and cinematographic intertext: their lavishly executed style imitates the aura of glamour photography and the black and white lighting aesthetics of the Hollywood studio system. Secondly, the technique is not that of the ink drawings familiar to the comics industry, but rather that of the wash drawings (*dessin au lavis*) more characteristic of press illustrations, wherein in hindsight it is possible to recognize a black and white precursor of what Thierry Groensteen will identify around 1990 as the "direct color" aesthetics that blurs the boundaries between drawing, inking, and colorizing.[16] Thirdly, the panel and page composition, although not always as original, is very different from the comics model, and borrows many elements from the typographical and visual design experiments of photographically illustrated press.[17]

14. See Giet, *Nous deux 1947–1997: Apprendre la langue du coeur.*

15. For a more theoretical discussion of these issues, see Stanley Cavell, *The World Viewed: Enlarged Edition* (Cambridge, Mass.: Harvard University Press, 1979), 101–108; Diarmuid Costello, "Automat, Automatic, Automatism: Rosalind Krauss and Stanley Cavell on Photography and the Photographically Dependent Arts," *Critical Inquiry* 38/4 (2012): 819–54, which contains full bibliographical references to all relevant publications pertaining to our discussion.

16. *Couleur directe/Direct Color*, ed. Groensteen (Thurn: Kunst der Comics, 1993). This work is the catalogue of an exhibition for the Hamburg Comics Convention.

17. See Danielle Leenaerts, *Petite histoire du magazine Vu (1928–1940): Entre photographie d'information et photographie d'art* (Brussels: Peter Lang, 2010).

These visual innovations fully match the no less important shifts in *subject matter*, which can be described on two levels. On the first level, it is clear that the link with cinema is stylistic as well as thematic: there exists an almost seamless transition from film to *drawn novel*. What does the latter borrow (and steal) from the former? Everything, ranging from storyline to decor, from erotic and risqué imagery to upper-class fantasies, from dialogue to the signs of luxury and exoticism that appealed so strongly to the poverty-stricken audiences in postwar Italy and France. On another level, and more importantly perhaps, the *drawn novel*'s subject matter combines the rules of the generically pre-determined Hollywood productions. All *drawn novels* are melodramas, although this equivalence is by no means a rigid one,[18] and what is most striking is the mix of melodrama and detective fiction, on the one hand, and more or less covert eroticism, on the other. The influence of *noir* cinema is unmistakable.

Thirdly and finally, the *drawn novel*'s visual and thematic characteristics would have remained unsuccessful or uneventful had they not interacted with the third pillar of any medium definition, namely the *host medium*, which covers a wide set of parameters, ranging from publication format to publication policy and culture. What is new in the *drawn novel* is neither the idea of serialization nor that of a niche audience, but the dynamic twist given to "niche serialization" thanks to a format that allows for, on the one hand, tabularity (the serial is not a daily or weekly *strip*, but a number of *pages*) and on the other, chapter structure (the serial is no longer a succession of small units cum cliffhangers, but larger sections allowing for less linear narratives). Moreover, the contrast between the highly innovative *drawn novel* and the less surprising, even worn-out genres and formats that complement it between the covers of the women's magazines, can only underline the qualities of the new (the *drawn novel*) in contrast to the old (the literary melodrama installments).

DRAWN NOVELS, PHOTO NOVELS: BOUNDARIES, FAMILY RESEMBLANCES, CONFUSIONS

Obviously it is possible to analyze the shift from the *roman dessiné* to a new genre, the *photo novel*, in a genealogical perspective, provided one manages to fine-tune the description of the genre's transformation

18. See Altman, *Film/Genre*, and Moine, *Les genres du cinéma*.

within a framework that is oriented toward the medium's complexity. Genealogy builds a strong story, but its over-simplistic nature can be problematic, and it can include problematic elements. One may wonder for instance why the *drawn novel* is almost absent from the study and history of comics. Even if this history still has many other lacunae,[19] the near-invisibility of the *drawn novel* remains intriguing. By extension, one can ask whether the genealogical presentation of the *drawn novel* does not suffer as a result of a linear and teleological approach to the medium of comics, whose history does not really fit the schema of a "young" form growing into adulthood.[20] Last but not least, one may also wonder what happened with respect to the broader historical and cultural context, which only appears as a backdrop in the perhaps exaggeratedly mono-medial definition of the *drawn novel* as outlined above. A more sophisticated approach is necessary, which stresses not only the permanent internal changes and updates, but also the relationships with other media and the exchanges with the broader cultural and historical context.

The most salient feature of the *drawn novel* in this respect, both as an object and as a cultural practice, is obviously its close relationship to the *photo novel*. Our idea of what a *drawn novel* is depends largely on our idea of what a *photo novel* is, as if the *drawn novel* were nothing other than a *proto-photo novel*. Both media practices have been, at certain moments in time, not only competitors but almost twins. Both coexisted within the same cultural space, copying each other's form and content and vying for the same audience. It is this complex relationship, among other elements, that may explain why the genealogical approach misses its target, and lacks nuance and depth.

If the *drawn novel*'s institutionalization was almost instantaneous, it was nonetheless precarious, since the genre was to be challenged almost immediately by a major competitor, the *photo novel*, that appeared within a year. As such, the birth of the genre coincided almost immediately with its decline. The success of the *photo novel* dealt a blow to the *drawn novel*, which soon disappeared from women's

19. See for instance the material gathered by Dan Nadel in *Art Out of Time: Unknown Comics Visionaries, 1900–1969* (New York: Abrams, 2006).

20. Comics did not have to await their "adulthood" before producing masterpieces, such as those written and drawn by Rodophe Töpffer, Gustave Doré, Winsor Mcay, or George Herriman. Some media theorists, among them Stanley Cavell in *World Viewed*, defend similar positions.

magazines. *L'amorosa menzogna* (1949), a short documentary by Michelangelo Antonioni about the market for women's magazines in Italy, put it bluntly: the days of the *drawn novel* were over, Antonioni claimed, as it was now the *photo novel* that was all the rage.[21]

The reasons for this decline were economic, and related to cost-efficiency and Taylorized production rhythms. It was simply much easier and cheaper to produce *photo novels* than to create the equivalent number of drawn pages,[22] and from 1950 onwards the decline of the genre was inevitable. The two leading magazines, *Grand Hôtel* and *Nous deux*, that had until then resisted the attacks of the new *photo novel* journals, started publishing *photo novels* themselves, hence reducing the available space for the *drawn novel*, which would disappear completely by the end of the decade.

Initially the radical differences between the two were not clearly understood, with Antonioni's documentary insisting on the continuity between *drawn novel* and *photo novel*, as the same genre, but with different means of production.[23] Such blurring of boundaries has to be taken very literally: *drawn novels*, which claim to be adaptations of (non-existing) novels, present pictures with the intention of being seen as imitations of film stills, whereas in *photo novels*, the page composition and printing techniques, which were often poor and hardly sufficient to reflect the indexical sharpness of the photographic images, were intended to stress their proximity with the highly popular *drawn novel*. Thereafter, the two genres were to split: the *photo novel* was to develop its own standards, and become a highly standardized product, whereas the *drawn novel* would stick to its own principles, and vanish.

The intertwining of *drawn novel* and *photo novel* opens up a complex field of interrelationships that in many respects exceeds the classic genealogical approach, encouraging us to ask new and different

21. The film can be accessed via youtube: http://www.youtube.com/watch?v =1oMv4uIVNIs.

22. On the economic aspects of the competition between *drawn novel* and *photo novel*, see Minuit et al, *Nous deux*.

23. Cf. *L'amorosa menzogna*. But we should add that the same applies to the *photo novel* itself, which is often confused with a movie: see Fedrico Fellini's representation of the making of a *photo novel* in *The White Sheik* (1951), where the shooting of a *photo novel* has the trappings of that of a film rather than that of a *photo novel*. See Baetens, "The Photo-Novel: Stereotype as Surprise," *History of Photography* 37/2 (2013), 137–52.

questions inspired by a point of view that is no longer genealogical but archeological, in the Foucauldian sense of the word as applied to film history by Thomas Elsaesser, for instance. Taking the limits of the genealogical analysis of cinema as his point of departure, Elsaesser identifies a credo implicit in the following analysis in *Archaeology of Knowledge*:[24] "Archaeology does not imply the search for a beginning. [. . .] (It) questions the already-said at the level of existence [. . .] and it describes discourses as practices."[25] Elsaesser derives a threefold approach that aims to rethink the evolution of media in film studies: 1) instead of searching for an origin, one should study the fact that cinema has several origins, coming from several media; 2) instead of studying the history of cinema as a chain of units, one should map it as a network disclosing new but less foregrounded aspects; 3) instead of seeing the study of cinema as a mere description or reflection of a given corpus and a given practice, one should consider that a film studies archaeology produces a new vision of the medium and its relationships to other media, for example through the study of those forms of cinema that never enjoyed widespread success, or are no longer used.

Elsaesser's plea for a way of reading focuses on gaps, discontinuities, lacunae, and absences in order to elaborate different ways of writing history, leading him, for instance, to analyze the current hype of 3D cinema as an epiphenomenon of shifts in *sound* technology.[26] It is a perspective that echoes similar orientations and sensibilities within literary history as well as media history. Examples include William Marx's critique of linearity and teleology, as well as the rewriting of history's irrecoverable past by contemporary interrogations in various contributions that have put notions such as "arrière-garde" and the past's opacity on the research agenda.[27] For the comics field itself, Thierry Smolderen's related hypotheses and observations clear the

---

24. Michel Foucault, *The Archeology of Knowledge* (London: Routledge, 2002 [1969]).

25. Quoted in Thomas Elsaesser, "Early Film Theory and Multi-Media: An Archaeology of Possible Futures?," in *New media, Old Media: A History and Theory Reader*, ed. Wendy Hui Kyong Chun and Thomas Kennan (New York: Routledge, 2006), 17.

26. Thomas Elsaesser, "The 'Return' of 3-D: On Some of the Logics and Genealogies of the Image in the Twenty-First Century," *Critical Inquiry* 39/2 (2013): 217–46.

27. *Les arrière-gardes au XXe siècle*, ed. William Marx (Paris: PUF, 2009 [2004]), and MDRN, *Modern Times, Literary Change* (Leuven: Peeters, 2013).

way for a reading of this medium as a polygraphic—a term that one can read as the graphic, visual equivalent of Bakthine's notion of polyphony—dialogue with the visual and literary culture of its times.[28]

TOWARD AN ARCHAEOLOGICAL APPROACH

The analysis of the *drawn novel* can also benefit greatly from the shift from genealogy to archaeology. If we follow the research agenda set out by Elsaesser, it is possible to put aside concerns on origins: who was the first to come up with the idea of the *drawn novel*?; who was the first to produce one?; who first published a *drawn novel* before all others?; where might we place analogous experiments in other fields? Likewise such an approach can nullify questions on how the *drawn novel* superseded comics, before being superseded itself by the newer *photo novel*. Instead, archaeology helps envision the *drawn novel* as a format that has multiple histories, for instance as a hybrid verbo-visual practice that can be seen both as a medium and a genre. As a medium, it belongs to the field of comics, of which it offers a special generic actualization (the melodrama). As a genre, it belongs to the field of melodrama, of which it offers a special mediatization (comics).

This mutual inclusion of genre and medium should not come as a surprise. On the one hand, medium as channel or support is part of any definition of genre: a genre combines semantic and syntactic features, but in terms of its medium, it is never neutral. On the other hand, genre as a subject matter category is part of any definition of medium: a medium is, as Stanly Cavell has shown, the automatic alliance of sign structures, subject matter, and technological support. The *drawn novel* is neither a medium nor a genre, it is both, and one that can twist like a Moebius strip from one aspect to another. This reciprocal containment may encourage us to disentangle medium from genre, but from an archaeological point of view it is more promising to accept this complexity and to use it as a point of departure for a new reflection on the *drawn novel*'s heterogeneity.

The intersection and partial overlap of genre and medium jeopardizes the homogeneous structure of either notion, both internally and externally. In the first case, that of internal heterogeneity, both

28. Thierry Smolderen, *Naissances de la bande dessinée* (Brussels: Les Impressions Nouvelles, 2009).

genre and medium prove to be a mix of (more or less) specific and (more or less) non-specific elements. It is of course this mix that explains why cross-mediality or cross-genericity is always possible, though never easy. Each genre or medium can be adapted into another genre or medium, but this adaptation is never a mechanical or neutral operation. In the second case, that of external heterogeneity, all genres and media, even those that might crave specificity and uniqueness, are always open to other genres and media. This is what happens with the *drawn novel*, whose handmade images dramatically imitate the visual poetics of the film still and glamour photography. The same process applies to the "competing" *photo novel*, whose machine-made images inevitably imitate the page layout of the *drawn novel*.

In a different register, that of the genre rather than that of the medium, the same logic can be observed when the melodrama of the *drawn novel* and, to a lesser extent, the *photo novel* is completed, troubled, and eventually displaced by, for example, crime fiction or detective stories. It is possible to transfer this interpretation of the *drawn novel* in particular to comics in general. Here as well, it is often difficult to ascertain where one form begins and another ends. Where do press cartoons end and comics begin, for instance? Are abstract comics another form of comics or are they actually paintings? Is Lichtenstein a visual artist or a comics artist? Are Tijuana bibles comics or pornographic drawings? Is graphic production studied as "direct color" an example of comics, or rather something else such as landscape painting or poster art?[29]

A second aspect of archeological research aims to criticize commonplaces that are applied to a given genre or medium. In the case of the *drawn novel*, what we know in general points to the following three characteristics: 1) it is a form of *storytelling*; 2) it illustrates the world of *melodrama*; 3) it is a work of *fiction*. But all these claims are open to debate.

That the *drawn novel* is a narrative form cannot be denied. Yet the observation that a medium or genre contains a mix of specific and less specific elements allows for alternative readings. In a sense, these new readings are all applications of the Derridean principle of

29. See Groensteen, *Couleur directe*.

the *parergon*, whereby what appears to be a detail is less a supplement than something that might represent the secret or hidden core of a given work or practice.[30] The *drawn novel* is not entirely devoted to storytelling as it contains multiple other aspects, such as the focus on the body, male as well as female, which in certain sections occupies the full attention of the reader, regardless of its contribution to the unfolding of the storyline. This body, moreover, is not always a body in motion, as one would expect in comics where the need to suggest movement through fixed images is a key feature, but a body adopting certain, often very clichéd poses, which increase the gap between the body as spectacle, as object of an eroticized gaze, and the body as a carrier agency for narrative information. Finally, the body is not infrequently divided, one may even say disintegrated, into body parts, which may generate other non-narrative meanings and ways of reading. The example of the *drawn novel* makes clear that the opposing term to "narrative" is not, as is often argued, "abstraction," a simplification that in the field of comics has become a stereotype.[31]

The *drawn novel* is clearly not a form of abstract comics, but it does exemplify another strand of non-narrativity, which is *non-sequentiality*, and given the importance in comics studies of the concept of "linearity" versus "tabularity," this is far from being a detail. The emphasis on the body, but also on the creation of a specific way of looking at the body, on the one hand detaches certain images from the narrative flow, while on the other reduces the need to read the images in a precise sequential arrangement. The highlighting of the body and the preference given to pose rather than to motion reshuffle the page-composition at the moment of reading and foreground a type of non-sequentiality that challenges the basic rules of visual storytelling.[32] In a *drawn novel*, linearity and sequentiality are present, but other reading paths are also instigated as the temporal structure of reading a *drawn novel* is definitely not that of watching a movie.

30. See Jacques Derrida, *The Truth in Painting*, trans. Geoff Bennington and Ian McLeod (Chicago: University of Chicago Press, 1987).
31. See *Abstract Comics*, ed. Andrei Molotiu (Seattle: Fantagrapics, 2009), and Baetens, "Abstraction in Comics," *SubStance* 40/1 (2011): 94–113.
32. On the role of tableau and pose in melodrama, see Peter Brooks, *The Melodramatic Imagination* (New Haven, CT: Yale University Press, 1976).

This intertwining of sequentiality and non-sequentiality does not however mean that the story is absent from the *drawn novel*, quite the contrary. Since the *drawn novel*'s melodramas are variations on traditional subject matter, the story it tells is often already known by the reader, who is aware in advance of what is about to happen. The new elements of the plot, the variations on the age-old canvas, are told by the text, which one reads sequentially, and not by the images, which can be read in a number of possible orders. The intertwining in question means instead that narrative and storytelling are not necessarily the core values of the *drawn novel*. In other words, attention should equally be placed elsewhere, *viz* the fascination with the sexualized body.

A second general claim made with respect to the *drawn novel* is that it belongs to the world of melodrama, more specifically to the subculture of women's comics, a term coined by analogy with the no less stereotypical qualification of the filmic melodrama as women's movies or weepies. Here as well, the archaeological insistence on the *drawn novel*'s heterogeneity helps put into question a number of strongly gender-biased ideas on the relationships between content, style, and readership. It is not enough, however, to suggest that the *drawn novel* was read also by men, although certain surveys of women's magazines give the staggering figure of 41% male readers.[33] There is direct and indirect historical evidence for this claim, as provided for instance by art-historical and sociological research on the reception of the melodrama in the postwar period.[34]

What is needed here is also internal, textual evidence, as can be inferred from the content and form of the *drawn novels* themselves. From this point of view it appears that the naïve gendering of the *drawn novel* as a hyper-feminine and tear-jerking form of melodrama is misleading. There may even be a mismatch between the imagined audience—100% female, with all the clichés brought by traditional visions of womanhood—and what the *drawn novel* is actually doing as a visual artifact. True, the dominant mode is the melodrama,

33. See Isabelle Antonutti, *Cino Del Duca: De Tarzan à Nous deux, itinéraire d'un patron de presse* (Rennes: PU Rennes, 2012), in particular 106 ff. Antonutti refers in particular to the sociological study by Evelyne Sullerot, *La presse féminine* (Paris: Armand Colin, 1965).

34. Many detailed and first-hand testimonies are given by Emiliano Morreale in his book *Così piangevano: Il cinema meló nell'Italia dagli anni cinquanta* (Roma: Donzelli, 2011).

however that term may be defined, but it is a *melodrama-plus*, a melodrama enriched and transformed by a number of twists and singularities that address a different readership. Firstly, the eroticization of the male and female body as mentioned, but also, and perhaps more importantly, a hint of violence and, above all, a dramatically developed play upon narrative pace. The nail-biting rhythm of certain *drawn novels* in undeniable, but should be noted in the context of the fact that classic melodramas in the tradition of Alexandre Dumas are known page-turners, and often such weekly installments contain as many dramatic events as a whole novel. Speed, violence, sexuality, and of course the fascination with the representation of modern technology—protagonists have professions such as aviator and engineer—all seem to appeal also to a male audience. Or they at least shatter the naïve belief in the *drawn novel* as a cultural practice catering to the needs of a certain type of non-emancipated women. Melodrama becomes once again what it has been at various points of its history: another word for action-driven and fast-forward storytelling, closer to what we today define as "hard-boiled" than to Jane Austen.

Thirdly and finally, awareness of the *drawn novel*'s internal tensions also brings to the fore its nonfictional elements, which are often discarded as the ultimate example of unrealistic escapism. What strikes in the *drawn novel*'s subject matter is the dominating presence of history and daily life. *Drawn novels* can be read as portraits of an era, or even as documenting mental and ideological representations. The supposed first example of the *drawn novel*, *Anime incatenate* (*Souls in Chains*), whose success was to make it a model for ensuing publications, is among many other things a study of the European perception of America, a hotly debated issue given the clash between the fascination with US science, technology, way of life, and culture (or the lack thereof), on the one hand, and deeply rooted suspicion, on the other. Most remarkable in this regard is the philo-American stance of *Souls in Chains*. This was allegedly an adaptation of an American novel (in fact nonexistent) with claims of its having already been translated into eight languages, but presented with gravitas to the reader via the representation of America as the site of modernity and success, in the prewar sequences as well as in those situated during and after the War. The primary storyline of *Souls in Chains* begins just before the War and ends during the Liberation. In France, where the translation of this *drawn novel* was a smash hit, this philo-Americanism stood as an important ideological statement in the immediate aftermath of the Allied liberation, an event that, paradoxically, had in fact only sharpened anti-US feelings.[35]

In order better to understand the presence of the "real" (documentary, reportage, current events) within the fortress of escapism and exoticism that the *drawn novel* continues to represent in the mind of many scholars, it can be useful to remind ourselves of the distinction in English-language criticism between two types of fiction: the *novel*, which foregrounds realism, and the *romance*, which is based on the internal verisimilitude within a given fictional universe.[36] The *drawn novel*'s melodrama is definitely not, as is often too hastily stated, "romance only"; it is a cultural form torn between novel and romance, and this duality undermines the conventional view of the melodrama as pure fantasy. In the postwar years of great political and social tensions (including many forms of ethnic cleansing), the *drawn novel* reflects no less the will to represent the real than the desire to flee from it. The *drawn novel* is mind-numbing day-dreaming as much as it is eye-opening social testimony.

The last strand of archaeological inquiry as sketched by Elsaesser orients us toward the reading of genre and formats as discourses. This discursive approach implies the shift from an *essential* view—what is a medium, what is a genre?—to a functional or *functionalist* view: what do media and genres do, what is their impact on the cultural field when they are used as communicative tools in the ongoing dialogue between encoding and decoding? Rather than representing a certain state of affairs, discourses are structures that are being made, that are discussed, imposed, contested in particular contexts. In that sense, discourses are related to agency, and their value is less descriptive than performative or, if one prefers a more traditional term, rhetorical. Such a view on cultural practices as discourses has become increasingly important in recent research. It underlies for instance the genre theory defended by Rick Altman and many others today, who add a pragmatic dimension to the classic analysis of genre in terms of mere syntax and semantics. More generally, the same view is also the foundation of many theories of culture. Promoting the idea

35. See the landmark publication by Philippe Roger, *The American Enemy*, trans. Sharon Bowman (Chicago: Chicago University Press, 2006 [2002]).

36. For a broader discussion of this distinction within the larger field of popular literature in the French context, see Matthieu Letourneux , *Le roman d'aventures* (Limoges: PULIM, 2010).

of culture as rhetoric, Michael Carrithers argues, for instance, that culture—the way in which we use stories, images, metaphors, myths, and so on—is not only a passive representation of a world view, but an active attempt to make sense of what disrupts our normal way of being in the world.[37] The *drawn novel* as genre or medium can therefore be seen as a form of rhetoric. The very act of using, naming, applying, changing, forging something like the *drawn novel* is a way of voicing a fascination with modernity, even if the *drawn novel* itself is not new at all: comics, melodrama, film, serialization, true confessions, all of these already existed. The making of a genre, and the subsequent use of a genre label, are a way of culturally, medially, shaping an answer to what Carrithers calls the "vicissitudes of life." It is, in other words, less an event in itself than a way of trying to make sense of what is really an event, namely of something that disrupts the habitual paradigms.[38] Defining culture as discourse, as rhetoric, is not a way of dehistoricizing it, but of offering a new historical reading that exceeds the constraints of genealogy proper.

37. *Culture, Rhetoric, and the Vicissitudes of Life*, ed. Michale Carrithers (Oxford: Berghahn, 2009).

38. On the notion of "event," see François Dosse, *Renaissance de l'événement* (Paris: PUF, 2010).

CATHERINE LABIO

The Inherent Three-Dimensionality of Comics

The history of comics is inseparable from the history of its publication formats. In English, the term "comics" refers, depending on the context, to a global, intermedial genre, or its North American variant, or specific formats such as the newspaper strip or the comic book. In French, the term *"bande dessinée"* can mean comics in general, or the Franco-Belgian tradition and its sphere of influence in particular, or, within that tradition, a distinctive publication format: the approximately 30 × 23 cm (12 × 9 inch), 48 – 64 page, color, hardcover *album*. Initially an offshoot of Hergé's codification of *Les aventures de Tintin*, the *album* played a significant role in giving *bande dessinée* its distinct identity in the decades following World War II and contributed to the success of the genre. By the late 1970s, however, *bande dessinée*'s popularity was at a low ebb. A number of authors saw the almost universal imposition of the standard *album* by a handful of mainstream presses as both a symptom and a cause of *bande dessinée*'s decline. In response to these authors, large publishing houses launched more experimental periodicals and imprints. This was not enough, however, to stem the tide of the genre's decline or to answer the demands for greater creative freedom. In the 1990s authors started a number of independent presses.[1] These included, most famously, the Paris-based L'association, launched in 1990, which made it its

1. See Ann Miller, *Reading* Bande Dessinée: *Critical Approaches to French-Language Comic Strip* (Bristol: Intellect Books, 2007), 33–70; Bart Beaty, *Unpopular Culture: Transforming the European Comic Book in the 1990s* (Toronto: University of Toronto Press, 2007); and *La bande dessinée en dissidence: Alternative, indépendance, auto-édition/Comics in Dissent: Alternative, Independence, Self-Publishing*, ed. Christophe Dony, Tanguy Habrand, and Gert Meesters (Liège: Presses universitaires de Liège, 2014).

YFS 131/132, Bande Dessinée: *Thinking Outside the Boxes*, ed. Laurence Grove and Michael Syrotinski, © 2017 by Yale University.

84

mission to abandon the "48CC" publishing standard (48CC stands for 48 pages, in color, and *cartonné*, namely, hardbound).[2] Its books were emphatically of varying lengths and sizes. Drawings were in black and white. Covers were soft.

Jettisoning the 48CC standard that had become synonymous with *bande dessinée* became a defining feature of the 1990s small press movement. As a result, a basic tenet of the Brussels-based collective Frémok (FRMK), created in 2002 following a merger of the Belgian and French publishers Fréon and Amok, which had both been launched in the early 1990s, is that each book be "a true art object, singular and unique."[3] Its experimental and affordable Flore series consists of relatively small (20.5 × 13.5 cm), softcover, intimate, and poetically allusive booklets, some four-color, some not, that draw on traditional printmaking techniques. In contrast, Paz Boïra's *Ces leurres et autres nourritures terrestres/These Lures and Other Nourishments*, a one-off co-published by FRMK and Le signe noir in 2008, looks like a small sketchbook (12 × 17 cm); it is bound by a hard cover that imitates leather binding with gold-leaf embossing, and these design decisions were well suited to a wordless sequence of red, green, and blue single-page watercolors that evoke the watery origins of the world.

FRMK's flagship series is called "Amphigouri." Paradoxically (with respect to the notion of series), yet aptly (in view of the heterogeneous nature of amphigories), most of the books in the series are "hors-collection." Physical characteristics vary markedly from one volume to the next. Dominique Goblet's *Les hommes-loups/Wolfmen*, for example, is a large (26.5 × 21 cm), beautiful, four-color, hardbound volume that consists in the main of full-, double-, and half-page reproductions of previously exhibited mixed media works. *Les hommes-loups* demonstrates that both the walls of the art gallery and the pages of the book lend themselves to exploring the narrative possibilities of visual juxtapositions.[4] The book accentuates these modal parallels by adding elements traditionally associated with *bande dessinée*, including the sequential ordering of panels and the presence of text and image. In addition, the physical characteristics of

2. [Jean-Christophe] Menu, *Plates-Bandes* (Paris: L'association, 2005), 25–31.

3. http://www.fremok.org/site.php?type=P&id=267. Translations are mine unless otherwise noted.

4. See Dominique Goblet's interview by Carmela Chergui in https://almanak.files.wordpress.com/2010/05/frmkcom_hommes-loups.pdf (April 2010).

Les hommes-loups—its size, binding, and full-color reproductions—underscore the aesthetic and socio-cultural similarities that obtain between the world of comics and the world of art. They are also thematically apt: the hard covers contain the (human) wolves inside, along with the primal fears they evoke.

In contrast to *Les hommes-loups*, Éric Lambé's *Le fils du roi/The King's Son* is both beautiful *and* raw (Fig. 1). It is unusually large, 33 × 33 cm, dimensions that correspond to the size of the sheets used for the original artwork. Its pages are printed on uncoated paper. Its upper and lower covers consist of rough cardboard, the back edges of which are left untreated. Its top, bottom, and fore edges are stained

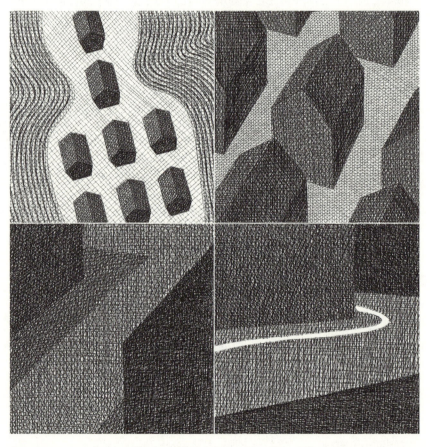

Fig. 1. Eric Lambé, *Le fils du roi/The King's Son* (Brussels: FRMK, collection Amphigouri, 2012). Courtesy of Eric Lambé.

a dark blue. It has no back cover (the stitching is visible underneath a layer of adhesive). Overtly singular, both conceptually and materially, *Le fils du roi* is a highly aestheticized object that pushes the boundaries of comics. Even its price—33 euros—obeys an aesthetic rather than a market logic by echoing the book's dimensions. Unsurprisingly, much of the original artwork has been exhibited. At the same time, any self-conscious appeal to the aura of the *objet d'art* is undercut by the affordability of the object, the author's exclusive reliance on workaday dark blue and black ballpoint pens, and his determination to give the reader an experience that negates as much as possible the difference between reproduction and original: "The format is quite similar to that of the original sheets of paper while the print techniques—four pantones: two blues, two blacks—reproduce very faithfully the way in which I worked with the blue and black ballpoint pens."[5] The work thus meets philosophical as well as formal requirements. Part drawing pad, part codex, it acknowledges and collapses the distinction between originality and reproduction, art and *bande dessinée*, the high and the low.

Le fils du roi suits FRMK's identity as a press that blends highly refined printing techniques with a brutalist aesthetic and pays close attention to the material elements of *bande dessinée*. Other small publishers have also pushed the formal limits of the genre, to the point where it is not always possible to tell the difference between a *bande dessinée* and an artist's book.[6] Hécatombe, based in Geneva, is a publishing platform that does not impose any publishing format on its authors, even within the context of a particular series. The core of its philosophy is "a vision of the book that does not distinguish between content (*contenu*) and physical appearance (*contenant*)."[7] In the case of the *Fanzine carré* series, for instance, the only constraint—in the Oulipian, or, rather, Oubapian sense of the word—is the square.[8] The third volume in the series, *Un fanzine carré numéro C* (2013), thus explores permutations of the square and the number 3 (Fig. 2). It is a

5. Eric Lambé, http://www.fremok.org/site.php?type=P&id=268

6. Catherine Labio, *From Bande Dessinée to Artist's Book: Testing the Limits of Franco-Belgian Comics*, catalogue of the exhibit held at The Center for Book Arts, April 19 – June 29, 2013 (New York, NY: The Center for Book Arts, 2013).

7. "Dossier de presse: Un fanzine carré numéro C," http://unfanzine.com/wp-content/uploads/2013/06/ddp_fznc_sub.pdf, [8].

8. OuBaPo, or Ouvroir de Bande Dessinée Potentielle, founded in 1992, is the *bande dessinée* version of OuLiPo.

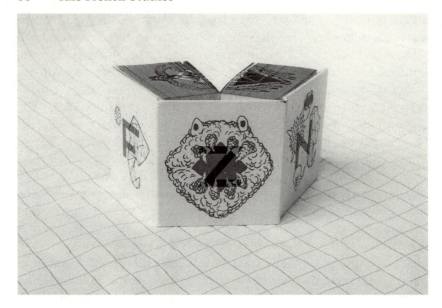

Fig. 2. Collectif, *Un fanzine carré numéro C* (Geneva: Hécatombe, 2013). Courtesy of Hécatombe.

heavy, 9 cm cube, printed in a numbered, limited edition of 999, no two of which are exactly alike. The six sides of the cube are all made to look like front book covers: different motifs are printed on the hard upper, lower, and back covers and on the three edges. In addition, each motif is drawn from a series of ninety-nine drawings and six glyphs chosen "according to a precise algorithm" for the edition to consist of 999 unique copies.[9] Each book is in turn "a 900-page block of graphic novels, subdivided into 9-page parts bringing together 90 stories in a narrative clash between two sets of authors."[10]

Only some of the ninety stories echo the formal constraint of the square/cube. In addition, because of its weight, size, and shape, *Un fanzine carré numéro C* tends to frustrate the reading process. *Contenant* trumps *contenu*. *Un fanzine carré numéro D* (2014), which comes in a limited edition of 500, unifies these more effectively. It measures 23 × 23 cm and consists of three twenty-page, wordless, and abstract comics by Ibn Al Rabin, Thomas Perrodin, and Yannis La

9. http://hecatombe.ch/shop/en/accueil/16-un-fanzine-carre-no-c-978294043 2110.html
10. Ibid.

Macchia that play on the motif of the balloon. There is no paratext of any kind (essential bibliographic information is provided on a sticker affixed to a clear and disposable plastic wrapper). In a manner befitting its experimental nature, both graphically and narratologically, *Un fanzine carré numéro D* is unbound. Its pages are folded in half to form a square *cahier* held together by an elastic band.

Also published by Hécatombe, Yannis La Macchia's *Quinze cases* (2014) consists of fifteen small (8 × 6 cm), silk-screened cards/panels that come wrapped in a matching four-sided case and can be played, according to Hécatombe, to form "approximately 3,554,027,500,000 different stories."[11] *Quinze cases* makes plain that the reader plays an active role in constructing a story. Moreover, it points to the move away from the codex that is also a hallmark of the recent history of artist's books and has allowed authors affiliated with *micro-éditions* to continue pushing the limits of *bande dessinée*. The Genevan press B.ü.L.b comix is another case in point. From 1997 to 2013, they published the 2[w] collection, a series of 26 sets of accordion-shaped mini-comics labeled A – Z and typically published in editions of 500. All but the earliest 2[w] sets consist of five two-color mini-comics by five different authors. Each comic is an accordion book that was folded manually and measures 4.5 × 3.5 cm when closed. Each set comes with a two-part matching box that can be assembled by the reader to store and protect the books. The box is not merely functional, however. It underscores the three-dimensionality of the comic book, both in terms of its material features and of the active and intimate role the reader plays in its reception. More generally, it signifies, in admittedly counterintuitive fashion, the "thinking outside the box," or emphasis on the comic as object, that has defined a number of recent comics experiments in and outside Europe.[12]

*   *   *

Even codices like *Le fils du roi* and *Un fanzine carré numéro C* proclaim their three-dimensionality. The reader is acutely aware, at all times, of their physical properties, their weight, their size, the way they feel to the touch. This emphasis on the material features of comics has led some *bande dessinée* producers to "think outside the

11. http://hecatombe.ch/shop/en/accueil/8-quinze-cases-9782940432097.html
12. Labio, *From Bande Dessinée to Artist's Book*, 29–33.

book" and open *bande dessinée* to other forms of individual and collective artistic expression, including sculpture, installation art, scenography, and dance. *Bande dessinée* drawings have not only left the pages of the book for the walls of the art gallery, the museum, and the auction house, they have also moved into three-dimensional spaces that allow for ever more complex explorations of the materiality of *bande dessinée* and its dynamic and performative dimensions.[13]

The launch of Marc-Antoine Mathieu's [S.E.N.S.] or, more accurately, the pictogram ➡, a *bande dessinée* published by Delcourt in 2014, was thus accompanied by two art installations. From 28 November 2014 to 4 January 2015, the Huberty-Breyne Gallery in Brussels exhibited a series of original drawings featured in ➡, as well as a number of "para-codexical" drawings, sculptures, and a video titled *Mille feuilles*.[14] A few months later, from 21 May to 11 October 2015, the Lieu international des formes émergentes (LiFE) in Saint-Nazaire, located in a submarine base, hosted *S.E.N.S.*, a vast installation that invited visitors to walk through four distinct spaces: the Entrance, the Corridor, the Sand Room, and the Floating Images Room. The occasionally disorienting immersive experience appealed to the senses of sight, hearing, touch, and proprioception.[15]

Mathieu's ventures into the world of art are secondary to his *bandes dessinées*. The sculptures exhibited in Brussels extend the graphic explorations of time, space, and architecture of *Mémoire morte* (2000), and the same themes are central to the *Julius Coren-*

13. The relationship between the world of comics and the world of art has become increasingly complex. For example, museums dedicated to *bande dessinée*, the Centre belge de la bande dessinée and the Musée de la bande dessinée, can be found in Brussels and Angoulême, and the Musée Hergé opened in Louvain-la-Neuve in 2009. Original *planches* and related artifacts are routinely exhibited in galleries around the time of a book's launch. Auctions of original *bande dessinée* drawings by classic and contemporary artists keep setting records. On 24 May 2014, for instance, a 1937 india ink drawing of the end papers used for some *Tintin* albums sold for €2,654,400, or, US$3,617,947: http://www.artcurial.com/fr/asp/fullCatalogue.asp?salelot=2546+++++++1+&refno=10487011

14. The video and related materials can be found at http://www.hubertybreyne.com/expositions/marc-antoine-mathieu-s.e.n.s.-bxl/

15. See Nick Nguyen's review in *European Comic Art* 9/1 (Spring 2016): 113–16, Pascal Krajewski, "La Filature," https://lelifesaintnazaire.files.wordpress.com/2015/06/life_sens_mamathieu_texte_lafilature_pkrajewski_v2.pdf), and Sylvain Huet's film, *Avis d'éclaircies* (23 June 2015) at https://lelifesaintnazaire.wordpress.com/archives/saison-2014–2015/sens/

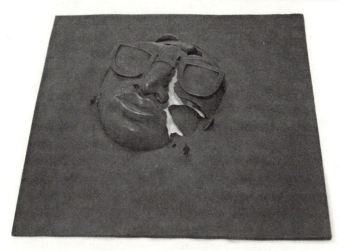

Fig. 3. Marc-Antoine Mathieu , *S.E.N.S. sculptures: Le héros creux*, 2014, bronze. Courtesy of Marc-Antoine Mathieu (c/o Galerie Huberty-Breyne-Paris, Bruxelles).

tin Acquefacques series, especially *Le processus* (1993) and *La 2,333ᵉ dimension* (2004), in which Julius is trapped, respectively, in a third dimension and a flat, two-dimensional world (Fig. 3). Similarly, the visitor's experience of the Saint-Nazaire installation imitated the halting, multi-directional path of the protagonist of ➡, a book that depicts, abstractly and wordlessly, one man's perambulation in a world of arrows.

By contrast, Nicolas Robel's *Limbo – Forever Halo*, a multimedia installation exhibited at the Fumetto International Comix Festival held in Lucerne in March–April 2012, did not grow out of a book project. Unlike the Floating Images Room, which invited the wandering visitor to ponder, like the protagonist of ➡, what direction to take, Robel's *Limbo – Forever Halo* brought the very possibility or desirability of *errance* into question by drawing visitors into a sunless space and time, in which two skateboarders intersected endlessly under a misshapen disco ball.[16] Against the walls forty-eight skateboard decks functioned as strips, each with five to seven brightly painted panels (*cases*) consisting of drawings and single words found on old

16. See Nguyen's review, *op. cit.*, for a description of one visitor's experience in the Floating Images Room.

maps and in trekking guides. The boards were arranged symmetrically in an endlessly modifiable sequence that sidestepped narrative linearity. In the background repetitive musical sequences echoed a symmetry that went nowhere, forever.[17]

While Mathieu's and Robel's installations amplified and thereby drew visitors' attention to the three-dimensionality and corporeality of comics and their reception, they also obeyed the logic of linearity, be it the directional arrow or the infinite loop. As other artists have shown, however, the logic of the line is not essential to comics. Tobias Schalken, co-author of the Dutch comics series *Eiland* (1997–), also creates paintings, sculptures, videos, and multimedia installations. It is impossible to tell where one medium ends and another begins. It does not even matter, for example, whether the panels that make up the last page of "A Love Supreme," published in *Eiland* 3 in 2000, were created before or after *Untitled (Horse)*, a sculpture dated 2006 (Figs. 4 and 5).[18] Chronology does not determine medial primacy, which may explain why Schalken does not date his sculptures on his own website. His interest in magical realism, coupled with his rejection of media hierarchies, trumps linearity. Book, body, and sculpture are one.

Nowhere is the three-dimensionality of comics more evident than in the relationship between comics and architecture. I have argued elsewhere that, across comics traditions, the conventional format of the comics page is structured in a way that evokes the façade and cross-section of the quintessential home.[19] The palimpsestic presence of the home on the page plays an essential role in making the comic readable and draws attention to the fact that reading a comic is a physical and dynamic act. The reader/viewer is invited to dwell in the page. As Ian Hague has argued in his study of *Comics and the Senses*, "the reading of a comic [. . .] constitutes a performance."[20] Comics creators' awareness of the performative nature of the act of

17. The exhibition catalogue is a handcrafted skateboard, silkscreened in three colors. See http://www.bulbfactory.ch/nicolas/expos.php#id=album-55&num=1 and http://www.bulbfactory.ch/nicolas/limbo.php#id=album-55&num=16

18. Tobias Tycho Schalken, "A Love Supreme," in Stefan J.H. Van Dinther and Tobias Tycho Schalken, *Eiland* 3 (Antwerp: Bries, 2000), 40.

19. Labio, "The Architecture of Comics," *Critical Inquiry* 41 (2015): 312–43.

20. Ian Hague, *Comics and the Senses: A Multisensory Approach to Comics and Graphic Novels* (New York: Routledge, 2014), 5.

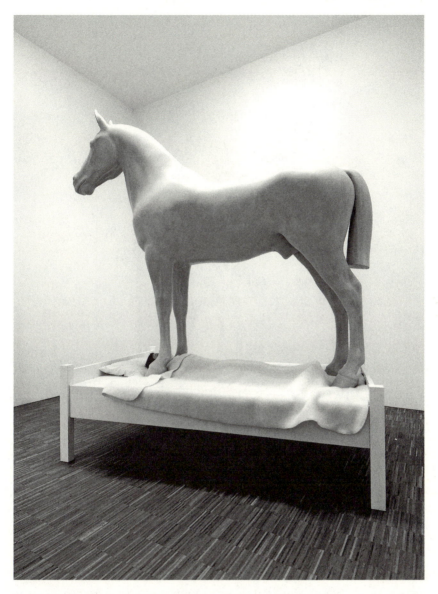
Fig. 4. Tobias Tycho Schalken, *Untitled (Horse)*, 2006, silicone, hair, polyester, mixed media. Courtesy of Tobias Tycho Schalken.

Fig. 5. Tobias Tycho Schalken, "A Love Supreme," in Stefan J. H. Van Dinther and Tobias Tycho Schalken, *Eiland*, vol. 3 (Antwerp: Bries, 2000), 40. Courtesy of Tobias Tycho Schalken.

reading has allowed them to step outside the book while remaining within the *bande dessinée* tradition, even when most of the features customarily associated with the form are nowhere to be found. François Schuiten's numerous forays into scenography are a case in point. The co-author, with Benoît Peeters, of the architecturally rich, multimodal, and ongoing *Cités obscures* series (1982–), Schuiten designed the stage set and costumes for a 1999 production of Rossini's *La Cenerentola*, in which the various protagonists emerged from a gigantic motorized book. He also drew up the plans for the Belgian pavilion of the Hanover World's Fair (2000), which involved the active participation of visitors, who intermingled with mannequins. More recently, he created the scenography of Train World, a Belgian railroad museum that opened in Schaerbeek, a Brussels borough (*commune*), in September 2015. Train World intersperses historical objects with multimedia and hands-on installations in order to immerse the public in "a kind of magical spectacle" (*une sorte de féerie*).[21]

Mathieu's, Schalken's, and Schuiten's projects underscore the links between the body of the book and the body of the reader. Keenly aware of the spatial, embodied nature of comic art and its reception, they have explored the similarities between the experience of reading a comic and moving in space. They have shown that while the flat, two-dimensional arrangement of panels on the page may be central to any definition of the form, comics are also three-dimensional entities that the reader can see and touch as well as enter. Reading a comic is a subjective and dynamic experience that allows viewers/readers to project themselves into a physical object and inhabit imaginary spaces that are partly of their own making. Comics-inspired installations merely amplify the three-dimensionality of comics and the somatic dimensions of the reading experience.

One should therefore not be surprised by the proliferation of multimedia installations and cross-media collaborations in which *bande dessinée* authors have recently been involved. In 2002 Thierry Van Hasselt collaborated with choreographer Karine Ponties to create *Brutalis*, the title of a solo performance by Ponties, with visuals and set design by Van Hasselt, and of a co-authored book published by FRMK that explores the relationship between a dancer's moving body and the fixed matter of the page. On stage Ponties's body inhabited Van Hasselt's paintings. In the book the artist's thick strokes, reminiscent of impasto techniques, show the dancer's body as it becomes one with the page. Both 2002 productions could stand alone, but enhanced one another by allowing for a mutual exploration of the relationship between dance and the visual arts, a relationship maintained by the book's continuing existence.[22]

Ponties's "feeling that regardless of its form, writing always originates in the body" has led to another collaboration with Van Hasselt.[23] *Holeulone*, a piece for two male dancers that premiered in 2006 and has been reprised on several occasions, stages the interior life of

21. François Schuiten, quoted in http://www.rtbf.be/info/regions/detail_train-world-plus-qu-un-musee-une-experience-qui-retrace-l-epopee-du-rail-belge?id=9086553

22. See interviews by Van Hasselt and Ponties at http://www.fremok.org/site.php?type=P&id=137 and http://www.fremok.org/site.php?type=P&id=136

23. Karine Ponties, "Everything Is a Question of Translation" (2003) http://www.damedepic.be/Public/Article.php?ID=3816

Fig. 6. Karine Pontiès, choreography, and Thierry Van Hasselt, animated ink, *Holeulone*. Photograph by ©Wilfrid Roche. Reproduced by permission of Wilfrid Roche and Dame de Pic/Karine Pontiès.

one man and his imaginary twin. During the performance, choreographed by Ponties, Van Hasselt's moving images, or "animated ink," are projected onto and become indistinguishable from the dancers' bodies (Fig. 6).[24] *Holeulone* has led in turn to a return to the book in the form of two "translations" of the performance staged by Ponties's company, Dame de Pic: *Heureux, Alright!* (2008), a text-image dialogue between Van Hasselt and writer Mylène Lauzon, who contributed text to the original performance by Dame de Pic, and Lauzon's *Holeulone* (2006), a book of poetry (without images). One can picture a continuous loop between stage and book.

*   *   *

As Bart Beaty has recently reminded us in *Comics versus Art*, comics artists have long struggled for recognition. For Beaty, even Chris Ware, arguably the most respected and celebrated cartoonist of his genera-

---

24. See http://www.damedepic.be/Public/Search.php?ID=3897&search=holeulone

tion, "reaffirms the supremacy of the art world relative to comics by maintaining and reinforcing existing prejudices about the inadequacies of a form presumed to be inexorably tainted by mass culture and its audiences."[25] The move away from traditional publishing formats and mass reproducibility and toward cross-disciplinary collaborations need not, however, be equated with a rejection of the popular origins of comics in general and *bande dessinée* in particular in favor of necessarily "higher" forms of artistic expression. First, one might argue, following Katherine Roeder, that Ware's work affirms instead, from within the very art institutions that have welcomed his work, the irreducibility and even superiority of comics.[26] One could also contend, after Walter Benjamin, that some of the *bande dessinée* experiments outlined above betray a bourgeois longing for the aura of the work of art rather than an avant-gardist, anti-bourgeois ethos. More importantly, the move away from the album—and from the codex more generally—substantiates Erwin Dejasse's and Charles Hatfield's claim that the art versus comics and independent or alternative versus dominant or mainstream dichotomies are becoming increasingly irrelevant in both Europe and North America.[27]

The relatively high status of Franco-Belgian *bande dessinée* has given the European version of this bilateral development a unique coloration. In France and Belgium the "Ninth Art" has been the subject of sustained critical analysis since the 1970s. Established museums are devoted to its study and promotion. This distinct reception history accounts in part for the relative ease with which *bande dessinée* has migrated to the world of art galleries and performance spaces. Indeed, it is telling that Beaty, whose earlier *Unpopular Culture* had documented the 1990s rise of French-language independent presses, chose to focus on American comics for *Comics versus Art*.

Within the world of *bande dessinée*, a further distinction operates: many of the key players in the small press movement, especially those

25. Bart Beaty, *Comics versus Art* (Toronto: University of Toronto Press, 2012), 222.

26. Katherine Roeder, "Chris Ware and the Burden of Art History," in *The Comics of Chris Ware: Drawing Is a Way of Thinking*, ed. David M. Ball and Martha B. Kuhlman (Jackson, MS: University Press of Mississippi, 2010), 65–77.

27. Erwin Dejasse, "Le regard cosmopolite et rétrospectif de la bande dessinée alternative" and Charles Hatfield, "Do Independent Comics Still Exist in the US and Canada?" both in *La bande dessinée en dissidence*, ed. Dony, Habrand, and Meesters, 27–45, 59–77.

publishers and authors who have experimented with non-codexical forms of creative expression, work in Belgium and Switzerland, countries where the high-low distinction and related media hierarchies operate less forcefully than in France. Thierry Groensteen has argued that in France the rejection of the high-low distinction is a "petit bourgeois" phenomenon.[28] The claim is questionable: according to recent sociological studies, the most avid French readers of *bandes dessinées* are "upper managers and professionals."[29] Whatever its validity, it underscores Groensteen's lasting preoccupation with the legitimization of comics.[30] Belgian and Swiss authors are less wedded to a dominant literary or linguistic model and to the avant-gardist and revolutionary logics espoused by Groensteen and Jean-Christophe Menu, one of the co-founders of L'association.[31] Moreover, to the extent that they belong, unlike most French authors, to multilingual communities, they are less likely to privilege the textual over the visual, literature over the visual arts. In addition, because of their historical contributions to the genre, Belgian *bande dessinée* authors and presses in particular need not and do not, as Jan Baetens has observed, look for the "kind of symbolic gratification" that Groensteen and Menu worry about.[32] In its promotional literature FRMK thus does not seek to distance itself from its *bande dessinée* origins, but insists its founders were "all *bande dessinée* authors" and that it sits "at the avant-garde of *bande dessinée*."[33]

28. Thierry Groensteen, *Un objet culturel non identifié* ([Angoulême]: Éditions de l'An 2, 2006), 9.

29. Benoît Berthou and Jean-Philippe Martin, "Introduction," in *La bande dessinée: Quelle lecture, quelle culture?*, ed. Benoît Berthou (Paris: Éditions de la Bibliothèque publique d'information, 2015). See http://books.openedition.org/bibpompidou/1672, in particular paragraph 17. Also see, in the same volume, Christophe Evans, "Profils de lecteurs, profils de lectures," http://books.openedition.org/bibpompidou/1673, paragraphs 20–21.

30. This preoccupation is also in evidence in "Why Are Comics Still in Search of Cultural Legitimization?," trans. Shirley Smolderen, in *Comics & Culture: Analytical and Theoretical Approaches to Comics*, ed. Anne Magnussen and Hans-Christian Christiansen (Copenhagen: Museum Tuscanulum Press, University of Copenhagen, 2000), 29–41.

31. On avant-gardism in the small press movement, see Menu, *Plates-Bandes*, 11–17.

32. Jan Baetens, "Of Graphic Novels and Minor Cultures: The Fréon Collective," *Yale French Studies* 114 (2008): 95–115 (107). This volume, edited by Jan Baetens and Ari J. Blatt, is on *Writing and the Image Today*.

33. FRMK Newsletter (e-mail dated 11 January 2016).

This last claim is subtly but significantly different from Menu's 1980s decision to embrace the "literary and artistic avant-gardes of the twentieth century" such as surrealism and the Situationist International, that is, to embrace, not the "avant-garde of *bande dessinée*," but the "high" avant-garde.[34] Of course, FRMK's books do not look like traditional *bande dessinée* albums. FRMK does not see itself as rejecting *bande dessinée* from its portfolio of interests, however, but insists on maintaining its ties to it. It has embraced a capacious definition of *bande dessinée*, in part by refraining from always deferring to the categories of the literary and the aesthetic, including, as Baetens has pointed out, "the notion of an *auteur* who ultimately wields complete control over the artistic vision of the work."[35] Artists associated with FRMK have thus not only worked with other professional visual artists and choreographers, they have also collaborated with outsider artists in a center for persons with mental handicaps to create a series of graphic/narrative "confrontations" published by FRMK, in a format similar to that of *Les hommes-loups*, under the title *Match de catch à Vielsalm* (2009).

It is precisely a relative lack of concern with the status of their works vis-à-vis art and literature that has allowed some small Belgian and Swiss presses to retreat from the codex and even resist, as needed, the tyranny of the beautiful or, as in the case of *Le fils du roi*, some of the properties associated with it. More dependent on a certain idea (ideal) of art and literature, self-identified alternative French *bande dessinée* presses such as The Hoochie Coochie, Mauvaise Foi, Tanibis, Groinge, and L'Apocalypse remain committed to the conventional definition of the book.[36] Ultimately, however, while

34. [Jean-Christophe] Menu, "Préface," Barthélémy Schwartz, *Le rêveur captif* ([Paris]: Apocalypse, 2012), n.p.

35. Baetens, 103.

36. L'association has produced *BD* objects: Anne Baraou and Sardon's *Coquetèle* (2002), the multi-authored *Le ScrOUBAbble* (2005), and Baraou and Killoffer's *DoMiPo* (2009). *Coquetèle*, "a box holding three dice arranged in no particular order, with a comic panel on each side, which can be combined to make 1, 296 three-panel strips," was created on the model of *Après tout tant pis*, a "Bd-dés" (dice comic) by Baraou and Corinne Chalmeau (Paris: Éditions Hors Gabarit, 1991). These games anticipate some of the works published by Hécatombe, but are not essential to L'association's identity as a publisher. They are confined to its OuBaPo series, itself modeled after a literary avant-garde movement. See http://www.lassociation.fr/fr_FR/#!catalogue/collection/221/open/87, and Côme Martin, "Jeux OuBaPo et objets-BDs," *Du9* (2010), http://www.du9.org/dossier/jeux-oubapo-et-objets-bds/

socio-cultural factors must be taken into consideration when trying to understand the evolution of comics, even if the move away from the traditional album and the codex more generally was purely aspirational, it would, above all, reflect the inherent three-dimensionality of comics in general and *bande dessinée* in particular as well as the intimate and sensual nature of the relationship of reader/viewer to the comic book.

As Roger Sabin has remarked, American comic books "can be bent, rolled-up, roughly opened or whatever. They can be held in different ways: cradled in your hand or gripped at the edges."[37] Larger and hardcover, *bande dessinée* albums cannot be rolled up. Their physical attributes account in part for the historically higher status of *bande dessinée*: these books are clearly not disposable.[38] Even the many eminently forgettable albums that still make up the larger share of *bande dessinée* publications in any given year have a pleasing materiality. There is something satisfying about the way they feel to the touch, about the sound of one's fingernails tapping against the covers, and about the manner in which an *album* glides into place on a shelf. To people who have grown up with them, they have the evocative power of a madeleine. More importantly, together with the standard composition of the page and its two-dimensional trace of the façades of domestic architecture, the three-dimensional features of the *bande dessinée* album—its unique combination of size, shape, weight, and solidity—invite a corporeal projection by the reader into the book. Habit, which results from the standardization of the *bande dessinée* album (and the American comic book), has rendered its three-dimensionality almost invisible and easy to ignore. It is this feature, however, more than any sociological logic, that has allowed authors affiliated with presses like FRMK, B.ü.L.b comix, and Hécatombe to step outside the books they and their readers have long inhabited. In trying to defamiliarize the traditional *bande dessinée* album, they are bringing its inherent three-dimensionality home.

37. Roger Sabin, "The Crisis in Modern American and British Comics, and the Possibilities of the Internet as a Solution," in *Comics and Culture*, ed. Magnussen and Christiansen, 52.
38. Labio, *From Bande Dessinée to Artist's Book*, 7.

KEITH READER

Alain Resnais and *Bande Dessinée*

It was Jean-Luc Godard who, in a voice-over for his 1967 *Deux ou trois choses que je sais d'elle,* said: "It could almost be said that to live in society today is tantamount to living in an enormous comic strip." The *bande dessinée* or BD plays a minor but not insignificant role in Godard's *oeuvre,* one of many touchstones of his enduring love-hate relationship with American culture (for all that the genre's accredited pioneer, Rodolphe Töpffer, was—like Godard—Swiss). Godard's 1965 masterpiece *Pierrot le fou* makes reference to the then-popular strip *Les pieds nickelés,* while *Made in USA* of the following year incorporates Roy Lichtenstein-like BD inserts. By and large, however, the influence of *le neuvième art* on its modern-day predecessor-but-one (television occupies the intermediate place) is less pronounced than might have been expected. I can find no trace of direct quotation from or allusion to it in the pre-World War II films known to me, and not until the work of Walerian Borowczyk (the extraordinary though comparatively little-seen *Le théâtre de Monsieur et Madame Kabal* of 1967), and much later Sylvain Chomet, best known for *Les triplettes de Belleville* (2003) and *L'illusioniste* (2010), and Marjane Satrapi/Vincent Paronnaud's *Persepolis* (2007) did animated features other than for a child audience achieve any degree of currency.[1]

The towering exception to this—although he never made an animated film—is Alain Resnais, much of whose work in one way or another bears the imprint of BD. Resnais's interest in the medium, ignited in childhood and maintained uninterruptedly thereafter, led

1. Historically, however, we can point to the early Lumière films as having been influenced by 19th-century strips. See Lance Rickman, "*Bande dessinée* and the Cinematograph: Visual Narrative in 1895," *European Comic Art* 1/1 (spring 2008): 1–19.

YFS 131/132, Bande Dessinée: *Thinking Outside the Boxes,* ed. Laurence Grove and Michael Syrotinski, © 2017 by Yale University.

him to become one of the original editors of *Giff-wiff*, founded in 1962 as the journal of the Club des bandes dessinées. An index of what Bourdieusians might call the greater distinction of the medium in France compared to the US or the UK is provided by the fact that among *Giff-wiff*'s other founders and supporters were Raymond Queneau; Francis Lacassin, who later occupied the first chair of BD in Paris; the philosopher and sociologist Edgar Morin; and Delphine Seyrig, celebrated above all for her appearances in Resnais's films (*L'année dernière à Marienbad* of 1961 and *Muriel* of 1963). Resnais had already won recognition as one of France's leading film directors by the time of *Giff-wiff*'s foundation, and *Nuit et brouillard*, his 1955 documentary on the concentration camps ten years after the end of the war, is credited as an important influence on Art Spiegelman's graphic novel *Maus*, initially serialized between 1980 and 1991.

'Giff-wiff' refers to an imaginary amphibious animal living on pearls and tapioca, who first appeared in the *Journal de Mickey* in 1935. Lacassin invokes the genre's supposed influence on Fellini, Marker, and Rivette, despite which it had some difficulty gaining widespread acceptance, as can been seen by the banning of the legendary *Barbarella* strip in 1965. BD appears at this time to have been widely regarded as simultaneously trivial—doubtless because of its associations with a child readership—and pernicious, so that the Club des bandes dessinées and *Giff-wiff* had a twofold battle to fight.[2]

Resnais was quick to perceive the affinities between BD and film, for Lacassin avers that for him "comics discovered and used close-ups, cinemascope images, and tracking shots well before cinema did."[3] Various plans for BD adaptations—including *Mandrake the Magician*, *Dick Tracy* and *Spider Man*—came, however, to nothing, Resnais in the end perceiving the graphic novel as too endemically un- or even anti-realistic for these to work.

His only film to incorporate BD into its diegesis is *I Want to Go Home* (1989), from a screenplay by the renowned cartoonist Jules Feiffer for whose theatrical work Resnais had expressed particular admiration. Despite Feiffer's participation and a cast including

2. On the development of the *bande dessinée* at this time, see Laurence Grove, *Comics in French: The European Bande Dessinée in Context* (Oxford: Berghahn, 2010 and 2013).

3. François Lacassin, *Pour un neuvième art: La bande dessinée* (Paris: UGE/10–18, 1971), 444.

Gérard Depardieu, the film was poorly received in France. Resnais himself considered it a partial failure, largely owing to his "unwillingness to take on the full scope of comics' intertextual dimension."[4] The film did not secure distribution in either the US or the UK, so that not until its release as part of a Resnais DVD box set in 2010 did it become widely available in English-speaking countries. It can be assigned to the sub-genre of culture-clash comedy, getting a good deal of mileage out of the greater regard in which the graphic novel is held in France than in its homeland. Thus, to quote Emma Wilson : "For Alain Masson, *I Want to Go Home* is a film about the American vision of French culture."[5]

The leading character, cartoonist Joey Wellman (played by Adolph Freed, screenwriter of Stanley Donen and Gene Kelly's 1952 *Singin' in the Rain*), is visiting Paris for what appears to be the first time, and is surprised and flattered by the esteem bestowed on his work there, demonstrated by the holding of an exhibition devoted to him in the prestigious locale of the Place des Vosges. Wellman has created a cartoon character, Hepp Cat, whose name refers back to the hipster jazz sub-culture of the 1940s, and who intervenes regularly in the action—the only time a BD character has actually appeared in a Resnais film. Joey's daughter, Elsie, is the first character we meet, on board an airplane to Paris where she is to pursue her study of Flaubert with the distinguished professor Christian Gauthier (Gérard Depardieu in his second and last Resnais feature). The culture-clash comedy here is generational as well as transnational, for Elsie appears somewhat disdainful of the graphic novel and of the US provincial capital (Cleveland, Ohio) she is leaving behind—an inversion of the more usual situation in which older generations favor more distinguished art-forms than their juniors. The cultural mix is complicated when it turns out that Gauthier, at whose country house in Normandy father and daughter spend a weekend, is a BD enthusiast and a great admirer of Joey's work. Joey and Elsie become closer and, in a classic role-reversal, he expresses a wish to stay in France while, cured of her infatuation with Gauthier, she returns home. Our last sight of

4. Deborah Walker-Morrison, *Le style cinématographique d'Alain Resnais, de Hiroshima mon amour (1959) aux Herbes folles (2009)* (Lewiston: Edwin Mellen Press, 2012), 205.

5. Emma Wilson, *Alain Resnais* (Manchester: Manchester University Press, 2006), 166.

her is on the plane back, reading a graphic novel by Will Eisner (who supposedly coined that term), as is her French neighbor on the plane, himself a cartoonist.

The slightly schematic nature of the role-reversals and cultural inversions in *I Want to Go Home* doubtless accounts for its commercial and artistic failure; it appears too French for an American audience and too American for a French one. Yet it still merits attention as the first French feature known to me to give the graphic novel such prominence in its diegesis. Resnais's Alan Ayckbourn adaptations *Smoking* and *No Smoking* (1993) are, as their origin suggests, primarily theatrical, with echoes of the silent cinema in the use of intertitles and a self-consciously tinny piano accompaniment. Yet their use of only two actors, both pillars of Resnais's work—Pierre Arditi and Sabine Azéma—to play nine characters, has overtones of the stylization often characteristic of the graphic novel, as does the clearly studio-shot and resolutely two-dimensional evocation of the Yorkshire countryside, most marked in the intertitles that punctuate the films. Louis Guichard and Pierre Murat in *Télérama* indeed paid tribute to the films' "superb mixture of comics and theatrical artifice."[6]

Azéma appeared in ten of Resnais's films and was his partner and, from 1998 until his death in 2014, wife—indeed they chose to get married in Scarborough, the Yorkshire seaside resort where Ayckbourn lives and works and where Resnais first introduced himself to the playwright in 1989. The partnership between Resnais and Azéma is one of the most fruitful and celebrated actor/director collaborations in French cinematic history. That is not to say that it invariably met with critical approval, for J. Hoberman in *The Village Voice* describes her as Resnais's "reliably irritating muse," and thus presumably responsible for the "insufferable [. . .] cutie-pie modernism" of what was to be his last film but two, *Les herbes folles* of 2009.[7] Azéma has not always appeared in the frequently comic, or at least comically-inflected, roles she was to play for Resnais. As the aristocratic war widow in Bertrand Tavernier's *La vie et rien d'autre* (1989) she could indeed be described as a tragic heroine. For Resnais, however, her act-

6. Louis Guichard and Pierre Murat, "Alain Resnais en six chefs-d'oeuvre," *Télérama* (16 March 2014): http://www.telerama.fr/cinema/alain-resnais-en-six-chefs-d-oeuvre,109847.php

7. J. Hoberman, "Alain Resnais Does his Carrot-topped Muse no Favors in *Wild Grass*," *The Village Voice* (22 June 2010): http://www.villagevoice.com/film/alain-resnais-does-his-carrot-topped-muse-no-favors-in-wild-grass-6393849

ing tends to be characterized by an often manically twittering acting style—which is what so irked Hoberman—that might be seen as having antecedents in female cartoon characters going back to the 1930s, such as Betty Boop or Popeye's *amour* Olive Oyl. This style of acting is present too in *Smoking* and *No Smoking*, particularly in Azéma's roles as Sylvie (where her stylized hopping and jumping evoke the world of the BD) and Celia, unhappy wife of the inebriate headmaster Toby, whose *pièce de résistance* is a farcically hysterical breakdown while she is making preparations for the village fête, culminating in her attacking and biting her secret admirer, the gardener and handyman Lionel. BD influence, of a generic rather than (so far as I am aware) directly citational kind, is discreetly apparent throughout the film, as witness the sky, shot like a graphic-novel frame, that accompanies Lionel's declaration of his love to Celia, or the cartoon-like identities—as when Lionel appears disguised as a gorilla—that the characters periodically assume.

Resnais's place in the pantheon of cinematic auteurs might be thought to rest above all on a certain hieratic, even solemn quality, as in the early masterpieces *Hiroshima mon amour* (1959) and *L'année dernière à Marienbad* (1961). Yet there is arguably a degree of neo-surrealist playfulness at work in the latter film that is picked up and amplified in his later work (the magnificent, and often underrated, *Mon oncle d'Amérique* of 1980—the first of Depardieu's two feature appearances for him—is a case in point). This reaches its apogee in *Smoking/No Smoking*, whose play with stylization and the assumption and exchange of roles in this writer's view rank them among the best of Resnais's work. The influence of *bande dessinée*, often underrated because of that medium's perceived lack of gravitas, is, I hope I have shown, a key factor in this.

III. BD and Modern France

ANN MILLER

Consensus and Dissensus in *Bande Dessinée*

The relationship between art and politics, maintains Jacques Rancière, is not a passage from fiction to reality, but between two ways of producing fictions. The dominant fiction is the consensual fiction, which denies its character as fiction.[1] His definition of the prevailing consensus is succinct: globalization has imposed the image of a homogeneous world ruled by market forces, over which the nation has no control and to which it must simply adapt, entirely obscuring any "dissensual horizon."[2] But, says Rancière, "the consensual fabric of the real" can be torn.[3] There is another way of producing fictions that "contribute to drawing a new landscape of the visible, sayable and doable."[4]

The first part of this essay will consider a spate of recent comics that have offered behind-the-scenes accounts of political campaigns in France, in which the "reality" that we are promised turns out to consist of the permanent fabrication and adjustment of consensus, a process that is uncritically, indeed admiringly, portrayed. It will then briefly sample from some of the many examples of caricature in comic book format, along with an instance of parody, in search of a more polemical stance.[5] The final section of the essay argues that an album by Étienne Davodeau exemplifies art as dissensus.

---

1. Jacques Rancière, *Le spectateur émancipé* (Paris: La Fabrique, 2008), 84. Gregory Elliott's translation, *The Emancipated Spectator* (London: Verso, 2010) does not include the chapter "Les paradoxes de l'art politique" (The paradoxes of political art), from which quotations in this essay are taken. Translations from that volume are therefore my own.
2. Ibid., 75–76.
3. Ibid., 85.
4. Ibid., 84.
5. Our discussion is limited to comic books (some of which were first serialized in magazines) and does not include single-image cartoons, with one exception (in rela-

YFS 131/132, Bande Dessinée: *Thinking Outside the Boxes*, ed. Laurence Grove and Michael Syrotinski, © 2017 by Yale University.

INSIDER AND OUTSIDER REPORTAGE

Modern strategies of communication and information have been likened by Rancière to the practice of the Scythians of ancient Greece, who used to put out the eyes of their slaves. Both, he says, are part of the police order (*la police*), the order that maintains social hierarchies.[6] No such distaste for "*la comm*" is in evidence in *Objectif Élysée* (*Destination Élysée Palace*), scripted by the political blogger Guy Birenbaum, and drawn by Samuel Roberts. It concerns the internal battles, from 2005 to 2006, within the Parti socialiste (PS) and the right-wing Union pour un mouvement populaire (UMP) over the selection of candidates for the presidential election of the following year. It invites readers to go "backstage at the presidential elections,"[7] and depicts politics as a game played by careerists whose rivalry consists of denigrating or grudgingly appreciating each other's "communication" skills. Dominique de Villepin, at that time Prime Minister in the ruling UMP, says of Nicolas Sarkozy: "His media management (*sa comm*) is frankly pathetic." In contrast, PS primary candidate Ségolène Royal's achievement in getting headline coverage in *Le Parisien* forces respect from her opponents: "Aha! That's media management (*de la comm*)!"

Ségo, François, Papa et moi (*Ségo, François, Papa and Me*), scripted and drawn by PS insider Olivier Faure, also sells itself as an insight into what goes on "backstage at the PS headquarters."[8] It covers the run-up to the 2006 PS primaries, in which candidates position themselves on the basis of opinion poll percentages: Dominique Strauss-Kahn's team accuses François Hollande of stoking rumors of a possible candidacy of Royal and Jack Lang only in order to "torpedo" Strauss-Kahn in the poll ratings, but it is around the photogenic Royal, focus-group favorite, that a media buzz develops.[9]

---

tion to the question of first- and second-degree readings). All translations from comic books are my own.

6. Rancière, *La mésentente* (Paris: Galilée, 1995), 53–54. *Dis-agreement*, trans. Julie Rose (Minneapolis: University of Minnesota Press, 1999), 29–30.

7. Guy Birenbaum and Samuel Roberts, *Objectif Élysée* (Paris: Seuil, 2007), front cover. The book is unpaginated.

8. Olivier Faure, *Ségo, François, Papa et moi* (Paris: Hachette, 2007), back cover.

9. Ibid., 86; 126.

A further insider account was produced in the two-volume *Quai d'Orsay*, the second of which won the prize for best album at Angoulême in 2013.[10] Scripted by Abel Lanzac, the pen name for Antonin Baudry, who had been a speechwriter for de Villepin and responsible for "elements of language" (*éléments de langage*), or less euphemistically, sound bites, it covers the period between 2002 and 2004 when de Villepin was Foreign Secretary. Renamed "Alexandre Taillard de Vorms," but unmistakably recognizable, he is portrayed as a charismatic figure who sweeps in and out of rooms dispensing abstractions and quotations from Herodotus, to be crafted into policy statements by his downtrodden advisors. The wit of both Lanzac's dialogue and Christophe Blain's graphic line distinguishes the book from the blandly-drawn, pedestrian efforts of Faure and Birenbaum/ Roberts, but its view of politics as a matter of expertise in rhetoric makes it ultimately no more critical. Although de Vorms is depicted as excessive, even monstrous, the fascination that he exerts over the authors is obvious, and de Villepin apparently loves the book.[11]

In seeking a tearing of the consensual fabric, in Rancière's term, we may look to some comics artists who are not quite so dazzled by their subject matter. Mathieu Sapin follows Hollande's presidential campaign of 2012 in *Campagne présidentielle*.[12] He puts himself in the frame, in the tradition of gonzo reportage begun by American print journalists during the 1960s and subsequently taken up by comics artists, most famously Joe Sacco. Sapin's outsider status is compromised, however, and he is forced to be a somewhat timid gonzo, because he is embedded with the campaign (along with the novelist Dan Franck, two film crews, and a roomful of bloggers and tweeters). The campaign team trades off access against "discretion," and he is constantly in danger of being absorbed into the party machine. He maintains a certain distance by making it clear how stage-managed is the whole operation of which he is a part, including Hollande's bid to exploit the aura of François Mitterrand. Sapin not only draws the TV image of the ex-president's would-be political descendant "alone"

10. Christophe Blain and Abel Lanzac, *Quai d'Orsay*, (Paris: Dargaud, 2009 and 2012).

11. Abel Lanzac, interviewed by Olivier Cariguel, "Le tourbillon du pouvoir" (*The Whirlwind of Power*), *Revue des deux mondes* (July-August 2012): 64–90 (69).

12. Mathieu Sapin, *Campagne présidentielle* (Paris: Dargaud, 2012).

on a contemplative stroll with Mitterrand's son and grandson, but also the "reverse shot" of film crews primed to capture this apparently intimate moment. Sapin has an eye for the absurd: by the following page, Hollande has progressed from claiming the mantle of Mitterrand to actually wearing his trademark wide-brimmed hat. By 2015, though, when he produces *Le château, une année dans les coulisses de l'Élysee* (*The Fortress, a Year Behind the Scenes at the Élysée Palace*),[13] Sapin is personally granted permission by Hollande to spend six months exploring the workings of the presidential residence, and assumes the role of in-house comics artist, offbeat but deferential. A scene in which royal hagiographer Stéphane Bern arrives at the Élysée to film a program serves as a (possibly unwitting) *mise-en-abyme* of Sapin's own project.

Martin Vidberg's blogs for *Le monde* have been brought together in four volumes under the overall title of *L'actu en patates* (*News with Potato-heads*), a reference to his minimalist drawing style.[14] In the second of these, he covers the 2012 presidential campaign. Like Sapin, he puts himself in the frame, and, like him, he is dependent on the goodwill of the various press offices. However, he solves the problem of political and professional ethics (*déontologie politique*),[15] by declaring himself unqualified to comment on the politics and opting to assess each party on its presentational qualities.[16] Invited to Hollande's investiture as candidate, he declares that "the *mise-en-scène* seems very successful" and embraces the PS practice of using "Mitterrandien" as a term of approval.[17] Europe Écologie makes a virtue out of the poor speaking skills (signifying "humility") of its candidate, Eva Joly, but hedges its bets by packing the stage with "stars." An uplifting introductory video is judged "touching" by party militants and "particularly successful" by Vidberg.[18] There is a noticeable absence of any such razzamatazz in the campaign of the Nouveau parti anticapitaliste (NPA), whose name indicates its non-consensual stance. Vidberg remarks on the unlikelihood of political "stars" being

---

13. Mathieu Sapin, *Le château, une année dans les coulisses de l'Élysee* (Paris: Dargaud, 2015).

14. Martin Vidberg, *Jusque-là tout est normal* (*So Far Everything is Normal*) (Paris: Delcourt, 2012).

15. Ibid., 20.

16. Ibid., 55, 67.

17. Ibid., 25, 27.

18. Ibid., 68.

prepared, like Philippe Poutou, to stand out in the freezing cold car park of a Peugeot factory. However, he also notes that most workers do not even bother to look up at the NPA candidate. For these workers, as much as for Vidberg himself, it would seem that any "dissensual horizon" has vanished.

That horizon is brought sharply into view in Jean-Yves Duhoo's *Soigne ta gauche (Keep Your Left Hand Up)*,[19] an exception among these comics reportages in its refusal of the "consensual fiction." It covers a slightly earlier period, focusing on the PS between 2003 and the primaries in 2006. Duhoo too follows the gonzo convention of appearing in the frame, but he determinedly remains an outsider. His observations of meetings and rallies (the merchandizing of red rose-logoed mugs, T-shirts, and soap standing as metonym for a party run as a marketing operation) are interspersed with another narrative, the grand leftist narrative now said to be over, described by Rancière as "a vision of the world revolving around class struggle, and (. . .) a vision of politics as a practice of conflict and a horizon of emancipation."[20] For Duhoo, this takes in revolutions from 1789 onwards, recounted in inventive visual ways (including board games), and the life and assassination of Jean Jaurès, socialist, pacifist, and internationalist. Duhoo revivifies the historical memory of this exemplary figure, ubiquitously but residually present in contemporary France as a street name, jostling up against more prominent brand names, like the multinational bank HSBC that looms large in Duhoo's drawing of the avenue Jean Jaurès in Paris's nineteenth arrondissement. In contrast, Duhoo has a derisive take on the cult of Mitterrand. Among the bizarre collection of official gifts displayed in the Musée du Septennat at Château-Chinon is an oil painting in which the former PS president resembles his UMP successor Jacques Chirac, an indication of the interchangeability of their politics. The "consensual fabric of the real" is brought under strain by Duhoo's implicit comparison between the managerialism of recent PS politicians and the historical vision of their predecessors, and is further stretched by his inclusion of sequences portraying interviews with people who do not line up with the neo-liberal orthodoxy. The pages that set out these

19. Jean-Yves Duhoo, *Soigne ta gauche: Un reportage dessiné sur le PS* (Paris: Seuil, 2007).
20. Rancière, "In What Time Do We Live?" in *The State of Things*, ed. Marta Kuzma, Pablo Lafuente, and Peter Osborne (London: Koenig Books, 2012), 9–39 (12).

dissenting positions are framed by a thick red surround. Within one
of these areas of red, Duhoo appears at his drawing table, where he
accidentally (?) spills ink over a book about Mitterrand. The fiction of
Mitterrand, arch-adaptor to "reality," as hero of the left, is symbolically erased (Fig. 1).[21]

FROM REPORTAGE TO CARICATURE

Our search for dissenting political comics now leads us from reportage to caricature of politicians and their milieu, although the bound-
ary between these two categories is necessarily blurred by the nature
of the comics medium. The "graphic shorthand" of the comics artist
allows not only for instant recognizability of the subject portrayed
but also for a social and moral critique.[22] As we have suggested, this
critique is blunted in most of the albums discussed above. The Bi-
renbaum/Roberts and Faure books deploy an insipid realism that is
devoid of satirical intent. Blain's line is more selective, homing in
on salient traits, but it arguably mythologizes de Vorms/de Villepin,
depicted as extravagant but seductive. If Vidberg's reduction of his
characters to potato-heads tends to undermine their dignity, Sapin's
clear-line drawings display a certain benevolence toward their subjects, including Hollande, tubby but composed. Duhoo's treatment
of contemporary PS politicians in his reportage is considerably more
acerbic. His vignette of the demagogue Arnaud Montebourg, for example, giant of stature and giant of ego, is merciless, and certainly a
moral portrayal.

We have categorized another group of comics as caricature rather
than reportage, even though some are based on journalistic investigation, because their tone is satirical throughout. There is, of course, a
long history of caricature in comics format: as Thierry Smolderen has
demonstrated in his work on origins, one strain of this hybrid medium can be traced back to the work of eighteenth- and nineteenth-
century political cartoonists such as Thomas Rowlandson and George

21. For a review of Duhoo's work, see Julien Bastide, "Éloge de Jean-Yves Duhoo"
(*In Praise of Jean-Yves Duhoo*), *Du9* (October 2007) http://www.du9.org/dossier/
eloge-de-jean-yves-duhoo/
22. Harry Morgan, "Graphic Shorthand: From Caricature to Narratology in
Twentieth-Century *Bande dessinée* and Comics," *European Comic Art* 2/1 (Spring
2009): 21–39.

Fig. 1. Jean-Yves Duhoo, *Soigne ta gauche: Un reportage dessiné sur le PS* (Paris: Seuil, 2007), 35. © Seuil, 2007.

Cruikshank.[23] Certain figures have proved particularly attractive to caricaturists: Louis-Philippe, famously drawn as a pear by Charles Philipon in 1835, or Jacques Chirac disguised as an eagle by Got and Pétillon in the 1970s,[24] prefiguring his appearance as the same rapacious bird in the *Bébête Show* of the following decade.

However, with the arrival on the scene of Sarkozy, something of a caricature industry, baptized "Sarkaricature" by Mark McKinney, began to be generated.[25] *La face karchée de Sarkozy* (*The Hidden/Water-Cleansed Face of Sarkozy*) (a reference to his boast about cleaning out the social housing estates with a water cannon),[26] appeared in 2006, the year before he became president. Researched by the journalist Philippe Cohen, scripted by Richard Malka and drawn by *Charlie Hebdo* cartoonist Riss, it detailed a political career built on opportunism and serial betrayals, underpinned by a political philosophy that amounted to "I'm going to screw them all" (*Je vais les niquer tous*), reiterated as a running gag throughout. The same authors followed up with two more albums, *Sarko 1er* (*Sarko I*),[27] a Napoleonic comparison that became an inevitable motif of Sarkaricature,[28] and *Carla et Carlito ou la vie de château* (*Carla and Carlito or Luxury Living*),[29] in which the eponymous presidential couple enjoy lavish rewards for the tax breaks with which Sarkozy had bribed the rich. Other (semi-) factual exposés followed, such as *Sarkozy et ses femmes* (*Sarkozy and his Women*) and *Sarkozy et les riches* (*Sarkozy and the Rich*), scripted by *Nouvel Observateur* managing editor Renaud Dély and drawn by Aurel, emphasizing respectively the extent of the president's emotional instability and his incestuous relationships with the very wealthy.[30] Sarkozy was a gift to caricaturists, a walking caricature as the *Charlie*

23. Thierry Smolderen, *Naissances de la bande dessinée, de William Hogarth à Winsor McCay* (Brussels: Les impressions nouvelles, 2009).

24. Got and Pétillon, *Le baron noir* (*The Black Baron*), Le Matin 1976–1981.

25. See Mark McKinney, "Sarkaricature," *Contemporary French and Francophone Studies* 16/3 (2012): 357–69.

26. Philippe Cohen, Richard Malka, Riss, *La face karchée de Sarkozy* (Issy-les-Moulineaux, Vents d'Ouest, 2006).

27. Cohen, Malka, Riss, *Sarko 1er* (Issy-les-Moulineaux, Vents d'Ouest, 2007).

28. See McKinney, "Sarkaricature," 365.

29. Cohen, Malka, Riss, *Carla et Carlito ou la vie de château* (Issy-les-Moulineaux, Vents d'Ouest, 2008).

30. Renaud Dély and Aurel, *Sarkozy et ses femmes* (Grenoble: Glénat, 2010); *Sarkozy et les riches* (Grenoble: Glénat, 2011).

Hebdo cartoonist Luz points out,[31] and his comics persona soon took on a life of its own, enacting wholly invented, even if quite plausible, scenarios. These include Luz's own *Les Sarkozy gèrent la France* (*The Sarkozys Run France*), and *Robokozy*, in both of which *Sarkozysme* is portrayed as the reign of intimidation and vulgarity even more deliriously uninhibited than the attested real-life instances.[32]

Sarkozy's successor, Hollande, Monsieur Normal, offered less immediately promising material for caricature, eschewing the populist language and conspicuous display of wealth that had furnished a ready-made verbal and visual vocabulary for the depiction of Sarkozy.[33] He was largely spared by *La gauche bling-bling* (*The Bling-bling Left*) scripted by journalists Aymeric Mantoux and Benoist Simmat, and drawn by Philippe Bercovici,[34] an excoriating denunciation of the venality of PS politicians from Mitterrand onwards, in which Hollande is portrayed merely as a complicit apparatchik, even if he is not averse to making discreet tax-minimizing arrangements of his own. In *Hollande et ses deux femmes* (*Hollande and his Two Women*), by Dély and Aurel,[35] he is depicted simply as a hapless doormat, and the satirical venom is reserved for the two women who dominate him, Royal and Valérie Trierweiler. The graphic treatment of the former is particularly cruel, following a long tradition of anti-feminist caricature of female politicians (Fig. 2).[36] In the two-volume *Moi, Président* (*When I'm President*) (a reference to Hollande's famous rhetorical flight in a televised debate with Sarkozy) scripted by France Info journalist Marie-Ève Malouines and drawn by Faro,[37] the children's-book graphic style is fairly gentle toward Hollande, and it is Trierweiler who is demonized, drawn with permanently resentful,

31. See the interview with Luz by Vincent Bernière in "La BD entre en politique" (*Comics Goes into Politics*), special edition of *Beaux arts magazine* (2012): 22.

32. Luz, *Les Sarkozy gèrent la France* (Paris: Les Échappés, 2009); *Robokozy* (Paris: Les Échappés, 2010).

33. McKinney, "Sarkaricature," 360.

34. Aymeric Mantoux, Benoist Simmat and Philippe Bercovici, *La gauche bling-bling* (Paris: 12 bis, 2012).

35. Renaud Dély and Aurel, *Hollande et ses deux femmes* (Grenoble: Glénat, 2013).

36. See Hélène Chenut, "Anti-feminist Caricature in France: Politics, Satire and Public Opinion, 1890–1914," *Modern & Contemporary France* 20/4 (November 2012): 437–452.

37. Faro and Marie-Ève Malouines, *Moi, Président* (Paris: Jungle, 2013 and 2014), back cover.

Fig. 2. Renaud Dély and Aurel, *Hollande et ses deux femmes* (Grenoble: Glénat, 2013), 106. © Glénat, 2013.

twisted features. Hollande does, though, suffer from the comparison with Mitterrand, the politicians' politician, whose ghost repeatedly makes winged apparitions, taunting the current incumbent for his failure to impose his authority on his ministers, the media, or the women in his life. By 2014, and the second volume, Hollande's ineptitude at controlling press coverage, as well as his private deceptions, had become emblematized by the crash helmet in which he had been ignominiously photographed on his way to visit his lover Julie Gayet. This element of visual vocabulary, in McKinney's term, would henceforth cling to his cartoon persona, and it makes an obligatory appearance on the cover of this volume.

We might imagine that these often brilliant exercises in exaggerating the moral flaws and weaknesses of the powerful and in laying bare their hypocrisy would amount to a form of political intervention, even if their frequent misogyny would logically have the opposite effect, that of keeping women in their place. But, in any case, Rancière cautions us by posing the question of the efficacy of political art. We think that art is political, he says, if it "ridicules ruling icons," and we persist in believing that "art makes us revolt by showing us revolting things," as if we learn from the portrayal of virtues and vices.[38] Rancière does not accept that the efficacy of art is about

38. Rancière, *Le spectateur émancipé*, 57.

transmitting messages, offering models or counter-models of behavior.[39] There is, then, no guarantee that these assuredly "revolting" images will move us to political action.

Moreover, Rancière raises a further difficulty: "the pedagogical model of the efficacy of art" presupposes that the political message of a work of art can be read off it, as if there were a continuum between production and perception; his example is a set of war photographs, which, he points out, call forth a number of divergent political and non-political responses.[40] It is worth considering whether this objection can be applied to comics. Photographs, especially if uncaptioned, can, of course, be polysemic. This very issue is thematized in *Moi, Président*, in relation to the problem of image control: Hollande is concerned that a paparazzi photograph in which he appears to embrace Strauss-Kahn will be put into circulation, and will be misinterpreted. A *Paris Match* cover featuring Trierweiler and Hollande is read by PS senator François Rebsamen as an image of a man of destiny and his supportive partner, but by a furious Trierweiler herself as offering visual evidence of Hollande's boredom with her. The comic can disambiguate the (redrawn) photographs, both by reframing (along with the Strauss-Kahn photograph, we see the context in which it was taken: the disgraced ex-minister had ambushed Hollande, out for a stroll along the *quais*) and by adding text (as Hollande confides in Rebsamen, the *Paris Match* cover is drawn twice, with thought balloons from the couple corroborating first one interpretation and then the opposing one) (Fig. 3). More generally, as we have noted above, the "graphic shorthand" of the comics image tends to indicate moral approval or disapproval: the vulpine features of Sarkozy, as drawn by Riss, Aurel, or Luz, manifestly signify greed and ruthlessness in drawings that are laser-guided to meet their target. However, although their message seems unambiguous, these comics still fall into what Rancière calls the "representational logic that seeks to produce effects by representations."[41] The relationship between artistic production and political mobilization is not, he argues, so straightforward.

39. Ibid., 61.
40. Ibid., 60.
41. Ibid., 43.

Fig. 3. Faro and Marie-Ève Malouines, *Moi, Président: Jusqu'ici tout va bien!* (Paris : Jungle, 2014), 27. © Jungle, 2014.

FROM REPRESENTATIONAL LOGIC
TO "CRITICAL ART"

There is another form of "critical art," Rancière says, that has combined representational logic with an aesthetic logic of shock and distancing. This is the Brechtian tradition that aims to promote reflection, while retaining an affective power that is translated into the ethical logic of the potential for revolt.[42] Rancière's examples of present-day "critical art" are strictly high-cultural and do not include comics; he refers mainly to installations in museums, although these may take the form of parodies of popular cultural forms such as manga or advertisements, intended to highlight "the power of the commodity, the reign of the spectacle or the pornography of power."[43] Parody, whether of specific images or of genres, has long been associated with comics.[44] It demands a "second-degree" interpretation, a requirement that may not always be obvious to the reader, who, in order to access

42. Ibid., 73–74.
43. Ibid., 76.
44. See Thierry Groensteen, *Parodies: La bande dessinée au second degré* (Paris: Skira Flammarion, 2010).

the second, ironical, meaning, must carry out the reframing that the artist declines to perform.[45]

An example is offered by the 15 January 2014 cover of *Charlie Hebdo*, drawn by Luz, following the revelations of *Closer* magazine about Hollande's affair with Julie Gayet. The single-image cartoon portrays the president standing in front of a tricolor, his penis hanging out, dripping with semen. The penis has been provided with a speech balloon containing the words "Moi président," referring to the anaphora that had suddenly made Hollande appear presidential shortly before the deciding round of the 2012 election. The cartoon may be read "at the first degree" as an indictment of Hollande for allowing his sexual impulses to distract him from his office, or as simple exploitation of the shock value of a crude depiction of the President, provocation for its own sake.[46] However, Charb, the late editor of *Charlie Hebdo*, questioned by the *Nouvel Observateur*, claimed a "second-degree" intention: "In fact, this cover is mainly intended to mock the other press titles that have covered this affair since the *Closer* revelations." *Charlie Hebdo* considered that the subject was not even newsworthy, he said, and was denouncing the "hypocrisy" of other newspapers.[47]

We might contend that the *Charlie Hebdo* image of Hollande, as a parody of mainstream press coverage, falls into Rancière's category of "critical art," its taboo-breaking effect stimulating critical reasoning as (and if) the "second degree" kicks in. But Rancière asks what happens when the "dissensual horizon," the critique of capitalism that once sustained critical art, is obscured by the contemporary context of consensus. When we have lost the forms of political struggle that offered a horizon for change, he contends, the types of parody that he describes, far from promoting dissensus, become self-perpetuating, and their indeterminacy (*indécidabilité*) becomes merely playful. They may even become part of the entertainment industry that they

45. Some cartoonists do perform just such a reframing: the British cartoonist Steve Bell, for example, often encloses parodies of right-wing news coverage within a drawing of a tabloid newspaper.

46. For a summary of debates around the interpretation of *Charlie Hebdo* images, along with debates around the separate but related area of free speech, in the wake of the massacre of cartoonists in January 2015, see Jane Weston, "Local Laughter, Global Polemics: Understanding *Charlie Hebdo*," *European Comic Art* 8.1 (Spring 2015): 6–14.

47. http://tempsreel.nouvelobs.com/politique/20140114.OBS2262/une-de-char lie-hebdo-sur-hollande-pour-dedramatiser-le-sujet.html

claim to be subverting.[48] In the case of the *Charlie Hebdo* cartoon, the frame within which we can reread the apparent sensationalizing of the President's private life as, instead, a critique of the celebritization of politics by the mainstream press relates to our knowledge of the history and ethos of the magazine itself; from its founding issue (under its original name of *Hara Kiri*) in 1960, it had set out to demolish the inanity and prurient timidity of the traditional French press.[49] This mission could be seen as a form of participation in the political upheavals of the period. In the twenty-first century, however, we can no longer reframe *Charlie Hebdo*'s exposure of the "reign of the spectacle" within the context of ongoing collective political struggle, that "horizon" having slipped out of sight. Does this mean that all that is left to us is "disenchanted parody"?[50] No, says Rancière. The loss of "certain things that were once self-evident" opens up the way for a whole set of "dissensual forms,"[51] as we will now see.

POLITICAL ART

The relationship between art and politics is not to do with the functionality of artistic production, according to Rancière. If aesthetic experience touches politics, it is because both can be defined as an experience of dissensus.[52] "Politics (*la politique*) is not about the exercise of power or the struggle for power."[53] Politics happens when those who are not normally seen or heard, who have no access to the "logos," the speech that counts, insist on taking up the place that democracy theoretically affords them as opposed to the place they have been assigned by the police order (*la police*).[54]

The role of political art, he proclaims, is the creation of new fictions. As we have seen, fiction for Rancière is not the creation of an imaginary world that is opposed to the real world. It aims rather to

48. Rancière, *Le spectateur émancipé*, 76–77. Rancière quotes an installation by Charles Ray, called *Révolution: Contre-révolution (Revolution: Counter-revolution)* that allegorizes this very indeterminacy.

49. Roxane Faissolle, "Hara Kiri en revue de presse" Dissertation, Aix-en-Provence: École supérieure d'art, 2009–2010. http://www.ecole-art-aix.fr/article4914.html

50. Rancièrè, *Le spectateur émancipé*, 84.

51. Ibid.

52. Ibid., 67.

53. Ibid., 66.

54. Rancière, *La mésentente*, 43–67; *Dis-agreement*, 21–42.

"change the reference system (*repères*) of what is visible and sayable, to show what was not seen, to show differently what was too easily seen."[55] Significantly for this essay, Rancière uses a number of terms that evoke the formal resources of comics. We have already quoted his reference to fictions that "draw a new landscape."[56] In defining the "distribution of the sensible" (*partage du sensible*), a term that recurs throughout his work in relation to the intersection of politics and art, he refers to the "delimitations (*découpages*) that define respective places and shares."[57] "Découpages" also has the specific meaning of "breakdown" in comics, the articulation of the sequence into separate and successive panels. Rancière further defines the "partage du sensible," in an article on the politics of literature, as "a partition of the visible and sayable (. . .) that frames a polemical common world."[58] Comics, can, of course, literally frame, and reframe, the world.

Étienne Davodeau is a prolific political comics artist. His many albums include *Rural! Chronique d'une collision politique* (*Rural! Chronicle of a Political Collision*),[59] a vision of the countryside not as a place of tranquility but of combat, that of an organic farm collective against the building of a motorway (for private profit) that will cut brutally through their land. Davodeau outlines his general method in the foreword. His framing is selective, and he does not pretend to objectivity: this is why he persistently includes himself in the frame.

We focus here on the multiple prize-winning *Les mauvaises gens* (*The People from Les Mauges/The Bad People*),[60] which, like most of Davodeau's albums, exemplifies politics as happening when "those who have no right to be counted as speaking beings make themselves of some account."[61] It is the story of the political education

55. *Le spectateur émancipé*, 72.

56. Ibid., 84.

57. Rancière, *Le partage du sensible, esthétique et politique* (Paris: La Fabrique, 2000), 12. *The Politics of Aesthetics*, trans. Gabriel Rockhill (London: Continuum, 2004), 12. Rockhill translates "sensible" as "sensible." An alternative translation would be "perceptible."

58. Rancière, "The Politics of Literature," *SubStance* 33/1, Issue 103 (2004): 10–24 (10).

59. Étienne Davodeau, *Rural! Chronique d'une collision politique* (Paris: Delcourt, 2001).

60. Davodeau, *Les mauvaises gens* (Paris: Delcourt, 2005).

61. Rancière, *La mésentente*, 49; *Dis-agreement*, 27.

of Davodeau's parents, Maurice and Marie-Jo, both brought up in a conservative Catholic milieu in the Vendée, a region with a famously counter-revolutionary past. They learn their place very early: both are forced to leave school for financial reasons when they turn fourteen. On two pages with identical layout, each made up of two vertical panels, the breakdown emphasizes the termination of their educational prospects. On the first of these, a panel in which Maurice gazes back toward his school is divided across the gutter from one in which the dark door of a machine shed looms over him (Fig. 4). A few pages later, a panel in which Marie-Jo leaves her school for the last time is separated off from one in which she stands in the shadow of the jagged outline of the shoe factory that awaits her (Fig. 5).

At the end of the 1950s, a young priest from the Jeunesse ouvrière chrétienne (Young Workers' Christian Movement) (JOC) arrives in the village, and encourages the young people not to be intimidated by the petty authoritarianism of their supervisors. Two panels showing a basketball game, not quite aligned across the gutter, suggest the jolting effect of people moving out of their allotted place, and the basket scored at the top of the next page expresses their exhilaration at standing up for their rights (Fig. 6). Davodeau's parents become involved in the setting up of union branches in their respective workplaces and take part in various militant actions that run counter to the tradition of docile obedience to bosses, including two demonstrations in 1962 and 1972, against a big local Catholic employer, Eram, that sacks workers who try to join a union. Over thirty years later, Davodeau interviews the priest, who had subsequently left the priesthood, and who tells him that even if the workers as well as the bosses were at that time all still practicing Catholics, there was a "rupturing of consensus" (*rupture de consensus*) over what was meant by "liberté" and "justice."[62] This is the very definition of "mésentente" given by Rancière, the disagreement that is the basis for political subjectivization, the process of becoming a political subject: it is a conflict between those who do not understand the same thing from the same words.[63]

In 1971, the Davodeaus join the PS, led by Mitterrand. Their son, from the standpoint of 2005, emphasizes the opportunism of the wily politician, describing him in a narrative voiceover as "the ex-Vichy

---

62. Davodeau, *Les mauvaises gens*, 137.
63. Rancière, *La mésentente*, 12. This section of the preface is not included in Rose's translation.

Fig. 4. Étienne Davodeau, *Les mauvaises gens* (Paris: Delcourt, 2005), 24. © Delcourt, 2005.

Fig. 5. Étienne Davodeau, *Les mauvaises gens* (Paris: Delcourt, 2005), 34.
© Delcourt, 2005.

Fig. 6. Étienne Davodeau, *Les mauvaises gens* (Paris: Delcourt, 2005), 53. ©
Delcourt, 2005.

functionary," who had managed to regain his political virginity.[64] This is not the perspective of his parents in the 1970s: the PS program that they enthusiastically support demands a break with capitalist society,[65] and the comic details the intensity and fervor of their lives as PS militants. The epilogue consists of the agonizing televised countdown to the result of the presidential election of 10 May 1981, which Davodeau further stretches out by intercalating a series of flashbacks and flash-forwards, delaying the announcement until the penultimate page. On the final page, the first panel shows Maurice, Marie-Jo, and their comrades celebrating what they believe to be a victory for radical change. The second, and last, panel consists of the pixelated close-up of Mitterrand on the television screen. A caption box contains Davodeau's dedication of the book to his parents (Fig. 7).

Is this political art? The subject matter concerns dissensus, and a process of political subjectivization, but does that make the album itself political? In an article in *Cahiers du Cinéma* in 2000, admittedly about film and not comics, but arguably with a more general application, Rancière distinguishes between the "real of fiction" and "political fictions of the real."[66] The "real of fiction" is made up of the "real of recognition," a surface documentarism that makes it credible, with characters falling into familiar categories of socio-cultural identity, and spiced up with the "real of surprise," the suspense mechanisms of fiction that breathe life into what is otherwise an inert, consensual object, in which politics is depoliticized. In contrast, the "political fiction of the real" is not consensual but polemical. It presents itself not as an enquiry into a truth, but into the formal means of constructing that enquiry.[67] It must change the relationship between the real and the fictional, the past and the present, History and stories.[68]

Like *Rural!*, the story of *Les mauvaises gens* is accompanied by the metanarrative of Davodeau's enquiry. He draws himself consulting his parents, and other militants, and making adjustments to fit with their recollections: his images clearly display the process of their own making (Fig. 8). However, we have seen that other comics gonzo reporters similarly show themselves at work, and, with the

64. Davodeau, *Les mauvaises gens*, 97.
65. Ibid., 117.
66. Rancière, "Il est arrivé quelque chose au réel" (*Something Has Happened to Reality*), *Cahiers du Cinéma* 545 (2000): 62–64 (63).
67. Ibid., 62–63
68. Ibid., 64.

Fig. 7. Étienne Davodeau, *Les mauvaises gens* (Paris: Delcourt, 2005), 184. © Delcourt, 2005.

exception of Duhoo's book, we would not describe the result as polemical. Moreover, *Les mauvaises gens* is not entirely devoted, unlike the films that Rancière uses as examples, such as Hervé le Roux's *Reprise* (1995), to questioning the way that "truth" comes into being.

We might, then, class his album as the "real of fiction." These militants are familiar to us from a now obsolete "leftist dramaturgy,"

40

Fig. 8. Étienne Davodeau, *Les mauvaises gens* (Paris: Delcourt, 2005), 40. ©
Delcourt, 2005.

in Martin O'Shaughnessy's term (i.e. the "real of recognition");[69] suspense is activated as we are made to share the tension of awaiting the election result (i.e. "the real of surprise"); and the ending is poignant but demobilizing, given the reader's knowledge that the joyous optimism was misplaced, since Mitterrand's presidency would see not a break with capitalist society, but the triumph of neo-liberalism. What Rancière calls "old-fashioned militantism" (*la vieillerie militante*),[70] can be consigned definitively to the past, the animation of the Davodeau parents and their comrades in the penultimate panel giving way to the frozen image of Mitterrand in the final one.

The album is, though, more complex than the above interpretation would allow. Instead of reading the final image as doubly depoliticizing (their story is all wrapped up by its happy end; History tells us that their victory was "really" a defeat), we can read it instead as a critique of, precisely, the depoliticization of politics. Paul Virilio has argued that the image made out of pixels is implicated in creating consensus and denies agency to the viewer.[71] The pixelated image of Mitterrand starkly represents the transition from dissensus to the consensual fiction that will be fostered by media coverage. But Davodeau's album as a whole resoundingly demonstrates both that dissensus will, in fact, continue past that frozen moment, and that comics can be a vehicle for political art. This is achieved through the disruption of time frames.

For Rancière, temporality is key to the replacement of the grand leftist narrative, which gave a "sense of the intelligibility of our lived world and a sense of its possible transformation,"[72] by a new dominant narrative that "proclaims the global triumph of world capitalism and global liberal democracy."[73] Under this new narrative, time works as a principle of impossibility: there are "things you can no longer do, ideas in which you can no longer believe, futures that you can no longer imagine."[74] "This is what 'consensus' means: the

69. Martin O'Shaughnessy, *The New Face of Political Cinema: Commitment in French Cinema Since 1995* (Oxford: Berghahn, 2007), 2. For a discussion of Rancière's article in relation to cinema, see 31–33.

70. Rancière, "Il est arrivé quelque chose au réel," 62.

71. See Paul Virilio, *The Vision Machine*, trans. Julie Rose, (Bloomington: Indiana UP, 1994), 75–76.

72. Rancière, "In What Time Do We Live?," 14.

73. Ibid.

74. Ibid., 12.

monopoly of the forms of description of the perceptible, the thinkable, and the doable."[75] But, he insists, there have always been forms
of political action that construct a "dissident temporality."[76] Examples occur within the diegesis of *Les mauvaises gens*. The workers
in the shoe factory resist attempts by the bosses to speed up their
output: the temporally indeterminate gutters between the repetitive
gestures made by Davodeau's mother can, therefore, be understood as
sites of struggle. Furthermore, Marie-Jo defies her boss by insisting on
taking her annual leave at the same time as her husband. And Maurice recalls the events of May 68: there was a factory occupation, time
for discussion, even if the defeat of a divided left led to the enforced
restoration of everyday routines.

The role of a politics of art also concerns temporality, says Rancière: it "intertwines different times within little machines or *dis-
positifs*, that construct other possibilities of looking at the present."[77]
He borrows the term "heterochrony" from Foucault, and defines it as
"a redistribution of times that invents new capacities for reframing a
present."[78] This intertwining of different times is exactly what Davodeau offers. The flashbacks and the two flash-forwards that distend
the narration of the 1981 sequence showing the televised election
countdown are not mere suspense mechanisms but recount another
story. The flashbacks give us glimpses of Davodeau's own troubled
education, itself interwoven with the account of a campaign, begun
three months before the May 1981 election, for a state school to be
built in an area exclusively served by private religious schools, a campaign in which the teenage Davodeau was enlisted to design posters.
The two proleptic panels show, firstly, the struggle still being waged
in 1985, as a symbolic foundation stone is laid (while the 2005 caption informs us that the school was never built, a somber note that
jars with the excitement of the build-up to the result in the surrounding panels), and secondly, the adult Davodeau at his drawing board,
producing, we assume, the album we are reading (Figs. 9a and b). The
period of the presidential election and the artificial tension of the
countdown coexist, we understand, with other temporalities: one in
which people were demanding access to state education for their chil-

75. Ibid., 27.
76. Ibid.
77. Ibid., 34.
78. Ibid., 36.

dren, and one in which a young man became politicized and went on to create polemical art. The image of Mitterrand's electoral victory, which, with hindsight, we read as a betrayal of the aspirations of the left, is thereby reframed by Davodeau within different chronologies, that of a continuing grass-roots fight for equal educational rights, even if ultimately thwarted, and that of his own apprenticeship in, and practice of, comics as politics.

More generally, throughout the album Davodeau offers new ways of seeing the present through recurring representations of a "dissensual horizon." *Les mauvaises gens* opens on the optical point of view of the three-year-old Marie-Jo as she careers, in a tiny cart, toward the celebrations of the Liberation in 1945, and that *élan*, stalled by her stultifying job, returns when, on a JOC camping trip, she looks out toward the line where sea meets sky, a metaphor for the "chance for emancipation" (*possibilité d'émancipation*) now opening up.[79] Other images of horizons follow, including those that feature in the sequence where Maurice stands as a candidate in local elections in 1979, with no expectation of winning, in order to show that "local dignitaries, aristocrats, and industrialists are not the only ones entitled to exercise power."[80] There is one panel in which the horizon lies ahead not of any character, but of the reader. As Davodeau drives to meet the militant JOC priest who had come to his parents' village at the end of the 1950s, he crosses a bridge, horizontally bisecting the panel. Although the discussion will take him back in time to a culture of militancy, the car travels from left to right, conventionally an indication of forward progress in a comic. And the reader is offered the straight ahead perspective of the road under the bridge (Fig. 10): past, present, and future are brought together, a diagrammatic representation of Rancière's "new landscape of the visible, sayable, and doable."

CONCLUSION

This article has argued that the new genre of political reportage in French comics has often failed to challenge the notion of politics as the deal-making of the powerful; that while the capacity of the medium for caricature has been deployed with a moral purpose, the ridi-

79. Davodeau, *Les mauvaises gens*, 63.
80. Ibid., 171.

178

Fig. 9a Étienne Davodeau, *Les mauvaises gens* (Paris: Delcourt, 2005), 178–79. © Delcourt, 2005.

179

Fig. 9b. Étienne Davodeau, *Les mauvaises gens* (Paris: Delcourt, 2005), 178–79. © Delcourt, 2005.

Fig. 10. Étienne Davodeau, *Les mauvaises gens* (Paris: Delcourt, 2005), 133.
© Delcourt, 2005.

culing of politicians is not in itself a political act; and that the critical intent of parody may be missed in a climate of consensus where the prospect of societal transformation has been closed off. It then offered a reading of Davodeau's *Les mauvaises gens* as a project of reframing the present and keeping open a dissensual horizon of possibilities for change. Rancière refers to forms of art that "work at the crossroads of temporalities and worlds of experience," and that "distend or disrupt the time of domination."[81] What art form, we might ask, can achieve that better than comics?

81. Rancière, "In What Time Do We Live?," 37.

NIKOLA WITKO

Alternative *Bande Dessinée* and Anti-Consumerism: Laurence Grove Interviews Nikola Witko

How would you describe briefly yourself, your work, and your place in the contemporary BD scene?

As an independent author, although I have also worked with more mainstream publishers. . .

How do you see BD evolving, and how are you part of that?

Since what I consider BD's second golden age—its maturity in the early 90s and the emergence of publishing controlled by authors themselves (as in our case)—BD has reached a much higher level where all forms and narrative techniques are possible. Few people would have imagined such a range of possibilities fifty years ago, and it is quite flattering to think one has been part of this liberation.

More specifically, which past work do you feel most represents you, and what are your future plans?

I tend to think that despite their flaws and occasional awkwardness, early works often best express an author's personality (this is also often true in cinema and music). So the goal now would be to rediscover that first vision, and to transcribe it using the technical mastery one has acquired, but this is easier said than done. Too much technique or reflection often kills one's natural instincts.

Can you outline briefly how the technical process of BD creation functions for you?

My original interest was in drawing, so learning about BD was also little by little learning to "abandon" drawing, or rather to give it less importance, to pay less attention to its aesthetic aspect so as to make

YFS 131/132, Bande Dessinée: *Thinking Outside the Boxes,* ed. Laurence Grove and Michael Syrotinski, © 2017 by Yale University.

Fig. 1. Nikola Witko, original artwork: *Afro*. Courtesy of the artist.

drawing support narrative. Story and drawing function binomially, and to give too much importance out of preference or passion to the latter can obscure a simple reading of the story. So at the moment I am working on simplifying, retaining only what is strictly necessary to bring the narrative to life, rather than on artistic embellishment and technique, which I tend to save for illustrations.

What is specific to BD as compared to other arts and media?

BD has, like literature, an almost infinite range of exploration and possibility, or at least this range is only limited by the author's imagination. Budget considerations or production difficulties are not really

Fig. 2. Nikola Witko, original artwork: *Alf*. Courtesy of the artist.

factors. Like film or theater, however, BD does leave less room for readers' imaginations because it already presents them with visual decor and images of characters. The zone of freedom for the reader is thus between the panels, and in the rhythm of reading. This rhythm can be so different from one work to the next that one could almost describe it as musical. Plus there is of course the pictorial element proper to painting.

It is this harlequin aspect of BD that I think explains why it was considered an inferior art form for so long. But I don't think this is true at all. To be in command of so many different elements and to assemble them into a coherent work, you need to have the balance of a tightrope walker. Or the skill of a puppeteer, making sure no one sees the strings.

Fig. 3. Nikola Witko, original artwork: *Bootleg*. Courtesy of the artist.

Fig. 4. Nikola Witko, original artwork: *Fakir*. Courtesy of the artist.

Fig. 5. Nikola Witko, original artwork: *Franky Dictator*. Courtesy of the artist.

Fig. 6. Nikola Witko, original artwork: *Gree*. Courtesy of the artist.

Do you, and BD in general, have a specific French identity?

BD in general is becoming more and more international. If each culture had its own BD and genre—manga, comix, Franco-Belgian BD—now graphic novels, autobiographies, BD-journalism, extreme graphzines, and so on have reached a certain maturity. . . and many borders, including those of storytelling, have been crossed. All of this is due in large part to artists who self-publish, who have been able to go beyond the expectations of commercial publishing to make BD a genuine means of expression. In this regard, France has played a major role, and I am pleased to have been part of that generation.

What is the role, if there is one, for academic study with respect to contemporary BD?

It is important to teach students how to read, and especially to think of BD not as a product, or a job, but as an art in its own right (not all

Fig. 7. Nikola Witko, original artwork: *Rodeo*. Courtesy of the artist.

Fig. 8. Nikola Witko, original artwork: *Wild Boar*. Courtesy of the artist.

the time, of course). There is such a wide range of possibilities, both graphic and narrative, that we have to start learning how to appreciate them.

How do you "think outside the box"?

Like other art forms before it, BD is now reaching the point where it has become abstract, conceptual even. However, this happened in a very short time-span if one refers to print-history, and a long time-span if one refers to the history of sequential images. Even though I don't like all BD, just as with music or any other art form, it does make me very happy to see that anything is finally possible with BD.

—Translated from the French by Michael Syrotinski

JEAN-YVES FERRI

Asterix and Modern France: Laurence Grove Interviews Jean-Yves Ferri

Describe briefly yourself, your work, and your place in the contemporary BD scene.

I think I am both at the classical end of the BD spectrum (with *Asterix*) and the contemporary end, with my own series (*De Gaulle, Le retour*

Fig. 1. Jean-Yves Ferri, original drawing for *Yale French Studies*. Courtesy of the artist.

YFS 131/132, Bande Dessinée: *Thinking Outside the Boxes*, ed. Laurence Grove and Michael Syrotinski, © 2017 by Yale University.

à la terre). Albums like *Le sens de la vis* are more stream of conscious-ness, with a more underground audience.

How do you see BD evolving, and how are you part of that?

From a creative point of view, even when I do contemporary BD, I play with the classical conventions (a strip of 3 or 6 frames, for example). So it is difficult to talk about evolution generally. From a commercial point of view, however, there has been an evolution: BD has become a big market, particularly in France. *Astérix* is different again, and a special case. It is a kind of national treasure (of the Chateauneuf du Pape or Roquefort kind).

More specifically, which past work do you feel most represents you, and what are your future plans?

Without a doubt *Retour à la terre*, because even though it is drawn by Larcenet, I am the scriptwriter, and make up the storyboards, and I completely identify with it, both in its minimalism and in a certain "naiveté" in the way it is handled. Among my current projects, right now I am in fact again working with Larcenet on a sort of "anthol-ogy of the comic strip" whose authors, as well as their works, will be invented.

Can you outline briefly how the technical process of BD creation functions in your case.

It depends on the series. For *Asterix*, I work on everything, up to and including the storyboard. Then Conrad does the drawings, and we exchange ideas throughout the whole process. After the inking, we oversee the coloring in. When I'm the one doing the drawing, I'm a traditionalist and work on paper. I don't use a table or graphic soft-ware, but I do use a computer to scan and touch up the lines, as well as to color in.

What is specific to BD as compared to other arts and media?

For me, what is specific about BD is the way it allows you to play with time. A page lays out before the reader's eyes a whole range of possibilities: going back to previous frames, comparing, accelerating, slowing down, and so on. I think BD is where one can best play with ellipsis too. BD is a selection of stills. This is even truer of BD that is humorous, whose effects are almost impossible to convey in film, for example.

Fig. 2. Jean-Yves Ferri, drawing for publication in the luxury edition of *Asterix and the Picts*. Courtesy of the artist.

Do you, and BD in general, have a specific French identity?

My type of humor (comic strips and cartoons) is quite Anglo-Saxon, that is, in its economy of words and effects. Before World War II there was a "French style" of cartoons (Capy, Gus Bofa), but it didn't really carry over into BD. The identity of BD since the 60s has rather been Franco-Belgian, less graphic, but more adapted to a frame-by-frame reading.

Nowadays authors are looking in other directions. *Asterix* represents a persistence of the Franco-Belgian style that Goscinny had perfected, but it is a slightly anachronistic phenomenon now.

What is the role, if there is one, for academic study with respect to contemporary BD?

I think it is important that the academy is taking BD seriously! Criticism of BD in the media is too superficial, or too verbose. BD deserves

Fig. 3. Jean-Yves Ferri, original preparatory drawing for a magazine publication. Courtesy of the artist.

better attention. The drawing element especially is greatly undervalued in France, or the teaching of drawing is devalorized.

How do you "think outside the box"?

I don't understand that question. I never think outside my box. I always think inside with some little holes to breathe.

—Translated from the French by Michael Syrotinski

IV. BD and the World Beyond

BILL MARSHALL

Imagining the First French Empire:
Bande Dessinée and the Atlantic

A page nearly halfway through Patrick Prugne's 2011 album, *French-man*, forms one starting point for this discussion. Alban Labiche is the eponymous young Frenchman who, through the manipulation of his aristocratic neighbor in Normandy, has been drafted into Bona-parte's armed forces and sent to New Orleans on the eve of the hando-ver of Louisiana to the United States in 1803. Having rescued a slave from arbitrary execution by his master, Labiche now finds himself a deserter and accompanying the gruff old French-Canadian fur trader Toussaint Charbonneau northwards toward St. Louis, where the latter is to join the Lewis and Clark expedition (which will of course open up the Pacific North-West for American exploration and settlement). The page (Fig. 1) asymmetrically and elliptically combines several procedures that contribute to the classic,[1] linear journey narrative but that have wider, even much wider, metonymic implications.

The layout consists of three strips, the first of which is a single panel that frames the two men and their mule in silhouette on the right, in an image dominated by the verdure of a forest landscape and stream, and punctuated by Alban's voice-off panel in three separate diagonal boxes. This and the two right-hand panels below are under-stood as being in the imperfect tense in terms of both the narration and the representative, repeated action they illustrate across different moments and sites: hunting deer, the encounter(s) with Amerindians (which thus is not a suspenseful prelude to conflict on the next page, but rather, through tense, links temporally to Alban's voiceover— "and my Normandy became even further away. . ."—and therefore

---

1. Patrick Prugne, *Frenchman* (Paris: Galerie Daniel Maghen, 2011), 35.

YFS 131/132, Bande Dessinée: *Thinking Outside the Boxes*, ed. Laurence Grove and Michael Syrotinski, © 2017 by Yale University.

Fig. 1. Patrick Prugne, *Frenchman* (Paris: Galerie Daniel Maghen, 2011), 35.

to the past, and the arrival on the next page of Alban's friend Louis in New Orleans, marking the distance in space and time that separates them). The smaller panels of the second and third strips recount, in the perfect tense, not only the narrative events of Toussaint revealing why he rescued Alban (his dislike for Americans), and killing a deadly snake, but also the developing mental state of Alban himself.

Established modes of analysis of *bande dessinée* take the reader a certain way: the motif of the men in long shot or at the side of the panel, to be understood as dwarfed by the immensity of the American landscape, forms one of the basic aspects of the *tressage* of the text, and is much repeated, as is that of the frequently dominant place of a wild animal—bear, bison, eagle, squirrel, vulture—in a panel. In addition, the narrative structure of the tale could not be simpler, in its combination of disrupted equilibrium, quest journey, separation and reunion, heroes and helpers. The genre is clear, that of the *BD historique* (historical BD) that now forms such an important part of the industry, in terms of production, marketing, and institutions.[2]

And yet, the metonymic force of this page of *Frenchman* inevitably takes the reader or scholar further into realms of cultural history and intertextuality. The first encounter with Amerindians speaks to a history of representations that this text must navigate and within which it positions itself. At this point in the narrative, and within the layout, the Amerindians are as one with landscape, two framed from behind and two silhouetted in the distance against the forest, as their position in the final panel echoes those of the three figures in the first, who were merging with the natural scene, and with the hunted deer in the third. Although not focalized from Alban's point of view, here they form part of the imperfect tense of his narration, and of the start of his composition with this new landscape and its cultures.

Frenchman cannot help, then, but be located in a whole history of French cultural and literary encounters with the Americas and their indigenous inhabitants. Here it is a question of course not of the "truth" of indigeneity, but of the uses to which the indigenous, from his/her appearance in fifteenth and sixteenth-century texts that first

---

2. See "Bande dessinée: Histoire en cours—avec Pascal Ory," 27 September 2013, http://www.nonfiction.fr/article-6724-bande_dessinee_histoire_en_cours_entretien _avec_pascal_ory.htm. In the context of the role that *bande dessinée* has taken in pedagogy, note that the *Prix Château de Cheverny de la bande dessinée historique* was inaugurated in 2004 at the Rendez-vous de l'histoire de Blois.

harness the questioning cultural relativism the figure provides, is put for an artistic or intellectual project, and in the myths of popular culture. Roughly contemporaneous with the period in which *Frenchman* is set, Chateaubriand, drawing on his American voyage of 1791 in *Atala* (1801), *Les Natchez* (1826), and *Voyages en Amérique* (1827), weaves his way through pre-conceived pseudo-Rousseauist conceptions of *le bon sauvage* and of America as "nature" to emerge with a Christianized, "universalized" and fundamentally ethnocentric view of the merits of "natural" and "civilized" life. Tzvetan Todorov's often stinging analysis of Chateaubriand's procedure links this with an egocentrism that characterizes not only this author's hyperbolic Romantic subjectivity but, along with nationalism and the scientism he finds elsewhere, the emerging nineteenth century as a whole: "Is it not a form of violence—reserved exclusively to creator-artists—to be able to shape at will and as needed the identity of persons one has encountered?"[3]

Patrick Prugne's treatment of Amerindians is even-handed, however: their violence is provoked and justified by Louis's companions' cruel murder of a squaw; Louis himself becomes fully and definitely assimilated into the Pawnee tribe; one of a group of women has a point of view shot when she perceives the threatening silhouettes of four white men at the water's edge, a scene that opens the sequel, *Pawnee* (2013).[4] This points to perhaps a more important intertext. James Fenimore Cooper's "Leatherstocking" sequence of novels, including *The Last of the Mohicans* (1826), was immensely popular in France in the first quarter of the nineteenth century, influencing canonical writers such as Balzac (*Les Chouans*, 1829). Fenimore Cooper lived in Europe, including Paris, where he published several of his novels between 1826 and 1833, with *The Last of the Mohicans* immediately translated by the prolific Auguste-Jean-Baptiste Defauconpret. Whatever the racial politics of the novel in an American context (white superiority, Amerindian destiny as metaphor), Fenimore Cooper's legacy is that of contributing to the French fantasy-myth, elaborated through the nineteenth century, of "America," "le 'Far-West.'"[5] This myth

3. Tzvetan Todorov, *On Human Diversity: Nationalism, Racism and Exoticism in French Thought*, trans. Catherine Porter (Cambridge MA: Harvard University Press, 1993), 298.

4. Prugne, *Pawnee* (Paris: Galerie Daniel Maghen, 2013).

5. Fenimore Cooper's legacy has been long studied. See, for example, Margaret Murray Gibb, *Le roman de bas-de-cuir: Étude sur Fenimore Cooper et son influence*

continues through popular fiction (Gabriel Ferry; Gustave Aimard), and culminates in the phenomenon of Buffalo Bill's Wild West Show that toured Europe from 1886.

Crucially, while the influence of Leatherstocking/Hawkeye is palpable in Ferry's *Le coureur de bois* (1850), here the author, like Aimard in *Les trappeurs de l'Arkansas* of 1858, typically takes an individual who is French or of French descent and uses him as a *passeur* between cultures. The first official contacts between France and Quebec since the Conquest of 1759 did not take place until 1855, which led to more sustained cultural "rediscoveries" of the descendants of that first French overseas empire.[6]

Here is the ambiguity that tinges the exoticism of this cultural production: if Todorov defines the exotic as a (selectively) valorized Other, not a stable entity but "a country and a culture defined exclusively by their relation to the observer,"[7] then the question is raised of what becomes of the refracted exoticism that takes a "French America" not just as mediator but as its actual object of contemplation. In *Frenchman* and *Pawnee*, this adjacency, and indeed entanglement of self/other, strange/familiar, France/America, European/indigenous, is embodied not only by the cross-cultural Louis but of course by Toussaint Charbonneau himself, a real historical figure (1767–1843) one of whose Shoshone wives, Sacagawea (who accompanied him on the Lewis and Clark expedition), makes an appearance. (As an aside, Patrice Edde plays another fictionalized Toussaint in Alejandro G. Iñárritu"s *The Revenant* of 2015, a prolongation of the figure of the "Frenchie" in Hollywood cinema who has punctuated that sub-genre of the western, the northern forests movie, since the early-twentieth century.)

If Prugne is careful in interviews to argue for the effort of documentation that underpins his work,[8] the cultural circulations that inform it are also evident in his visual style. While the role of illustrations in the numerous editions of Fenimore Cooper's novels have an important history—for example the Belgian *bédéiste* René Follet's

en France (Paris: Honoré Champion, 1927); Georgina C. Bosset, *Fenimore Cooper et le roman d'aventure en France vers 1830* (Paris: Librairie Vrin, 1928).

6. For a more sustained discussion of cultural relations between France and Quebec in this period and following, see Chapter Four of my *Quebec National Cinema* (Montreal: McGill-Queen's University Press, 2001), 75–102.

7. Todorov, *On Human Diversity*, 264.

8. https://www.youtube.com/watch?v=DuDuoW8CTU8

contributions to a 1962 version,⁹—Patrick Prugne's eschewal of digital techniques in favor of a direct use of watercolor places him in a distinct lineage. Arguably more in vogue in Britain and the United States in the nineteenth century than in continental Europe, watercolor enables Prugne to establish ambiance through the depiction of changes in natural light according to time of day, shadow, and background, and to indulge in painterly, set-piece one-page or double-page panels (two in *Frenchman* and *Pawnee*, respectively), or, more commonly, half-pages or panels without text. It is sufficient to look at his depiction of foliage to see the resemblances to work by America's premier nineteenth-century watercolorist, Winslow Homer—see for example, *On The Trail* (1892), or *Sunlight and Shadow* (c.1872)—to understand that both artists are part of an Atlantic circulation of influences and of visuality. Homer, like many American artists, spent a year in Paris, in 1867, where he exhibited at the Exposition universelle.

Analysis of a second BD page enables further exploration of this Atlantic dimension. Patrice Pellerin's volumes for the *L'épervier* series are set in the 1740s, its eponymous hero is a privateer in the employ of the King of France, Yann de Kermeur, who captains a ship, *La méduse*. The first six-volume cycle of his adventures (1994–2005) has been followed by a second, of which three volumes have thus far (2016) been produced (2009–2015). A six-episode television adaptation was broadcast in 2011. This example is taken from the 2015 volume, number nine of the whole series (Fig. 2).¹⁰

Two large panels construct a symmetrical positioning of *La Méduse*: at top left, on the open sea and viewed toward the prow, its headsail obscuring the female figurehead; at bottom right, viewed toward the stern as it enters the harbor of Louisbourg in Canada, dwarfing the town's rooftops. With Yann's voice-off present in each, the right half of the top panel is taken up by three superimposed panels that provide a montage of him gazing (with desire—"the riches of this New World. All the riches. . .") at the mysterious Amerindian princess he has been ordered to transport. The last of the three superimposed panels has him in close-up ruminating about forgetting what he has left behind. This segues into the incrustation found in the second large panel, two superimposed panels, the second narrower

9. (Paris: Éditions des deux coqs d'or, 1962).
10. Patrice Pellerin, *L'épervier: Coulez la Méduse!*, vol. 9 (Paris: Soleil, 2015), 44.

Fig. 2. Patrice Pellerin, *L'épervier: Coulez la Méduse!*, vol. 9 (Paris: Soleil, 2015), 44.

and in close-up, of another love interest, Yann's cousin Agnès, locked in a dungeon in Brittany by the evil Marquis de Beaucourt who has trapped her into marriage, and who utters Yann's name in the single speech bubble of the page. This chimes with a favored device of Pellerin's, the contrastive play of light and shadow, openness (the ocean) and confinement, wide angle and close-up: "the fact of including a close-up or a narrow-angle shot in a wide-angle shot [. . .], of placing one in the other, will render the close-up closer and the wide-angle shot wider."[11]

The visual style and layout differ significantly from Prugne, in the more conventional use of (predominantly even) light and color; in the emphasis given to narrative, identification, and suspense by the use of incrustation to evoke distance and motivation; and in the emphasis of sea over land. *L'épervier* is a series about the ocean, in which sea battles and voyages structure the narrative, dominate the visuals and iconography, and in turn determine the meaning of what occurs—court intrigues, romantic betrayals, frame-ups of the lead protagonist—on land. Unlike *Frenchman* and *Pawnee*, which contain a double page of the conscripted Alban on board ship and a few panels of his and Louis's arrival in New Orleans harbor, four of Alban's sister Angèle disembarking off the east coast of the USA, *L'épervier* is less about "America" than the "Atlantic," with that ocean forming the series' crucible of meaning in terms both of its narrative peripeties and its wider mythology, and memory.

On the one hand, then, *L'épervier* partakes of the French tradition of the *roman maritime*. Analyzing the history but also characteristics of the genre such as the use of stock characters (captains, surgeons, cabin boys), the alternations of action on land and sea, and the ship as dramatic *huis clos*, Odile Gannier notes the confluence of determinants at its origins that propelled its success, which can be traced—for authors writing in French—from Eugène Sue through Gustave Aimard (once more), Jules Verne, and Pierre MacOrlan—to, arguably, the contemporary BD medium:

> The maritime novel flowers fully at a time when Romanticism is favoring a sentimental and metaphysical relationship with wide-open spaces whose forces surpass humanity, when Realism allows it a base of credibility, and when the vogue for the historical novel endows

11. Paul Chopelin and Tristan Martine, *Le siècle des lumières en bande dessinée: De poudre et de dentelles* (Paris: Karthala, 2014), 302–303.

a certain type of maritime adventure with legitimacy and abundant subject-matter.[12]

On the other hand, in Pellerin, legitimacy is also partly sought through a process of documentation that manifests itself stylistically. On this page from *Coulez la Méduse!* the ship, especially in the closer view provided on the bottom right of the second panel, is portrayed in meticulous detail, as it is throughout the series, a level of detail which includes the varying deployment of the sails. Pellerin's source is the abundant work of the naval architect Jean Boudriot, who, working closely with the Musée de la marine, published the four-volume *Le vaisseau de 74 canons* (1973–1977).[13] Pellerin's procedure thus contributes to the ongoing assertion of (cultural) legitimacy of the BD as art form, to the "credibility" of the text in relation to its narrative extremes, and thus to an "effect of the real," in Barthes's terms, in which the signified of the signifying detail connotes "reality" as much as if not more than its designated object.[14]

Frenchman, *Pawnee*, and the *L'épervier* series are examples of the much larger field of the *BD historique*, as we have seen, but within that the number of albums and series that deal with the French North American empire and/or the Atlantic is abundant and significant. Indeed, already Prugne, in collaboration with the scriptwriter Tiburge Oger, had produced in 2009 *Canoë Bay*,[15] an Atlantic and North American treasure hunt narrative whose cabin boy protagonist is a survivor of the Acadian deportations. There are antecedents: *L'épervier* grew directly out of the work Pellerin did on the *Barbe-rouge* pirate series that began in 1959 (which had various authors, starting with Jean-Michel Charlier and Victor Hubinon), although the classification as "historical" would here be elusive. The breakthrough text was François Bourgeon's *Les passagers du vent* (five volumes, 1980–1984, with a sequel, *La petite fille bois-caïman*, in two volumes, 2009–2010),[16]

12. Odile Gannier, *Le roman maritime: Émergence d'un genre en Occident* (Paris: Presses de l'université Paris-Sorbonne, 2011), 14.

13. Jean Boudriot, *Le vaisseau de 74 canons: Traité pratique d'art naval* (Grenoble, Éditions des quatre seigneurs [collection "Archéologie navale française"], 1973–1977).

14. See Roland Barthes, "L'effet de reel," in Barthes et al., *Littérature et réalité* (Paris: Seuil, 1982), 81–90.

15. Prugne and Tiburge Oger, *Canoë Bay* (Paris: Galerie Daniel Maghen, 2009).

16. François Bourgeon, *Les passagers du vent*, 5 vols. (Paris: Glénat/12bis, 2009); *La petite fille bois-caïman, livre 1* (Paris: Glénat/12bis, 2009); *La petite fille bois-caïman, livre 2* (Paris: Éditions Delcourt, 2014).

which we shall examine momentarily. Indeed, its success led the Glénat publishing house to inaugurate its magazine and collection *Vécu* devoted to the *BD historique*. But there is also, for example, the massive series *Les pionniers du nouveau monde* (Jean-Marie Charles, Ersel, Maryse Charles, twenty volumes, 1982–2015), which depicts its French and French-Canadian characters suffering the upheavals wrought by the Franco-British conflicts of the mid-eighteenth century (Acadian deportation, French and Indian War).

Writing of *Les passagers du vent*, Matthew Screech attributes the vogue for the *BD historique* from the 1970s/1980s onward as evidence of a French identity crisis: "The boom in historical *bandes dessinées* is very much in keeping with the popular desire to rediscover identity by re-connecting with a common past."[17] If we see these series in terms of *national* culture, we might proceed to analyze them as we might any historical fiction, such as a costume drama or heritage film. As Homi Bhabha has argued, the relationship between the origins ("common past," in Screech's terms) and present of any "national people" is problematic. There is a—temporal—split between that pedagogy of origins and the need to elaborate, repeat, and reproduce the nation, in all senses: "In the production of the nation as narration there is a split between the continuist, accumulative temporality of the pedagogical, and the repetitious, recursive strategy of the performance."[18]

The people of the origins, in the *énoncé* of the fictional past, are also both "us" and not "us," they are the same *and* different. In "national" romances set in the past, for example, the heterosexual couple may not be able to achieve stable form (beyond the obstacles inherent to the romance genre) because of the past's pastness: *Un long dimanche de fiançailles* (Jeunet, 2004) is one example (for most of the film at least, until its ambiguous ending: the life-long love between the protagonists is prevented by World War I); *Titanic* (Cameron, 1997), may, on a "world" or, literally, Atlantic level, be another, the couple destroyed not just because of the sinking but because of the class rigidities of 1912; or else, in *Ridicule* (Leconte, 1996), the main protagonist's goals (for social justice, technical progress), are prevented by

17. Matthew Screech, *Masters of the Ninth Art: Bandes Dessinées and Franco-Belgian Identity* (Liverpool: Liverpool University Press, 2005), 194.
18. Homi Bhabha, "DissemiNation," in *Nation and Narration*, ed. Homi Bhabha (London: Routledge, 1990), 297.

the injustices of the eighteenth-century *ancien régime*. In these cases, audiences look at the past via an intervening event (post-1945 peace and security in Europe, 1960s sexual revolution or counter-culture, 1970s feminism and after, the French Revolution) that evaluates the texts' protagonists as "lacking" in the gains that came after.

This argument works up to a point with *Frenchman* and *L'épervier.* Alban's life is disrupted by the injustice of Napoleonic conscription, persistent feudal hierarchy, and the institution of slavery; the Angèle-Louis couple is consequently prevented from forming. Yann de Kermeur suffers in turn from court intrigue, the *ancien régime* class system, and the penal institution of the galleys. However, the argument around the "lack" bound up with the national narrative could cut both ways: the "lack" is in the present, in the form of a lost empire, although this would be to neglect the contemporary reality of French in the Americas represented by, among other spaces, Quebec and Guyane.

Many of these BD protagonists are "modern" *avant la lettre*, or so it would seem. In the case of Yann L'Épervier (this being de Kermeur's epithet name), any temporal split, lack, or difference is overcome via hyper-masculinity. Pellerin argues he is ahead of his time, but still of his time: his experience in the galleys can explain, or at least contribute to, his desire to defend slaves and the weak.[19] But what if the perspective were here de-centered from the national to the transnational, to the Atlantic space as a crucible of the modern, and also as a variation—or variations—on "Frenchness" that are not about a lost empire but a lost sense of plural, mobile, diasporic identities within French culture, of crossings and *métissages*? Yann—Breton, growing up in Guyane adjacent to indigenous peoples including his friend Chacta who accompanies him on his voyages—would epitomize this, as well as Louis, with his "becoming-Amerindian." The problematic becomes then not one of *re-membering* in which a national plenitude is sewn together, but a dispersal of memory/memories, which emphasizes transformative lines of flight across the Atlantic and through the Americas.

Les passagers du vent offers further insights into these arguments, as it is so bound up with memory, especially but not only the *contested* memory of the slave trade. It is worth situating 1980, the year

19. Chopelin and Martine, *Le siècle des lumières en bande dessinée*, 312.

of the first volume, in relation to that memory, and the way in which Bourgeon's *oeuvre* contributed to creating a new momentum, which helped bring the trade more center-stage in public memory and the public sphere. Bourgeon builds on renewed work by historians, such as Serge Daget, who edited Jean Mettas's repertoire of French slave-trading expeditions that appeared in 1978, and Pierre Pluchon, whose *La route des esclaves* was published in 1980. The vast majority of historical works written on the French Atlantic slave trade have been published since that date, and this production has accompanied, and been accompanied by, a politics of memory and commemoration. The main slave trading port, Nantes, has experienced a journey from a refusal by the municipal council to support a conference on the Code Noir in 1985, through a new policy of recognition and re-branding which saw a major exhibition on the trade in 1992, the erection of a commemorative sculpture (torn down by vandals) in 1998, and the inauguration of a memorial garden and walkway—the Mémorial de l'abolition de l'esclavage—in 2012. In 2001, a law was adopted that recognized the slave trade as a crime against humanity, and since 2006 the 10th of May has been the official national day of commemorating the trade and its abolition. None of this is to establish a causal link with *Les passagers du vent*: rather, it is to position Bourgeon's texts within the ongoing re-negotiation in France of relations to the colonial and slave-trading past.

Les passagers du vent achieves its evocation of that past, still rare in popular cultural forms of the time, in two potentially contradictory ways. The first is, as in Pellerin, a work of documentation, and indeed a proclamation of documentation, as in the peritexts of volume 3, *Le comptoir de Juda* (1981). Here are to be found: the 1776 plan of the Saint-Louis fort in "Juda" (present-day Ouidah in Benin, where the protagonists spend most of volumes 3 and 4), which Bourgeon found in the Archives nationales and which he then reproduces in a three-quarters size panel;[20] and cross-sections of the imagined slaver ship, the *Marie-Caroline*, based on the *Marie-Séraphine*, found in Mettas's repertoire and the subject of further advice from Jean Boudriot. In addition, the dialogue at times reveals itself to be a product of research on eighteenth-century debates, along with their ambiguities and contradictions: a page dominated by discussion—and by small panels of

20. Bourgeon *Les passagers du vent*, vol. 3, 21.

faces and speech bubbles save for the larger top panel that groups the men and one woman as brandy is served—between the ships's officers and the emancipationist Isabeau;[21] the ship's surgeon who regards the trade as barbaric but inevitable, but who nonetheless is making notes, helped by Isabeau, that are ultimately destined for Jacques Pierre Brissot, one of the founders in 1788 of the Société des amis des Noirs.[22]

Secondly, the saga is as reliant on the tropes of maritime adventure fiction, and its contradictions, as is *L'épervier*. Indeed, this is where it decisively differs from the more straightforwardly didactic project of BD artist Serge Diantantu, whose *Mémoire de l'esclavage* series was published between 2010 and 2015. Here, however, a strong female teenage protagonist, Isabeau, leads the reader through a narrative, taking place in 1781 and 1782, of identity switches, loss of social status, loves lost with both women and men (her rather weak *compagnon* is obliged to leave definitively in volume 5), with female rather than male nudity to the fore, along with exile in England, a voyage in the triangular Atlantic slave trade that ends in Saint-Domingue, voodoo, wild animals, and slave mutiny. The latter, unlike in Mérimée's 1829 short story, *Tamango*, which ends with the victorious slaves unable to navigate a now drifting ship, ends in defeat for the revolt but nonetheless shows the slaves to possess agency and strategic skills, is even partly focalized by them (for example, panels on page 4 of volume 4 of *Les passagers du vent*), and is led by two women.

These two approaches cease to seem antithetical if we reflect, beyond questions of the "effect of the real" and the cultural legitimacy of the BD form, upon the workings of, and labor upon, memory. The works of both Bourgeon and Pellerin can be seen as "memory-images," in the sense that "archives" are raided that are both literal (the work of documentation) and cultural (the repertoire and repository of images, fictions, and genres from which these authors draw). It is indicative how the fluid terms "repertoire" and "archive" slide so easily between history (we recall the title of Mettas' work), memory, and fiction (the "archives secrètes"—presented as such, with "gaps"—of Yann L'Épervier that tell his backstory).[23]

This explains the self-reflexiveness about memory that pervades the late sequels to *Les passagers du vent*, *La petite fille bois-caïman*

21. Ibid., 14.
22. Bourgeon *Les passagers du vent*, vol. 2, 47–48.
23. See Pellerin, *L'épervier: Archives secrètes* (Paris: Dupuis, 2006).

(in two volumes, 2009 and 2014). Set in war-torn Louisiana in 1862 to 1863, they feature an equally assertive but resolutely confederacy-supporting descendant of Isabeau, "Zabo," who, having lost her mother and sibling as a result of the conflict, sets off from New Orleans for the relative safety of an ancestral plantation on a remote bayou. She is accompanied by, and argues with, a French republican photojournalist, whose presence obliges and permits an explanation of the difference between a Creole and a Cajun: "Not French from France, but I am *French* [in English in the text], yes! Creole in other words!"[24] This text is much more pluralized linguistically, with extensive use of untranslated Creole in the Saint-Domingue sequences, and of Cajun French in those set in Louisiana.

At the plantation Zabo discovers her 98-year-old great-grandmother, the original Isa/Isabeau. Via portraits, Isabeau's written memoirs, and her own oral narration, the story is told of her life since Saint-Domingue in the 1780s: the move to Louisiana working as a naturalist's artist, her marriage to his son, the dramatic loss of her mixed-race daughter, and her disfigurement due to a family member's betrayal. The final sequences of each woman's story are eloquent about time and memory. A page features three top panels that progressively pull out from Isa's position as she watches the torrential downpour from the gallery of her swamp cabin, to an aerial image of the Mississippi delta illuminated by the dying sun: here the standard poetic trope linking time with flowing water, and the dark open sea—featured in a single panel on the following page—with death, is complicated by the delta image,[25] where time flows in linear fashion but also gets caught in complicated backwaters that return upon themselves, branch out, and make surprising connections. The final panel of the volumes, occupying the lower two-thirds of the page, has the younger, now safe Zabo framed at a table, quill in hand, wearing the amulets given her by Isa, writing in a notebook, the reader assumes, the words we see in the dialogue box at the bottom of the panel. She is in a library or study where books encased behind mesh form the background of the image in three partial rectangles; she gazes out of frame, to bottom right, leading the reader's eye beyond the page. This narration had explicitly begun (after a completely text-free two-page hiatus when Zabo discovers the floodwater and the death of Isa, and

24. Bourgeon, *La petite fille bois-caïman, livre 1*, 23.
25. Bourgeon, *La petite fille bois-caïman, livre 2*, 63–64.

canoes away from the cabin) three pages earlier, but implicitly the entire two volumes could be understood this way, ending with Zabo writing the narrative we have read.

Given the links made here between the individual and collective, including those shared archives and repositories of memory that are books and libraries, it is pertinent to ask in the context of these BD texts, whose cultural memory is present or represented? A brief excursion into a *BD historique* in Quebec, where Glénat set up a subsidiary in 2007, may shed light. Jean-Sébastien Bérubé's four-volume series, *Radisson* (2009–2012),[26] takes as its subject the life of explorer and trapper Pierre-Esprit Radisson (c. 1636–1710). The text has elements relevant to a pedagogical "origin" of a French-Canadian people in the brief glimpses we get of seventeenth-century Montreal, Quebec City, and Trois-Rivières, but Radisson is above all a bizarre choice as the subject of a nationalist project, notorious for his collaboration with the English and his role in the Hudson's Bay Company, and the author of unreliable memoirs. In the BD texts, he embodies therefore certain fundamental uncertainties of Quebec identity, particularly with regard to the Amerindians, presented here in the pluralism of their different cultural groups. Patterns and rhythms of adjacency and differentiation have characterized that relationship over the centuries, although debates in recent years have seen an assertion of the view of French-Canadians as settler colonia*lists* rather than as colon*ized* subjects, the prevailing argument of 1960s nationalism.[27] Traditionally, the difference represented by the adjacency of Amerindian and French-Canadian identity has been managed symbolically by the unifying hyper-masculinity of the *coureur de bois* figure, escaping in individualist manner the restrictions of the *ancien régime*: indeed in volume 3, Radisson remarks, "You see, in this country, we are both masters and servants."[28] In Bérubé's series, Radisson, while heterosexually active, is marked especially by youth and mobility. As the sovereignty project in Quebec sits on the backburner, and as younger generations are marked by a plurality of cultural references or "inter(re)ferences" which free "English" from

26. Jean-Sébastien Bérubé, *Radisson: D'après l'autobiographie de Pierre-Esprit Radisson*, 4 vols. (Montreal: Glénat, 2009–2012).

27. See Audra Simpson, *Mohawk Interruptus: Political Life Across the Borders of Settler States* (Durham: Duke University Press, 2014).

28. Bérubé, *Radisson*, vol. 3, 30.

166   *Yale French Studies*

the colonial reference,[29] Radisson/*Radisson* could be seen to embody renewed elaborations of the performance of Quebec identity in terms of the mobile modernity of the *transfuge*.[30]

It is a commonplace of BD historiography that the relationship with American culture is a perennial reference point, be it in terms of resemblance or disengagement.[31] At the same time, as we have seen, the history of French (popular) cultural engagements over the past two hundred years has frequently involved a fantasy "America," a sometimes exoticized vessel into which could be poured Franco-French dilemmas and preoccupations. The Quebec geographer Jean Morisset, scourge of both Quebec and metropolitan French cultural nationalism, has lambasted metropolitan French culture for this myth-making that resolutely excludes, for example, its own creolized, *canadien* offshoot: "Real America could not exist in French in the eyes of France, precisely for fear of its dream of America turning into an indecipherable nightmare speaking *joual* or Creole."[32] The texts by Prugne, Pellerin, and Bourgeon examined here permit a certain pluralization and even dissipation of the national "we" across time and space, even as it is so implicated in the slave trade, and interpellated, by Isabeau in *Le comptoir de Juda*.[33] The oceanic crossings and that distance in time and space all contribute to a problematization of the same/other relationship, historical memory, and French cultural identities. The texts are characterized by continuing tensions between the French Atlantic as the nostalgic space of a national pastness or a convocation to identity debates concerning (pre-republican) difference and hybridity; as accompanying the colonial enterprise or proposing nomadic *déracinement*; as proposing fixed, "major" positions of mastery, or minor, even utopian takes on mobility. It could be

29. See Jocelyn Létourneau, *Passer à l'avenir: Histoire, mémoire, identité dans le Québec d'aujourd'hui* (Montreal: Boréal, 2000).
30. A further relevant Quebec BD corpus of texts is to be found in the work of François Lapierre, whose *Chroniques sauvages* (2011) and two-part *Sagah-Nah* (2002, 2004) spin magic realist tales in seventeenth-century New France from the Amerindian protagonist point of view, mixing myth, skepticism, and anticlericalism.
31. See Pascal Ory, "Mickey go home! La désaméricanisation de la bande déssinée (1945–1950)," *Vingtième Siècle* 4 (octobre 1984): 77–88.
32. Jean Morisset and Eric Waddell, *Amériques: Deux parcours au départ de la Grande Rivière* (Montreal: L'Hexagone, 2000), 271.
33. "We snatch in their thousands each year men, women, and children from their land and family, for them to soak with their blood and tears products we perhaps don't even need" (Bourgeon, *Les passagers du vent*, vol. 3, 14).

argued that this Atlantic corpus within the *BD historique* represents one the of the few French cultural "realms" or "sites of memory" in Pierre Nora's terms (and we recall the very "hexagonal" nature of the *lieux de mémoire* project), in which there is a memorial investment in the first French overseas empire in North America, alongside the very official Commission franco-québécoise des lieux de mémoire communs (*http://cfqlmc.org/*), and the enthusiasm for transatlantic genealogy. Michael Rothberg has pointed out the fallacy of the assumption in Nora and Maurice Halbwachs that "there are as many memories as there are groups, but that each group possesses a coherent language of remembrance." Rather, the French Atlantic *bandes dessinées*, in their aesthetic contradictions and ambiguities, might be seen to contain, like the pattern of the Mississippi delta and its swamps on the fringes of the ocean itself, hints of "knots of memory," "rhizomatic networks of temporality and cultural reference that exceed attempts at territorialization (whether at the local or national level) and identitarian reduction."[34]

34. Michael Rothberg, "Introduction: Between Memory and Memory: From *Lieux de mémoire* to *Noeuds de mémoire*," *Yale French Studies* 118–119 (2010): 3–12 (7).

MARK MCKINNEY

Photography's Other Territories in Séra's *L'eau et la terre*

SÉRA'S TRANS-ARTISTIC COMICS[1]

In May 1975 Phouséra Ing, his siblings, and their mother, a French-woman, arrived in France as refugees escaping from the Khmer Rouge, whose mass murders, torture, and brutally misguided national development policies killed some 1,700,000 Cambodians. Phouséra's Cambodian father, Ing Phourin, who had been a high official in the Cambodian government before the arrival of the Khmer Rouge, was killed by them. Phouséra eventually trained in Paris as a fine artist. He has created paintings and sculptures under the names Phousséra and, more recently, Séra, also the pen name with which he signs his comics.[2] Working alone and in collaboration with other cartoonists, Séra has published several graphic novels, beginning in 1983.[3] His

1. I am deeply grateful to Séra for generously sharing much with me over the last two decades, beginning when we first met in Paris in summer 1996. Early in what has become a long research project on (post-)colonialism and comics, I benefitted from Séra's extensive knowledge of the wide field of *bande dessinée*, which he freely shared with me. Then and at several points since, Séra has also discussed his own art with me. He has likewise very kindly and generously provided several documents that have allowed me to understand better the wide range and the meanings of his art. Séra also generously gave permission to reproduce the illustrations in this article.

    I am also very grateful to Hugo Frey, Dominique Le Duc, Laurence Grove, the International Bande Dessinée Society (IBDS), and the staff of the French Institute of London, especially Magali Laigne. I read an earlier version of this essay at the IBDS conference organized by Hugo, Dominique, and Laurence at the Institute in 2007. Magali later kindly sent me a recording of a roundtable in which Séra participated at the Institute on 21 October 2007. I warmly thank Laurence and Michael Syrotinski for giving me the opportunity to publish an article on Séra's beautiful and intelligent art.

    2. *Séra, en d'autres territoires*, ed. Eric Joly and Dominique Poncet (Montrouge: P.L.G, 2006), 24.

    3. Ibid., 18–21.

YFS 131/132, Bande Dessinée: *Thinking Outside the Boxes*, ed. Laurence Grove and Michael Syrotinski, © 2017 by Yale University.

L'eau et la terre: Cambodge 1975–1979 (Water and Earth: Cambodia 1975–1979), published in 2005, is the second volume in a series that now has three.[4] The first, *Impasse et rouge: Cambodge 1970–1975 (Impasse and Red: Cambodia 1970–1975)*, was published in 1995 and 2003, in two versions with significant differences.[5] The third volume, *Lendemains de cendres: Cambodge 1979–1993 (Morrows of Ashes: Cambodia 1979–1993)* was published in 2007.[6] Together, the three books cover the historical period from before the victory of the Khmer Rouge, through the Khmer Rouge regime's rule, to its fall and aftermath. *Séra, en d'autres territoires (Séra, in Other Territories)*, a retrospective exhibition of his paintings, was held from 3 February to 31 March 2006 in Première Station—Espace d'art contemporain, an art exhibition space in a subway station in Paris.[7] Séra is also a long-time contributor to the comics periodical *P.L.G.* He has taught graphic art at the Sorbonne for many years, and now travels periodically from Paris to teach in Cambodia.[8]

Interviewers of Séra have noted that his cartooning is influenced by painting and sculpture.[9] He has also described the importance of photography to his art. Séra's trans-artistic creation makes his comics exemplary for studying relationships between comics and other arts. Here I focus on photography's role in *L'eau et la terre*, a complex and powerful graphic narrative that deals primarily with the Khmer Rouge genocide. Artistically manipulating photographs, whether by painting directly on them or by digital transformation, or both, constitutes one of the most important, haunting ways in which Séra represents the trauma of the Cambodian genocide.[10] It is also manifested in the violent deaths, murder mysteries, and eroticized bodies found

4. Séra, *L'eau et la terre: Cambodge 1975–1979* (Paris: Guy Delcourt, 2005). All translations from French are mine.

5. Séra, *Impasse et rouge*, preface by Jacques Tardi (Paris: Rackham, 1995); Séra, *Impasse et rouge: Cambodge 1970–1975* (Paris: Albin Michel, 2003).

6. Séra, *Lendemains de cendres: Cambodge 1979–1993*, preface by Bernard Kouchner (Paris: Guy Delcourt, 2007).

7. Joly and Poncet, *Séra, en d'autres territoires*, 64.

8. Ibid., 54, 64, 67–73.

9. Ibid., 24.

10. Cf. Adrien Genoudet, *Dessiner l'histoire: Pour une histoire visuelle*, preface by Pascal Ory (Paris: Le Manuscrit 2015), 161–68. Séra kindly brought Genoudet's work to my attention in early 2016. I read Genoudet's chapter after completing this essay. Our analyses converge on several points, as I indicate throughout.

in virtually all of his comics, even those not ostensibly about the genocide.[11] In recent years his art has deservedly received increasing attention in France, Cambodia, and beyond. For example, in 2010 the film company Vivement lundi! released a documentary by Céline Dréan on Séra.[12] Adrien Genoudet, a French historian, also recently published a chapter on Séra's comics.[13] Séra's works have been prefaced by important figures associated with comics, Cambodia, or human rights: the first edition of *Impasse et rouge* by Jacques Tardi, *L'eau et la terre* by Rithy Panh, and *Lendemains de cendres* by Bernard Kouchner.

HAUNTING PARADOXES OF PHOTOGRAPHY AND DRAWING, AUTO/BIOGRAPHY AND FICTION

Susan Sontag describes a well-known paradox in *Regarding the Pain of Others*, an essay on looking at certain kinds of images, especially war photography.[14] Through means both subjective and artistic, photography gives us the impression that we are confronting an objective reality of a most compelling and excruciating sort, and with little or no mediation or manipulation by man or machine, despite the fact that such images are virtually always subjectively created by the artist. Another paradox in Séra's work, noted in an interview with him, is that he has so far mainly chosen fictional comics instead of autobiographical ones to tell stories about important world historical events, even though he himself was caught up in that history, and despite the existence of a strong autobiographical trend in comics over the past few decades.[15]

Séra has categorically stated: "Watch out, *L'eau et la terre* is not at all an autobiographical narrative."[16] Séra's personal story is different from those of his characters in *L'eau et la terre* in crucial ways. By escaping from Cambodia to France he was spared having to live and die under the Khmer regime, which *L'eau et la terre* depicts. He has also explained that his eschewal of autobiography is a form of cultural and

11. Joly and Poncet, *Séra, en d'autres territoires*, 63.
12. Céline Dréan, *Séra le veilleur*, (Rennes: Vivement lundi!, 2010).
13. Genoudet, *Dessiner l'histoire*: 141–71.
14. Susan Sontag, *Regarding the Pain of Others* (New York: Farrar, Straus and Giroux, 2003).
15. Joly and Poncet, *Séra, en d'autres territoires*, 30.
16. Ibid., 11.

personal modesty.[17] Still, there are autobiographical, personal dimensions to Séra's historical fictions, as Tardi notes in his preface, even if they may not be immediately obvious to readers.[18] Séra borrows from autobiography and witness narratives by, for example, having some characters textually narrate their stories in the first person in *L'eau et la terre*.[19] Furthermore, that work includes an image (Fig. 1) of the last place where Séra's father lived in Cambodia, and where he was executed in 1978.[20] However, one only learns this by reading *Séra, en d'autres territoires*, where Séra reveals it.[21] He also connects his family history to the fictionalized stories of *Lendemains de cendres* through a double-page reproducing letters that Cambodian survivors of the genocide sent from Thailand to Séra's mother in France,[22] and then, after another of several maps that Séra includes in his comics about Cambodia, sixteen pages of watercolors and sketches that the artist made upon his return to Phnom Penh in 1993, eighteen years after his flight into exile.[23]

If Séra's goal had been to heighten the purely fictional effect of his *bande dessinée* stories, he might have told them without photographs at all, and excluded any trace of auto/biography or family history from them. Conversely, if Séra had wished to emphasize the purely historical, documentary character of his stories, he could have inserted, into his narratives, photographs of victims of the genocide that are not ostensibly touched up, placing them either within a story or in a dossier at a book's end, as some other cartoonists working on (post-)colonial history or genocide have done. To emphasize the historical and the real, Séra could have also explicitly incorporated auto/ biography into his narrative, say by recounting his family's flight from the Khmer Rouge, or clearly telling of his father's entrapment and death. Two works by French cartoonist Emmanuel Guibert are some of the best-known examples of comics in which auto/biography

17. Ibid., 30, cf. 64.

18. Séra, *Impasse et rouge* (Paris: Rackham, 1995), 4; cf. *Séra, en d'autres territoires*, 29, 74–75. Genoudet, *Dessiner l'histoire*, 163–68, provides other examples.

19. Cf. Genoudet, *Dessiner l'histoire*, 146, 170.

20. Séra, *L'eau et la terre*, 97; Jason Dittmer, "Our land: Berfrois interviews Séra," (2012), http://www.berfrois.com/2012/08/when-dittmer-met-sera/

21. Joly and Poncet, *Séra, en d'autres territoires*, 18, 34–35.

22. The letter may contain news about Séra's father, including his death; Séra, *Lendemains de cendres*, 106–107; Joly and Poncet, *Séra, en d'autres territoires*, 18.

23. Séra, *Lendemains de cendres*, 110–25; cf. Séra, *Impasse et rouge* (Paris: Rackham, 1995), 113–24; Genoudet, *Dessiner l'histoire*, 171.

Fig. 1. From Séra, *L'eau et la terre* (Paris: Delcourt, 2005), 97. © SÉRA.

and photography are brought together to tell histories of violent conflicts with worldwide ramifications. In *The Photographer*, by Guibert, Didier Lefèvre and Frédéric Lemercier, photographs by the titular photographer, Lefèvre, are directly inserted, almost untouched, into a comic-strip narrative to help tell the story of the Soviet war in Afghanistan.[24] Guibert has also published *Alan's War*, which reproduces several photographs of Alan Cope, who fought in Europe as an American G.I. in the Second World War, and of his friends, including an appendix presented like a photo album.[25] In both works by Guibert, photographs serve a more or less classic documentary function in the narrative, much like the one that Sontag describes.

Séra has explained his use of photographs as a way of avoiding the often colonialist visual clichés found in many other French and Belgian comics about Southeast Asia.[26] Yet of course photographs themselves may be or become just such clichés, through their initial composition or widespread circulation and reproduction. What then happens when Séra reworks historical photos in a way that calls attention to their artistic transformation and thereby to the fictionalized status of the photograph in the narrative? What happens when the artist inserts auto/biographical or familial traces into, or at the threshold of, a fictional text, but without explaining their relation to the fiction? The photograph (Fig. 2) presented as the most real or objective in *L'eau et la terre* is potentially autobiographical.[27] As the first image of the book, it occupies a prominent place, just after the cover illustration, and is the only one that appears not to have been transformed by the cartoonist. The photo depicts a happy moment, with three woman, a young child, and a dog. It is not part of the following fiction, but instead helps constitute the author's memorial dedication, along with the text below it, which states: "To the memory of those who had to begin a journey without the possibility of a return. . . ."[28] The photograph and dedication recall the beginning of the second volume of Art Spiegelman's *Maus*.[29] However, Séra's

24. Emmanuel Guibert, Didier Lefèvre, and Frédéric Lemercier, *The Photographer*, trans. and intro. Alexis Siegel (New York: First Second, 2009).

25. Guibert, *Alan's War: The Memories of G.I. Alan Cope*, trans. Kathryn Pulver, lettering Céline Merrien (New York: First Second, 2008).

26. Joly and Poncet, *Séra, en d'autres territoires*, 21.

27. Séra, *L'eau et la terre*, 4; cf. Joly and Poncet, *Séra, en d'autres territoires*, 1.

28. Cf. Genoudet, *Dessiner l'histoire*, 158.

29. Cf. Joly and Poncet, *Séra, en d'autres territoires*, 27.

À la mémoire de ceux qui ont dû prendre la route sans retour possible...

Fig. 2. From Séra, *L'eau et la terre* (Paris: Delcourt, 2005), 4. © SÉRA.

photo is devoid of names. Does it represent the artist in the arms of his Chinese nanny, whom he has described as being like a second mother to him?[30] Was it taken by his father, to whom Séra dedicated *Impasse et rouge*, the previous volume in the series? Does it show other members of his father's family? Together, the enigmatic photo and the textual reference to a tragic departure are haunting.

Sontag asserts that "[h]arrowing photographs do not inevitably lose their power to shock. But they are not much help if the task is to understand. Narratives can make us understand. Photographs do something else: they haunt us."[31] Of course this simple dichotomy is problematic, because narratives can haunt us, and photographs can

30. Ibid., 24, 64.
31. Sontag, *Regarding the Pain of Others*, 89.

help us understand. However, Sontag's remark is useful for helping us puzzle out how and why Séra uses photography in *L'eau et la terre*. Both haunting and explaining are important functions of war photographs and of narratives about wars, as Sontag suggests. As a sequential combination of words and images, *bande dessinée* is well-suited to describing the inexplicable, haunting nature of the trauma of war and genocide, as cartoonists such as Spiegelman have shown. Sontag ends her meditation on wartime images with a categorical denial that those who have not experienced war for themselves can really understand it.[32] Much of Spiegelman's and Séra's work attempts to apprehend and represent, for themselves and others, experiences of war and genocide that they did not undergo directly, but which have affected them deeply, which haunt them. What then is the specific contribution of photography to the haunting and explaining of *L'eau et la terre*, a graphic narrative? To answer this and explore the paradoxes just mentioned, let us look at a few more examples of how Séra uses photography in the book.

Sontag notes that some of the first war photographs, of soldiers killed during the American Civil War, included the rearrangement of dead bodies by the photographers to create certain dramatic effects.[33] The photographs shocked viewers.[34] This is the first example in a genealogy of manipulation and staged effects that Sontag lays out for us, in her dissection of photographic and drawn images of pain, suffering, and death. She observes that the odd thing is not the manipulative or fictionalizing activity of the news photographer, but instead our surprise and disappointment when we learn that the images were staged.[35] In order to create his fictional graphic narrative, and to heighten its dramatic effects, Séra, too, manipulates photographs and the stories attached to them. He rearranges images of human bodies and inanimate objects in a virtual manner, which is certainly physically different from, but nonetheless functionally akin to, the physical manipulation of real corpses by Matthew Brady's photographic team. Sontag describes how "the picture titled 'The Home of a Rebel Sharpshooter, Gettysburg' shows in fact a dead Confederate soldier

32. Ibid., 125–126.
33. Ibid., 51–55.
34. Ibid., 62–63.
35. Ibid., 55.

who was moved from where he had fallen on the field to a more photogenic site [. . .] and includes a prop rifle that Gardner leaned against
the barricade beside the corpse."[36]

Tea Kim Heang took one of the photographs that Séra borrowed.[37]
In *Requiem: By the Photographers Who Died in Vietnam and Indochina*, where it is reproduced, the photo is captioned "Siem Reap,
Cambodia, 1974. Cambodian girl with her Father's Rifle at a Marshal-
ing Point."[38] Séra changes several aspects of the photo, which transforms its historical setting and significance. The military backpack
carried by the girl and the rifle propped up against her have disappeared (Fig. 3). The image in *L'eau et la terre* helps represent the tran-
sitional period between the forced evacuation of Phnom Penh by the
Khmer Rouge beginning on 17 April 1975, after the fall of the Lon Nol
government, and the subsequent relegation of the evacuees to the
killing fields. Of course it is possible that Tea Kim Heang had propped
the rifle against the girl before taking the original photograph, but
by removing it Séra renders his image appropriate for representing
the vulnerability of a new kind of exile, after Cambodian military
resistance to the Khmer Rouge had been crushed. On the other hand,
he makes a Trans World Airlines bag more prominent in his image
than in the original photograph, perhaps to remind us of the connections between the United States and the previous period of Cambodian history, and of the abandonment by the outside world, including
the United States, of the Cambodians to the merciless and paranoid
Khmer Rouge leaders. Later in the graphic narrative, Séra uses an image of a high-flying jet to emphasize this last point.[39]

In addition to the important distinction between manipulating
real bodies and rearranging images of them, another major difference
between composing the Civil War photograph and Séra's use of the
photo by Tea Kim Heang is that the human subject is alive in both
this photo and the *bande dessinée* picture based on it. Elsewhere,
Séra moves us closer to photographs of the dead by incorporating into
his narrative some snapshots and posed photos from *Stilled Lives:*

36. Ibid., 54.
37. Séra, *L'eau et la terre*, 31.
38. Horst Faas and Tim Page, *Requiem: By the Photographers Who Died in Vietnam and Indochina*, intro. David Halberstam (New York: Random House, 1997),
282, 284
39. Séra, *L'eau et la terre*, 94.

Fig. 3. From Séra, *L'eau et la terre* (Paris: Delcourt), 31. © SÉRA.

Photographs from the Cambodian Genocide, although there too the people were alive when their pictures were taken.[40] Take, for example, a photograph captioned "Ben Savoeun and Three of her 15 Children: Ek Chandy (Age 8), Ek Chanda (Age 7) and Ek Phornny (Age 6) circa 1975."[41] Séra inserts it into his story via a sketch based on the photograph, and captions it "Ben Savoeun Family/Doc DCCAM- [i.e., the publisher of *Stilled Lives*]/Ben Savoeun and Three of her 15 Children/75/All Executed" (Fig. 4).[42] The red stamp, we later learn, is a "Chinese seal of validation of the Khmer Rouge for an execution."[43]

Together with the Khmer rouge slogan printed on top of the page and Séra's handwritten caption, the stamped sketch constitutes a damning indictment of Khmer Rouge violence, for how could three young children ever deserve to be executed? Séra's handwritten caption and the red stamps on the faces of the characters suggest that all four were executed. However, Séra's apparent source indicates that seven of Ben Savoeun's children (but not her) died during the Democratic Kampuchea period, but does not say which ones, nor how they died.[44] For example, did they die from malnutrition, disease, torture, or instead—as Séra indicates—by execution? Curiously, although in Ben Savoeun's autobiographical narrative she mentions the fact that one of her children was shot by the Khmer Rouge (but did this kill him?—she does not say), she says nothing about the deaths of her other children, although the authors indicate the seven deaths. Moreover, in a bizarre twist, she cannot conclusively identify herself in the photograph: "I don't know if the other person is me or not because I don't remember that sarong."[45]

The stamp, caption, and slogan on Séra's sketch erase some unsettling ambiguities from his source, in order to represent more forcefully the horrific toll of the Khmer Rouge regime. In his graphic novel, Séra changes the unexplained fate of Ben Savoeun's three children on the photo into certified executions. He thereby transforms

40. Wynne Cougill, *Stilled Lives: Photographs from the Cambodian Genocide*, with Pivoine Pang, Chhayran Ra and Sopheak Sim (Phnom Penh: Documentation Center of Cambodia, 2004).

41. Ibid., 3.

42. Séra, *L'eau et la terre*, 76.

43. Ibid., 109.

44. Cougill, *Stilled Lives*, 2–5.

45. Ibid., 4.

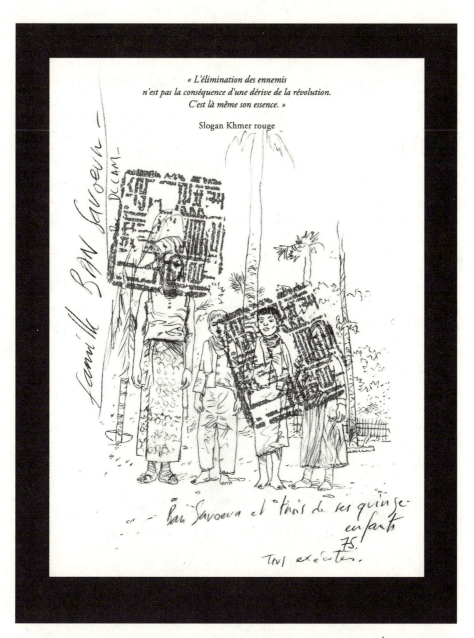

Fig. 4. From Séra, *L'eau et la terre* (Paris: Delcourt, 2005), 76. © SÉRA.

Ben Savoeun and her family into a synecdoche for the Cambodian people as a national family martyred by the Communist regime. The red, black, and white of Séra's image are all symbolic of this fate: the black of Khmer Rouge uniforms, the red of the Communist revolution (stated in the *rouge* [red] of Khmer Rouge), and the white as symbolic of death and mourning for Khmers and, or including, Séra.[46] At the same time, Séra provides a closure that has long been lacking for many Cambodians, including the artist himself: a confirmation that one's missing loved ones did indeed die in a specific way under the Khmer régime. The lack of adequate information surrounding the disappeared creates a mystery that makes more difficult the process of mourning and of reconstructing history, whether personal, familial, or national.[47]

Artists' sketches have sometimes constituted a mark of authenticity in graphic narratives about imperialism, colonialism, or genocide: they supposedly indicate the proximity of the artist to her or his historical subject. They may serve as evidence that an artist witnessed a source of the narrative, which therefore seems more real to the reader. Photographs have provided the same function with respect to graphic narratives, sometimes in conjunction with sketches. Séra told me that "the photo has one of the most intense emotional powers, and for the great majority of people, to find oneself before a photograph is to confront reality, what is or was."[48] Séra's sketch, based on a photograph of a woman who could be Ben Savoeun and three of her children, is designed to reinforce a historical effect.[49] Elsewhere in *L'eau et la terre*, one finds eerie images of faces looking out at the reader.[50] Séra deftly creates this effect by scanning photos, drawing images, and superimposing, coloring, and otherwise reworking them on a computer.[51] This appears to be the case with some of the final images in the book. One of the most forceful ones (Fig. 5) is based on a

46. Joly and Poncet, *Séra, en d'autres territoires*, 25; cf. Genoudet, *Dessiner l'histoire*, 157.

47. Cf. Genoudet, *Dessiner l'histoire*, 142–43, 158.

48. Séra, written personal communication, 1 April 2007.

49. Cf. Pierre Fresnault-Deruelle, "L'effet d'histoire," in *Histoire et bande dessinée: Actes du deuxième Colloque international éducation et bande dessinée, La Roque d'Antheron, 16–17 février 1979*, ed. Jean-Claude Faur (La Roque d'Antheron: Objectif promo-durance/Colloque international éducation et bande dessinée, 1979), 98–104.

50. Cf. Genoudet, *Dessiner l'histoire*, 151–58.

51. Joly and Poncet, *Séra, en d'autres territoires*, 30, 50–53.

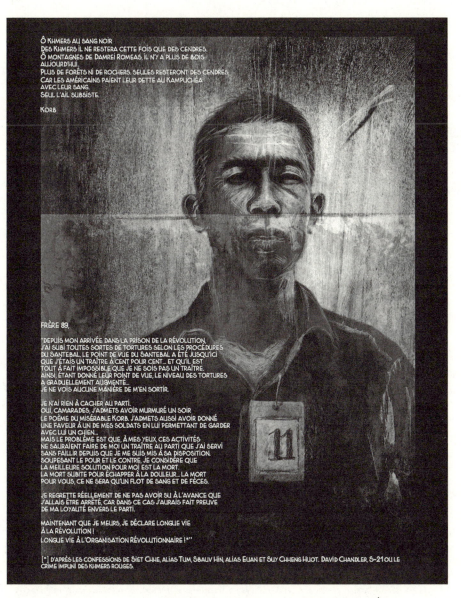

Fig. 5. From Séra, *L'eau et la terre* (Paris: Delcourt, 2005),103. © SÉRA.

photograph that Séra borrowed from *The Killing Fields*.[52] Of the photos reproduced in that book, showing the men, women, and children condemned to die at the S-21 Khmer Rouge prison, Sontag says that "the viewer is in the same position as the lackey behind the camera; the experience is sickening."[53] In a footnote, Séra indicates that the text that he associates with this man's face is in fact an amalgamation of excerpts from several confessions, all taken from the French translation of *Voices from S-21: Terror and History in Pol Pot's Secret Prison*, by historian David Chandler.[54] Séra's footnote imparts historical authenticity and credibility to the prisoner's voice in the text, but also marks it as Séra's own orchestration of sources.[55] Similarly, the image is a creative reworking by the artist: for example, he changed the prisoner's number from 412 to 11, and the color and texture of the image are very different from the original.

One of the photographers whom Séra cites as an inspiration is Sarah Moon.[56] He wrote to me that "Sarah Moon is one of the rare photographers who knows how to grasp what is situated between the real and the phantasm. She knows how to translate that frontier in the best possible way and to restitute it in all of its poetic fullness."[57] The final two pages of Séra's historical fiction frame the history of Cambodia as a nightmare remembered by an old woman (Figs. 6 and 7). She curses her two sons, who fought as soldiers on opposite sides, for having failed to prevent the destruction of both the US bombings that killed her parents and the Khmer Rouge massacres that decimated the rest of her family and killed both of the brothers.[58] Séra's source for the two images of the woman is again *Stilled Lives*,[59] as it is for at least the setting of the photo of her Khmer Rouge son.[60] The lighting on, and the artistic touching up of, the woman's face, the mottled pattern on her skin and on the floor, the brush-stroke pattern

52. Séra, *L'eau et la terre*, 103; *The Killing Fields*, ed. Chris Riley and Douglas Niven (Sante Fe: Twin Palms Publishers, 1996), 87.

53. Sontag, *Regarding the Pain of Others*, 61.

54. Séra, *L'eau et la terre*, 103; David Chandler, *Voices from S-21: Terror and History in Pol Pot's Secret Prison* (Berkeley: University of California Press, 1999).

55. Cf. Genoudet, *Dessiner l'histoire*, 147.

56. See, for example, Sarah Moon, *Vrais semblants* (Paris: Delpire, 1991).

57. Séra, written personal communication.

58. Séra, *L'eau et la terre*, 104–105.

59. Cougill, *Stilled Lives*, front cover, 9.

60. Ibid., 122.

Fig. 6. From Séra, *L'eau et la terre* (Paris: Delcourt, 2005), 104. © SÉRA.

Fig. 7. From Séra, *L'eau et la terre* (Paris: Delcourt, 2005), 105. © SÉRA.

of the space behind her, and the sepia coloring of all the images on these two pages help transform the double-page into a haunting space "between the real and fantasy."[61] In these two images, the old woman incarnates the older, popular Cambodian identity to which the book's title (*L'eau et la terre*), a transliteration of a Cambodian expression (*Teuk Dey*) refers.[62] She and other figures in *L'eau et la terre* look at and address us from a place that we could call *le presqu'au-delà* (the almost-beyond).[63] They proclaim that they are not yet dead, and appear to be the very image of the living dead.

"IN OTHER TERRITORIES": PHOTOGRAPHY AND COMICS UNDER THE THREAT OF DEATH

The cover illustration of *L'eau et la terre* (Fig. 8) is again a haunting image based on a photograph. The book's publication page informs us that it is "in homage to Sou Vichtih, who disappeared in 1975."[64] In his acknowledgements, Séra also expresses gratitude to Sou Vichith and twelve other photographers for having inspired him.[65] In his bibliography, placed after the conclusion to his historical fiction, Séra indicates that one of his sources is *Requiem: By the Photographers Who Died in Vietnam and Indochina.*[66] Listing one's historical and visual sources is a trend in French graphic novels about imperialism, colonialism, and genocide, and plays several important roles. It may have legal and artistic functions, because cartoonists thereby formally acknowledge the source of an image and their artistic debt. It also helps produce the history effect. Finally, it has a pedagogical function, by encouraging readers to learn more about the historical events and images behind the story, by reading other texts.[67]

Among the many modifications that Séra made in his cover illustration to the photograph taken by Sou Vichith, originally captioned

61. Séra, *L'eau et la terre*, 104–105.

62. Séra, written personal communication; Dittmer, "Our land: Berfrois interviews Séra".

63. Cf. Genoudet, *Dessiner l'histoire*, 154: "All these gazes that stare at us are gazes from a beyond (*un au-delà*), they are the witnesses who did not survive and who are here as though incarnated by the drawing of Séra."

64. Séra, *L'eau et la terre*, 112.

65. Séra, *L'eau et la terre*, 110; cf Genoudet, *Dessiner l'histoire*, 161.

66. Faas and Page, *Requiem*.

67. Cf. Genoudet, *Dessiner l'histoire*, 146–49.

Fig. 8. From Séra, *L'eau et la terre* (Paris: Delcourt, 2005), cover illustration.
© SÉRA.

"Near Phnom Penh, Cambodia, 1975," and published in *Requiem*,[68] the most significant is the replacement of what are apparently Cambodian government soldiers in the original, with armed Khmer rouge soldiers, on the left of the image, in the reworked version.[69] One of the soldiers is looking out at the viewer of the image, while the other looks toward the man walking down the road. This transforms the original photograph of a refugee, no doubt taken before the fall of Phnom Penh on 17 April 1975, into a much more disturbing image. The reader who returns to the cover image after having finished reading the book takes it to represent the forced emptying out of the cities by the Khmer Rouges, a process that led to the killing fields, where former city-dwellers died from overwork, malnutrition, torture, executions, and related causes. We might therefore see the refugee as walking toward his death. The white brushstrokes around his feet and his luggage look like a photographic halo, perhaps through a double exposure. They suggest movement, but also the ghost or spirit of the man.[70] This is the image of a (now) dead man walking.

Yet perhaps the most haunting aspect of Séra's reworked image is the look that the Khmer Rouge soldier gives the reader,[71] which sug-

68. Faas and Page, *Requiem*, 302–303.
69. Cf. Joly and Poncet, *Séra, en d'autres territoires*, 16–17.
70. Cf. Genoudet, *Dessiner l'histoire*, 154.
71. Cf. Ibid., 158.

gests that the reader/viewer of the book will witness the impending genocide and, like the man walking, risks being killed by the Khmer Rouge. The eerie effect is heightened by a reading of the short biography of Sou Vichith in *Requiem*:

> A photographer who worked for Gamma and AP, Sou Vichith and his wife and children took refuge in the French embassy when Phnom Penh fell, but they were forced out by the Khmer rouge. They began walking along Routes 5 and 6, where they were seen by Dith Pran headed in the direction of the killing fields. Dith Pran heard later that Sou Vichith died there.[72]

Séra's image implicitly follows or moves Sou Vichith from the position of photographer-viewer of the scene before the Khmer Rouge victory to that of condemned-viewed after it. In *Séra, en d'autres territoires*, Séra explained that he and his family likewise took refuge in the French embassy, and that he, his siblings and his mother—as French nationals—were allowed to stay at the embassy and then flee the country, whereas his Cambodian father was expelled from the embassy, remained in the country, and was killed.[73] The preliminary drawings for the dustcover are reproduced next to this part of the long interview, as though to emphasize the personal connections between the fates of Sou Vichith and Séra's family. Admittedly, the information in *Requiem* and the published interview of Séra are external to *L'eau et la terre*, but Séra clearly offers readers the opportunity to track down his sources and compare them with his graphic narrative. The gaze of one Khmer Rouge soldier is therefore directed at the reader, but also at the cartoonist drawing the image, and implicitly, by extension, at Sou Vichith, as the photographer who took the photo upon which the drawing is based. Séra puts himself as the cartoonist and we the readers, as well as the man walking, together in the position(s) of people watched by Khmer Rouge soldiers, and therefore about to die in the killing fields. We all thereby accompany Sou Vichith in his movement from viewer to viewed, from photographer to internal exile. Together under the deathly gaze of Khmer Rouge soldiers, we meet him walking along routes 5 and 6, toward the killing fields.

72. Faas and Page, *Requiem*, 315.
73. Joly and Poncet, *Séra, en d'autres territoires*, 16.

Séra's drawing, based on Sou Vichith's photograph, does what the photographer obviously could never have done. He could not have taken such a photograph of Khmer Rouge soldiers, and it could not have been sent out of the country to be published. The Khmer did not tolerate documentary photography of the type that Sou Vichith practiced, as Séra pointed out in describing the place of photography in *L'eau et la terre*:

> And so it is also a response that I send to the Reds. Photography, at the time, was completely forbidden. . . today that does not keep that weapon from turning back against them. A message addressed to that which, today, still thinks in positive terms about that period and that society.[74]

Photography in Séra's work is therefore also a weapon that he turns against the Khmer Rouge and those who continue to support their vision of society. In *L'eau et la terre* he moves it into other territories, where photography could not have existed, just as he imports images of those territories into France. He does so in order to tell stories that photographers were prevented from telling and, in fact, that photography on its own may not be able to tell. By inserting redrawn photographs into his graphic narrative, Séra hauntingly helps us understand the horrific mechanisms that produced the Cambodian genocide, and the haunting effects of his and its memory on the present.

74. Séra, written personal communication.

CHARLES FORSDICK

Haiti and Comics: The Search for (New Graphic) Narratives

In the defiantly entitled *Haiti Rising*, a collection of essays that appeared shortly after the earthquake of January 2010, the artist, musician, author, record producer, and general *provocateur* Bill Drummond wrote a chapter on the country's post-disaster art market. In this, he underlined—as have many others—the asymmetries of power on which this trade is based.[1] Drummond developed his analysis further, however, by suggesting—via the report of a conversation he claims to have had with the Grande Rue artists André Eugène and Louko (the second of whom died in the disaster)—that Haitian cultural producers actively exploit the various expectations of North American consumers, challenging and destabilizing in the process the notions of "authenticity" and of "art brut" often associated with external critical responses to the work of groups such as *atis rezistans*. In the same volume, also writing on the theme of "art in the time of catastrophe," the novelist Madison Smartt Bell illustrates a similar observation by recalling a French cartoon he has seen in the country:

> On the wall of a beach resort hotel near Cap Haïtien in the north of Haiti, there's a wicked little cartoon by a well-known French artist whose name I do not recall: a cheerful *blan* (foreign) customer is purchasing art from a couple of Haitian artists or artisans who are sawing off suitably sized sections of typical Haitian scenes from a plank, or a sort of endless *bande dessinée*, that recedes on trestles all the way to the horizon and probably beyond. The satirical intent of the drawing,

---

1. Bill Drummond, "What is this earthquake for?," in *Haiti Rising: Haitian History, Culture and the Earthquake of 2010*, ed. Martin Munro (Liverpool: Liverpool University Press, 2010), 174–82.

YFS 131/132, Bande Dessinée: *Thinking Outside the Boxes,* ed. Laurence Grove and Michael Syrotinski, © 2017 by Yale University.

of course, is to show that a lot of Haitian art is no more and no less than a market commodity. How bad, how diminishing, is that? The inexhaustibility also implied by the sketch might, at this point in the history of disaster, be encouraging.[2]

What is particularly striking in Smartt Bell's example—a *mise-en-abîme*, inserting a comic within a cartoon—is the way in which, on a number of different levels, comic art becomes both the medium and the message of his analysis. It is not only a means of reflecting on the resilience and strategic flexibility of Haitian cultural production, but also a way of illustrating —albeit obliquely—the processes of that production itself.

The equation of artistic creation with this "sort of endless *bande dessinée*" clearly introduces a humorous dimension in the discussion of the earthquake's impact on cultural production in Haiti. The evocation of the comic implies not only the continued co-existence of the artistic and the artisanal, of "high" and "popular" culture, but also betokens the creative ingenuity persistent among those artists seeking to supply external demand in the wake of disaster. Equally important for the purposes of the current article, however, is the specific deployment of the *bande dessinée* in this context, i.e., the resort to a graphic genre, juxtaposing text and image, whose visibility has (for reasons that will be explored below) increased in Haiti following the earthquake, but whose presence as an established and home-produced form in Haitian culture arguably remains still only nascent. As a reaction building on Smartt Bell's vignette, this article reflects on the ambivalent presence of the *bande dessinée* in a Haitian context. In part, it draws on the recent engagement with the comics form from a variety of postcolonial perspectives, welcoming this as a critical development in both postcolonialism and comics studies, but seeing it also as one from which Haiti (and indeed the wider Caribbean) has often been regrettably absent.[3] While there has been increasing attention in scholarship to postcolonial approaches to the *bande dessinée*, as well

2. Madison Smartt Bell, "Art in the Time of Catastrophe," in Munro, *Haiti Rising*, 166–73 (167).

3. Most of the current work on comics in Haiti and elsewhere in the French Caribbean is available on line. For a good overview, see Christophe Cassiau-Haurie, "La BD caribéenne francophone en mal d'auteurs et d'éditeurs," available at: http://www.africultures.com/php/index.php?nav=article&no=8066 [accessed 30 June 2016].

as to comics produced in "postcolonial" contexts more generally, the representation of Haiti in the genre has rarely been studied, and Haitian *BDs* similarly remain relatively neglected. By way of example of this oversight, a pioneering and critically incisive volume in this field—*Postcolonial Comics: Texts, Events, Identities*—provides a particular focus on sub-Saharan Africa and the Middle East, and as such reflects this general lack of engagement with *bande dessinée* in a Caribbean frame. The inherent challenge of the collection to postcolonialize the study of comic art nevertheless has clear implications for any attempt to study Haiti in this frame.

The current article seeks to explore ways in which this gap in scholarship might be addressed by: (i) exploring—in comparative and transnational frames—some of the key external representations of Haiti in comic form, especially in the USA and France, across a period of over 150 years; and (ii), by extension, considering the increasing importance of the *bande dessinée* in Haitian culture and society themselves. As such, it seeks to contribute to the on-going disruption of those understandings of studies of comic art that often privilege paradigms based on US-European production and manga. It suggests at the same time—through a focus on links between comics and key turning points in Haitian history and cultures (such as the Revolution of 1791–1803 or the 2010 earthquake)—that what Binita Mehta and Pia Mukherji dub "graphic interventions within specific moments of historical crises" can indeed permit new understandings of "postmodern trauma, the possibilities of solidarities and protest in transnational communities, or the politics of new visual technologies."[4] This is an approach inspired in part by that of the editors of *Postcolonial Comics* themselves, who suggest that research at the intersection of postcolonialism and comics requires the close attention to con/textualities (understanding *bande dessinée* as "instances of postcolonial textuality or as aspects of public culture in the postcolony") central to the current study. Such a critical approach invites at the same time a historical reflection on the questions of (re)definition, production, and representational asymmetries with which this article began.[5]

    4. "Introduction," in *Postcolonial Comics: Texts, Events, Identities*, ed. Binita Mehta and Pia Mukherji (New York and London: Routledge, 2015), 1–26 (13).
    5. Mehta and Mukherji, "Introduction," 2.

DAUMIER AND CHAM: HAITI AND NINETEENTH-
CENTURY FRENCH CARICATURE

As is often the case with Haiti, critical attention to self-representa-
tion tends to be eclipsed by a predominant interest in representation
from outside. The portrayal of Haiti in comic art—as well as the relative paucity of the production of *bandes dessinées* in the country itself—tend to encourage repetition of the same patterns evident in
the study of literature and historiography. In an acerbic article on
contemporary portrayals of the country, Michael Dash alludes to the
"(un)kindness of strangers," outlining the ways in which "[n]ot only
does Haitian history seem doomed to repeat itself, but [writers] on
Haiti seem destined to repeat each other."[6] These patterns of self-
referential representation, often dislocated from the place and culture they seek to portray, have a long history. In the aftermath of
its independence (1804) and the imposition of a crippling debt (1825)
that would contribute to the systematic underdevelopment of the
country, Haiti featured heavily in satirical illustrations in the French
press. Following the logic of Dash's analysis, these cartoons maligned
the country through racialized and often racist mechanisms of representation with little if any root in Haiti itself; and they also simultaneously diminished their subject—in an early historical illustration
of what Paul Farmer has called the "uses of Haiti"—via a process of
instrumentalization that used a detour via Haitian otherness to critique France itself.[7]

While for the most part not approximating formally modern
bande dessinée (they depend on the juxtaposition of text and image,
for instance, and do not deploy speech bubbles), images of Haiti circulated throughout the later nineteenth century as caricatures and
political cartoons, in particular drawing the Caribbean nation into
domestic discussions of the February Revolution as well as of the
abolition of slavery in 1848 and of Napoleon III's *coup* of 1851. Darcy
Grigsby has provided a detailed analysis of the representation of Haitian subjects in this period, considering the ways in which Haiti was

6. J. Michael Dash, "The (Un)kindness of Strangers: Writing Haiti in the 21st Century," *Caribbean Studies*, 36/2 (2009), 171–78 (171).
7. See Paul Farmer, *The Uses of Haiti* (Monroe, ME: Common Courage Press,
1994).

privileged in discussions of blackness in the body politic, and high-lighting the extent to which Faustin Soulouque, self-appointed emperor of the country for almost a decade from 1849, served as a means of ridiculing (now almost five decades after independence) Haitian aspirations to statehood.[8] Racist caricatures in publications such as *L'illustration* and *Le charivari* by artists including Cham were highly visible in the press, and led to an increasing elision of fictionalization and any sort of political reality.[9] Honoré Daumier also contributed Haiti-related material to *Le charivari*, using images of Soulouque throughout the 1850s to critique the regime of Louis Napoléon during the Second Republic and into the Second Empire, invoking—in Elizabeth C. Childs's terms—"the distancing mechanisms of the exotic to veil political criticism in seemingly safe and foreign terms."[10] Exploiting exaggerated and racialized facial features, and mimicking delusions of imperial grandeur, these images tended to treat Haiti as a detour in domestic concerns, a visual repository of received ideas about blackness and unimaginably precocious postcoloniality that (literally) denigrated the Haitian state while using it for oblique criticism of elements of French political culture.

As Grigsby notes, however, it was "not only the Haitian villain, but the Haitian hero [who] played a prominent role in Paris between the 1848 Revolution and the 1851 Empire."[11] As a result of the success of the play *Toussaint Louverture*, Soulouque was even briefly eclipsed in visual representations by Alphonse de Lamartine's eponymous protagonist, the leader of the Haitian Revolution and precursor of its independence. The drama had been written in 1840, but only made it onto the Parisian stage after the (second) legislative abolition of slavery in the French colonial empire in 1848, a process in which Lamartine—as Minister of Foreign Affairs—had played a key

8. Darcy Grigsby, "Cursed Mimicry: France and Haiti, Again (1848–51)," *Art History* 38/1 (2015), 68–105.

9. Cham was the pen name of Charles Amédée de Noé, the caricaturist and lithographer, one of whose ancestors is said to have freed Toussaint Louverture from enslavement. See Jean-Louis Donnadieu, *Un grand seigneur et ses esclaves: Le comte de Noé entre Antilles et Gascogne (1728 – 1816)* (Toulouse: Presses universitaires du Mirail, 2009).

10. Elizabeth C. Childs, *Daumier and Exoticism: Satirizing the French and the Foreign* (New York: Peter Lang, 2004), 111.

11. Grigsby, "Cursed Mimicry," 92.

role.[12] Recent critical attention to his play *Toussaint Louverture* has underlined the ways in which the work destabilized received notions of blackness, promoted anti-racist republicanism, and sought actively to challenge any self-congratulatory rhetoric of abolitionism by underlining the importance of the resistance of the enslaved, aspects that had already led certain contemporary critics to attack the drama as anti-French.[13] The popularity of Lamartine's work with Parisian audiences triggered a visual backlash by the caricaturists mentioned above, with *L'illustration*—previously a vocal supporter of abolitionism—producing two full pages of images in April 1850 that expressed astonishment at the play's success in the eyes of French audiences. In her discussion of this material, Grigsby highlights the focus on the representation of blacking up, exploring an actively parodic approach to the transformations this implies; but she stresses at the same time the continuing respect for the revolutionary Haiti of Louverture in contrast to the perceived farce of Soulouque's contemporary regime. Grigsby concludes: "Soulouque had been denied bivalency, the oscillation between villain and hero, but Toussaint had long been accorded a greater semantic density; here was a tragic black hero whose complexity matched that of blackface on stage."[14]

It is striking to see this over-determination of Haitian subjects present in another contemporary but little-studied engagement with Lamartine: Cham's comic version of his play in *Le Punch à Paris*. This appeared across six pages in April 1850.[15] A marker of the success—and perceived threat—of *Toussaint Louverture* is the extent to which the play was subject to parody. *Traversin et Couverture*, a dramatic rewriting by Varin and Labiche, was performed in April 1850, transforming Lamartine's work into a blend of melodrama

    12. On French abolition, see Lawrence Jennings, *French Anti-Slavery: The Movement for the Abolition of Slavery in France, 1802–1848* (Cambridge: Cambridge University Press, 2000).
    13. For recent discussions of the play, see Clint Bruce, "Displacing Dessalines, or the Transatlantic Geographies of Lamartine's *Toussaint Louverture*," *Romance Studies*, 33/3–4 (2015), 192–207, and Mouhamédoul A. Niang, "La dramaturgie lamartinienne ou le postcolonial avant la lettre: le marronnage comme résistance dans Toussaint Louverture," *Nineteenth Century French Studies*, 42/3 (2014), 190–205.
    14. Grigsby, "Cursed Mimicry," 100.
    15. Cham, "TOUSSAINT SALE FIGURE, pièce en vers et contre tout ce qui est blanc, mêlée de strophes, d'apostrophes et catastrophes," *Le Punch à Paris* 3 (1850), 65–69.

and farce,[16] and Cham actively contributed to this tradition with his graphic narrative "TOUSSAINT SALE FIGURE." The very title of the work echoes—with its reference to facial skin pigmentation—the referencing of blackface in other contemporary representations as well as (in pitching the parody "against everything that is white") the reading of the play as hostile both to white Frenchness and French whiteness. Cham's principal target would appear to be the play's author himself, for by April 1850 Lamartine was no longer in political office and had arguably deployed Louverture both as protagonist in defense of his own political legacy and as critique of his adversary Louis-Napoléon Bonaparte (soon to become Emperor Napoléon III). The sequence of Cham's images concludes with a three-quarter-page "philosophical caricature" of "M. Lamartine in self contradiction," which the satirist glosses along these lines: "Abolishing slavery in April 1848 – Selling the negro Toussaint in 1850."[17] Louverture—portrayed in an exaggerated parody of a French officer's uniform, with accentuated lips and pointed nose—is led by the dramatist via a rope around his neck to the offices of Lamartine's publisher, Michel Lévy. This reduction of revolutionary history to a more venally motivated farce is reflected in the main body of the narrative, where—across five rapidly sketched acts—Cham undermines any political intent in Lamartine's play by sending up its melodramatic dimensions. There is a tearful separation of Louverture from his niece Adrienne; a disguise scene in which the protagonist approaches, as a beggar, his sons recently returned from France (General Leclerc mistakes him for Robert Macaire, the fictional swindler previously created by actor Frédérick Lemaître, now portraying Louverture himself); and the execution of the revolutionary's nephew Moïse. The parody concludes with a comically chaotic compression of the Haitian War of Independence into two *cases*, in which Lamartine is added to the French casualties, and the reader is reminded of the illusion of black face on which the play depends: "With the play dragging on, so as to put an end to it, Toussaint grabs the black flag, crushes the whites, thrusts it in the author, and goes home to clean himself up."[18] Lamartine succinctly described Louverture in his play with the often repeated phrase: "That man is

16. See Charles Varin and Eugène Labiche, *Traversin et Couverture* (Paris: M. Lévy frères, 1850).
17. Cham, "TOUSSAINT SALE FIGURE," 69.
18. Ibid., 66.

a nation," but the dignity of his protagonist—for whom the choice between resistance and surrender achieves, as it would in the work of others such as C.L.R. James, tragic proportions—is in Cham's graphic representation trivialized, domesticated and reduced to caricature.

GRAPHIC REPRESENTATIONS OF
TOUSSAINT LOUVERTURE

As if in anticipation of the Eighteenth Brumaire the following year, Cham thus presents history repeating itself as farce, with Louverture himself claiming succinctly, as early as Act 2: "My role is ridiculous." The parody of Lamartine in *Le Punch à Paris* belongs, however, to a longer and more varied tradition of visual representations of Toussaint Louverture, stretching back to contemporary illustrations in biographies and eyewitness accounts written while the revolutionary was still alive (including iconic images such as Maurin's lithograph from 1837), and culminating in the recent creative engagement evident in the work of prominent contemporary artists of the African diaspora including Edouard Duval-Carrié, Lubaina Himid, and Kimathi Donkor.[19] Within that substantial corpus, Cham nevertheless inaugurated a narrative strand dependent on the sequential use of images integrated in various ways with text to tell the life story of Louverture—or at least to recount specific segments of his life and the turning points whereby it was structured.

Although not often read in terms of the structures of graphic narrative, a very different work, Jacob Lawrence's 41-panel life of Toussaint Louverture (produced in 1938 in the context of the Harlem Renaissance), has also been read as "similar to a comic strip."[20] The analogy is a good one for the series uses bold color and form, and

19. For a discussion of representations of Louverture, see Fritz Daguillard, *Mystérieux dans la Gloire: Toussaint Louverture (1743–1803)* (Port-au-Prince: MIPANAH, 2003); David Geggus, "The Changing Faces of Toussaint Louverture: Literary and Pictorial Depictions" (2013), available at: http://www.brown.edu/Facilities/John_Carter_Brown_Library/exhibitions/toussaint/index.html [accessed 30 June 2016]; and Helen Weston, "The Many Faces of Toussaint Louverture," in *Slave Portraiture in the Atlantic World*, ed. Agnes I. Lugo-Ortiz and Angela Rosenthal (Cambridge: Cambridge University Press, 2013), 345–73. It is significant that none of these studies includes a focus on comics.

20. Joanne Mattern, *Jacob Lawrence* (Edina, MINN: Abdo Pub., 2005), 18. Patricia Hills, who provides a useful overview of the series, also sees the panels of the work as "like storyboards for a movie, with his style giving each panel its dynamism." See 74.

deploys a sequential, story-board approach to its historical content. Images are juxtaposed with captions to provide an account of Haiti and its Revolution, beginning with the arrival of Columbus in 1492 and culminating in the crowning of Dessalines as emperor in 1804. In an account of a retrospective of Lawrence's work in 1987, Kay Larson links the apparent simplicity of the artist's work to the graphic genre, claiming: "at first glance these paintings resemble comic strips."[21] She goes on to tease out the complexity of a series of images that create a powerful narrative force through the use of simplified, flat shapes and collage-like images.

Lawrence's account of Louverture was produced in the aftermath of the US occupation of Haiti, and was one of the first to harness the narrative of revolution and emancipation to the African-American struggles emerging in the interwar years.[22] The panels deploy comic-book aesthetics to encapsulate the extreme brutality of the plantation regime (the scene of flogging in panel 10 is a striking illustration of this), but also to reflect the dynamism of rebellion and struggle (Bel-Argent, Louverture's charger, streaks across panel 21, evoking the assault on the English at Artibonite; panel 23 is dense with black troops bearing arms, on the march to capture San Miguel, reflecting the transformation of the once enslaved into a formidable fighting force; figureless, panels 31 and 32 use stark images of approaching vessels and burning buildings to suggest the arrival of Leclerc's counter-revolutionary forces in 1801 and Henri-Christophe's burning of Le Cap as he refused to surrender). Images also depict isolation and defeat, most notably the almost identical panels 37 and 39 reveal Louverture imprisoned in the Château de Joux: in the first staring through the bars of the cell, in the second lying dead on his bed.

Lawrence's work exemplifies the intertexuality often evident in literary and historiographic depictions of Louverture: several panels owe much to formal portraiture, and draw into their comic-book style a different aesthetics, that of the representation of martial prowess, evident in the magnificent profile of panel 20 (drawn from Maurin's 1837 image), and in panel 26 (a three-quarter portrait of Louverture

21. Kay Larson, "Bound for glory," *New York Magazine*, 19 October 1987, 112–13 (112).
22. On other examples of African-American artistic engagement with Haiti, see Krista A. Thompson, "Preoccupied with Haiti: The Dream of Diaspora in African American Art, 1915–1942," *American Art* 21/3 (2007), 75–97.

at the capture of Mirebalois, reminiscent of the earlier work of Edin-
burgh lithographer John Kay from 1802). As such, the series seeks to
bring the story of Haiti to wider audiences, and Lawrence's *Toussaint
L'Ouverture* is very much in the tradition of similar contemporary
endeavors, not least Orson Welles's production of *Voodoo Macbeth*,
staged in Harlem in 1936 as part of the Negro Theatre Unit of the Fed-
eral Theatre Project.[23] Subsequent black artists have developed Lawrence's approach to Haitian history through sequences of narrative
images, one of the finest examples of which is in the work of Lubaina
Himid. *Scenes from the Life of Toussaint L'Ouverture*—made up of
fifteen pictures, watercolor and pencil on paper—shows a series of
moments from the revolutionary's life, ranging from the domestic to
the martial.[24] Lacking the logic of linear narrative of Lawrence's series and incorporating characteristic flashes of humor ("who," asks
the caption to image 2, "will do the laundry?"), Himid's work forms
an integral part of her wider project: "challeng[ing] dominant and op-
pressive versions of history, and in so doing, continually seek[ing] to
rescue Black historical figures from an ever-threatening obscurity."[25]
As such, *Scenes from the Life* can be read in (if not necessarily as part
of) a wider corpus of comics and *bandes dessinées*.

These works often share pedagogical aims, but have different em-
phases especially when issues of gender are considered as Louverture
regularly serves in them as an exemplum of black masculinity. Mid-
twentieth-century examples of such an approach are also to be found
in the graphic art of the United States. The second issue of *Real Life
Comics*, released by Pines Publishing in 1941, included the life of
Louverture among what the publication's subtitle called "the adventures of the world's greatest heroes."[26] A further example is a *Golden
Legacy* issue, produced by Fitzgerald Publishing in 1966 on the "Saga
of Toussaint L'Ouverture and the Birth of Haiti," a comic reflect-

23. See Charles Forsdick, "'Burst of Thunder, Stage Pitch Black': The Place of Haiti
in US Inter-War Cultural Production," *Contemporary French & Francophone Studies/
SITES* 14/5 (2011), 7–18.

24. http://www.artscouncilcollection.org.uk/artist/himid-lubaina [accessed
30 June 2015].

25. See "Lubaina Himid MBE," available at: http://new.diaspora-artists.net/
display_item.php?id=43&table=artists [accessed 30 June 2015].

26. Such works complement representations in other visual media studied by
Lindsay J. Twa, in *Visualizing Haiti in U.S. Culture, 1910–1950* (New York: Routledge,
2014).

ing the ways in which the leader of the Haitian revolution was conscripted in graphic form as a role model for young African Americans.
In its hagiographic maneuvers, the *Golden Legacy* issue smooths out
many of the historiographic controversies of Louverture's life—including the motivations for, and strategies deployed as a result of, his
volte-face that led to a change of allegiance from Spain to France; the
ideological conflicts that underpinned his leadership of the final stage
of the Revolution, often known as the Haitian War of Independence;
the context of his arrest and deportation to France in 1802. The comic
adopts a heroic mode, casting Napoleon as villain and compressing
Dessalines's final push for independence into a concluding panel
dominated by a single frame in which a spectral Louverture overlooks
his faceless successor.

An even more striking example of the conscription of the Haitian
heroes to contemporary contexts is found in a 1985 French *bande
dessinée, Toussaint Louverture: Le Napoléon noir*, illustrated by
Pierre Briens and written by Nicolas Saint-Cyr.[27] Produced in the context of preparations for the bicentenary of the French Revolution, during whose celebrations there were even attempts to "pantheonize"
Louverture, the album contributes to contemporary revisionist efforts
to recruit the Haitian leader to a French republican narrative.[28] These
suggest that the Haitian Revolution was little more than a subsidiary
event in its overarching French counterpart and not—as scholars such
as Nick Nesbitt have recently claimed, through their studies of the
intersections between republicanism, anti-colonialism, and the will
to emancipation—a radical destabilization of the French revolutionary project and clear illustration of its limits.[29] Briens and Saint-Cyr
deploy the stylistic and technical features of contemporary *franco-
belge* production to offer a detailed overview of the shift from pre-
revolutionary Saint-Domingue to post-revolutionary Haiti (the book
ends with the country's re-adoption of this pre-conquest designation,

27. Pierre Briens and Nicolas Saint-Cyr, *Toussaint Louverture: Le Napoléon noir*
(Paris: Hachette; Edi-monde, 1985).

28. On Toussaint Louverture and the bicentenary of the French Revolution, see
my "The Black Jacobin in Paris," *Journal of Romance Studies* 5/3 (2005), 9–24.

29. On the interconnections between the French and Haitian Revolutions, see
C.L.R. James, *The Black Jacobins* (Harmondsworth: Penguin, 2001), and Nick Nesbitt,
Universal Emancipation: The Haitian Revolution and the Radical Enlightenment
(Charlottesville: University of Virginia Press, 2008).

the Taíno term meaning "land of high mountains"). Key events such as the Bois Caïman (the *vodou* ceremony often claimed to be the place at which the Revolution began) lend themselves to graphically lurid treatment, and gratuitously erotic imagery is deployed when, for instance, Louverture's rival Jean-Louis Villatte captures Governor Laveaux in his bed before temporarily imprisoning him in Cap Fran-çais. Repeated focus on the drumming of the formerly enslaved rebels lends itself to striking typographic treatment of the onomatopoeic sounds that result, but the album ultimately seeks to maintain a level of historiographic accuracy while privileging the French dimensions of the international struggle in the 1790s over the future of Saint-Domingue. The volume opens, for instance, with the arrival on board ship of news of the French Revolution, then focuses briefly on the harsh treatment of those free men of mixed ethnic descent such as Vincent Ogé who demanded equal rights for the colony's colored pop-ulation, but ultimately concentrates on the military and diplomatic aspects of the event that followed the outbreak of Revolution in Au-gust 1791. There is close attention in the final third of the volume to the War of Independence, which allows representation of the series of battles making up this final stage of the Revolution, but also a focus on the figure of Pauline Bonaparte, the wife of the leader of the French expedition Leclerc. The album concludes with a largely romanticized version of Toussaint's arrest and death, providing little reflection on the historiographic conundrum of the reasons for his capture, and us-ing a large *case* on the penultimate page to portray the iconic image of the Château de Joux, "his icy prison on a rock in the Jura."[30] The bru-tal final stage of the War of Independence—and the French struggle to reimpose slavery—is reduced to two panels in a single strip, and the final image of the volume appears to portray a street scene in modern Haiti, complete with drums, tropical fruit, and dancing. Louverture is locked into his frozen, early nineteenth-century grave; the contempo-rary country is represented as abstracted from its revolutionary roots; and the meanings of Haiti for contemporary France are conveniently evacuated.[31]

30. Briens and Saint-Cyr, *Toussaint Louverture*, 47.
31. On France and Haiti, see Forsdick, "Haiti and France: Settling the Debts of the Past," in *Politics and Power in Haiti*, ed. Kate Quinn and Paul Sutton (New York: Palgrave Macmillan, 2013), 141–60.

BEYOND LOUVERTURE: HAITI, THE
ENLIGHTENMENT, AND ABOLITION

Louverture has continued to attract the attention of graphic artists, with one of the most recent graphic representations being in the UK-published children's comic *The Phoenix*, in which the Haitian revolutionary appeared, as a "butt-kicking bookworm who fought the French, smashed the Spanish and bashed the British to found the first (and only) free republic of former slaves," in the series "Corpse Talk."[32] In this comic, inspired by the chat show format (the feature "brings the dead famous to life"), the focus is on Louverture's exceptionalism, manifest in his literacy and tactical sophistication. The Revolution is presented in five strips, with particular attention given to Louverture's change of allegiance from the Spanish to the French, and also to his capture and deportation. "Corpse Talk" seeks to compress Louverture's life into two pages, and may be read as a contribution to what is increasingly seen as the development of the revolutionary's global iconicity.[33] Notwithstanding its inherent playfulness, the comic strip may be seen to use the graphic form to present the spectrality of Louverture, the ways in which his embodiment of what Nick Nesbitt has called the "idea of 1804" continues to persist as a challenge to any system that seeks to limit the "universal right of all human beings to freedom as the positive capacity for self-determination on a global, and not merely local, scale."[34]

This reading is more explicit in the most recent graphic rendering of the Haitian Revolution: *Drums of Freedom: The Saga of the Haitian Revolution* (2015), by the Guyanese writer and illustrator Barrington Braithwaite.[35] Based on careful consultation of the rich historiography of the struggle for Haitian independence, and drawing in particular on C.L.R. James's *Black Jacobins*, Braithwaite provides in five chapters and an epilogue a densely detailed visual account that is perhaps the most nuanced representation of the Revolution produced in graphic art thus far. Like James, he offers a sweep of Haitian history, begin-

32. "Corpse Talk," *The Phoenix* 151 (2014), 24–25.

33. See Forsdick, "Toussaint Louverture in a Globalized Frame: Reading the Revolutionary as Icon," *Contemporary French & Francophone Studies/SITES*, 19/2 (2015), 325–34.

34. Nesbitt, "The Idea of 1804," *Yale French Studies* 107 (2005), 6–38 (7).

35. Barrington Braithwaite, *Drums of Freedom: The Saga of the Haitian Revolution* (New York: Davie Press, 2015).

ning with Columbus's arrival and Mackandal's eighteenth-century rebellion before shifting to a detailed account of the Revolution, the War of Independence, and their aftermath. Like James also, it locates Louverture's struggle within a wider Atlantic and intercontinental frame, underlining the pragmatic and testing choices—such as the order to execute his nephew Moïse on the grounds of rebellion—he was forced to make. The page presenting Louverture's death at Joux is rich in terms of iconography and text. Reminiscent of its theatrical staging by Edouard Glissant in *Monsieur Toussaint*, it portrays the dying protagonist surrounded by hallucinated images of his Haitian past. At the same time, it stresses the contrast between Louverture and Napoleon Bonaparte, with the former—to his death—"anchored to the tenets of liberty and equality," while the latter "sets the stage for the savage colonization of Africa, the brutal carnage of the trenches of WWI, and the final sum of the idolatry of racial supremacy in the macabre scourge that was Adolf Hitler."[36] Such historical analysis is extravagant, and a similar thesis by Claude Ribbe in *Le crime de Napoléon* led to controversy in France,[37] but Braithwaite deploys comic art to reassert the place of Haiti in world history while also suggesting reasons for the country's systematic silencing in the writing of that history: "The colonial world would bring Haiti to its knees economically, but she stands tall before the goddess of justice as the drums of freedom vibrate where ever enlightened souls dwell."[38]

Although Louverture does not—unlike Dessalines more recently in the work of Karl Heins Desroches (of which more below)—achieve the status of superhero, his persistent presence in comics and *bande dessinée*—as well as in other digital media such as video games (he appears, for example, as a character in *Age of Empires III: The War Chiefs*)—betokens a more general visibility of Haiti in recent popular culture, especially in the USA. The Revolution as seen in BD and comics is not, however, only recounted via an exclusive focus on his often exceptionalized character. More recent representations include the sixth and seventh volumes of Bourgeon's *Les passagers du vent*

---

36. Braithwaite, *Drums of Freedom*, 118.
37. See Claude Ribbe, *Le crime de Napoléon* (Paris: Privé, 2005).
38. For a discussion of the "silencing" of the Haitian Revolution, see Michel-Rolph Trouillot, *Silencing the Past: Power and the Production of History* (Boston, MASS: Beacon Press, 1995).

(2009, 2010),[39] evidence of a wider shift in French-language comics from an association of slavery with maritime history to an interpretation that allows the enslaved to become "the potential actors in their own freedom."[40] As the title of *La petite fille Bois-Caïman* suggests, the focus of the two albums is on Haiti and its revolution, but with these approached obliquely. Whereas the fifth volume of the *Passagers du vent* series, *Le bois d'ébène*,[41] had ended with the protagonist Isa apparently stranded in Saint-Domingue, the sixth and seventh (published a quarter of a century later, in 2009 and 2010 respectively), focus on her great-granddaughter Zabo, fleeing Civil War New Orleans to rejoin her family in the bayou. Reunited with her great grandmother, Zabo's narrative becomes entangled with flashbacks to 1780s Saint-Domingue and an account of the traumatic events surrounding Isa's experience of the August 1791 Bois Caïman ceremony. The two albums thus juxtapose accounts of the Haitian Revolution and the American Civil War, creating a transhistorical and transgenerational narrative in which the similarities between the two protatonists Isa and Zabo are located in a wider frame of multidirectional memory and hemispheric American history, with both of these developed in the context of Atlantic slavery and its aftermath.

FROM ZOMBIES AND 'VOODOO' TO THE HAITIAN EVERYDAY

These recent developments in BD portrayals of the Haitian Revolution and its wider context, especially in the work of Bourgeon, constitute a considerable development beyond other representations of the country and its history and culture in non-Haitian cultures, notably in North America. In a recent discussion of "finding Haiti in comic book literature," Edwin Magloire describes the way in which most US representations of Haiti—through Marvel figures such as Brother Voodoo, Sister Voodoo, and Doctor Voodoo—foreground cli-

---

39. François Bourgeon, *Les passagers du vent 6: La petite fille Bois-Caïman, livre 1*, and *Les passagers du vent 7: La petite fille Bois-Caïman, livre 2* (Paris: 12 bis, 2009).

40. See Philippe Delisle, "La traite négrière du XVIII siècle dans la bande dessinée 'franco-belge': d'une image édulcorée à une vision historico-critique," in *Le siècle des lumières en bande dessinée*, ed. Paul Chopelin and Tristan Martine (Paris: Karthala, 2014), 123–45 (137).

41. Bourgeon, *Les passagers du vent 5: Le bois d'ébène* (Grenoble: Glénat, 1984).

chés about *vodou* and zombification.[42] In one of the earliest examples he identifies—"Dead who swim" (1944)—the character Namor the Sub-Mariner reacts in this way to a reference to Haiti: "Haiti! Haiti! is famed among all the West Indian people for its zombies." Such an equation was perpetuated subsequently by Marvel in the supernatural superhero "Brother Voodoo" (the character Jericho Drumm, more recently known as "Doctor Voodoo"), who first featured in *Strange Tales* in 1973, and was associated primarily with New Orleans, although his travels took him to Haiti. The country's association with "voodoo" extends more widely, and Magloire identifies a reference to the Joker in *Batman: The Killing Joke* that seeks to explain the character's insanity through reference to possession by the Haitian *vodou lwa* Bawon Samdi, and also cites a character Medjine Parker, in the Lucifer series, a Haitian orphan accused by her adoptive father of having brought a "demon" with her to the US.

As Elizabeth McAlister has recently claimed, such representations are widespread:

> Zombies show up in pop songs and are stock characters in comic books and graphic novels. They appear in video games such as the *Resident Evil* series and in the *Resident Evil* movie spin-offs. Since 2000, about 100 movies and scores of video games have featured undead, cannibal zombies.[43]

Popular cultural manifestations perpetuate certain strands of the patterns of representation evident in the nineteenth century but further intensified by authors such as William Seabrook during the US occupation of Haiti.[44] The foundations of this tradition are to be found in quasi-anthropological literature, but its popularization occurred through Hollywood's embracing of the zombie theme in the interwar period.[45] These exogenous practices of description—reducing Haiti to

42. Edwin Magloire, "Finding Haiti in Comic Book Literature," 22 April 2016, available at: http://woymagazine.com/2016/04/22/finding-haiti-in-comic-book-literature/ [accessed 30 June 2016].

43. Elizabeth McAlister, "Slaves, Cannibals, and Infected Hyper-Whites: The Race and Religion of Zombies," *Anthropological Quarterly* 85/2 (2012), 457–86. See also Stephen O'Donnell, "The Revenant Signifier: The Zombie in Comics and Cinema," unpublished PhD thesis, University of Dundee, 2015.

44. See J. Michael Dash, *Haiti and the United States: National Stereotypes and the Literary Imagination* (New York: St. Martin's Press, 1997).

45. On this subject, see Franck Degoul, "'We are the mirror of your fears': Haitian Identity and Zombification," trans. Elisabeth M. Lore, in *Better Off Dead: The Evolu-*

images of barbarism and violence—remain widespread in comics,[46] although there is increasing evidence—including in *bande dessinée*—of an endogenous retort, transforming phenomena portrayed negatively, such as zombification and *vodou*, as symbols of a more "positive Haitianness."[47] A parallel reaction among visitors to Haiti is to be found in a form cognate to the *bande dessinée*, the *carnet de voyage*, where artists have increasingly counteracted the lurid representational tendencies of much previous (particularly North American) popular culture by developing more neutral observations of the Haitian everyday.

A number of *carnets de voyage* published around the bicentenary of the country's independence, such as *Titouan en Haïti* (2003) and Nicole Augereau's *Tap Tap Haïti* (2004), are to be read in relation to earlier graphic representations, but also as a corrective to a rich and often distortive tradition of Western travel writing on the country.[48] The sailor and artist Titouan Lamazou visited Haiti in the late 1990s, and produced a *carnet* in dialogue with the visual arts in Haiti, and also with a number of contemporary artists whom he met and with whom he worked (including André Pierre, Préfète Duffaut, and Louisiane Saint-Fleurant).[49] His volume opens with images of a series of *vévés* used in vodou ceremonies, but these are cited as graphic evidence of Haitian familiarity with "la chose graphique," and are drawn into a wider assemblage of sketches, photographs and other iconographic material assembled during the journey. Lamazou follows the linear progress of his journey—Port-au-Prince, Jacmel, Pestel, Cap Haïtien—juxtaposing images of the artists he encounters (and of their work) with the ethnographic and architectural material commonly found in *carnets de voyage*. He focuses on means of transport, not just the boats in which his professional interests meet, but also the

―――――――――

tion of the Zombie as Post-Human, ed. Deborah Christie and Sarah Juliet Lauro (New York: Fordham University Press, 2011), 24–38.

46. See, for example, a recent volume in the German Beserker series: Stephan Hagenow, *Todesgrüsse aus Haiti* (Esslingen: Gringo Comics, 2014).

47. Degoul, '"We are the mirror of your fears,"'38.

48. These volumes complement *Une journée haïtienne* (Montreal: Mémoire d'encrier; Paris: Présence africaine, 2007), an important collection of short stories edited by Thomas C. Spear, that similarly seeks to explore the ways in which everyday life in Haiti is no more exotic when understood on its own terms than that of any other location.

49. Titouan Lamazou, *Titouan en Haïti* (Paris: Nouveaux loisirs, 2003).

brightly-painted *tap-taps*, the collective taxis that often feature in accounts of urban Haiti.

The ubiquity of these vehicles is echoed in the title of a volume that appeared the year following Lamazou's *carnet*, Nicole Augereau's *Tap Tap Haïti*. Augereau—co-author also of a volume inspired by a stay in Marrakech, and currently listed by her publisher as preparing a book on the Haitian singer Manno Charlemagne—describes her stay in Haiti as a *stagiaire* at the *lycée français* in Port-au-Prince.[50] Unlike Lamazou, whose *carnet* mixes his own colorful and at times impressionistic paintings with photographs and other sketches, *Tap Tap Haïti* deploys a more conventional *ligne claire*, with pages split into *cases* of varying size, and with text juxtaposed with images which recount the artist's slow acclimatization to her surroundings. The narrative is more one of dwelling than travelling, and while there is an initial focus—in the section of the *carnet* following arrival in Santo Domingo—on streetscapes and movement around the city, the book's main section presents the stay in Port-au-Prince. The tone is often ambivalent and even ironic as Augereau describes the closeted and anxious existence of French ex-pats in the Haitian capital, as well as of tourists subject to physical restriction as their cruise ships land to the confines of Labadie. References to history, to the media, and (as in Titouan Lamazou's *Titouan en Haïti*) to local visual art open up the narrative, and observation of the linguistic and iconographic landscapes of the country reveal the ways in which traces of the past persist in the visual field of the present. As her *carnet* reaches its conclusion, Augereau is struck by the absence of *vodou* from her narrative, and the final pages contain an acknowledgement of her own "confused picture of voodoo based on a mixture of ignorance and curiosity,"[51] making a clear reference to the Western popular cultural representations to which this is linked. The concluding images—drawn from street art, inspired by contemporary artists including Hector Hyppolite, and also recalling images from Maya Deren's film *Divine Horsemen*—picture members of the *vodou* pantheon, and emphasize the historical roots of the religion, its political instrumentalization, and its contemporary manifestations. As with Lamazou's work, it is also possible to detect the impact of Haitian aesthetics

50. Nicole Augereau, *Tap Tap Haïti* (Poitiers: FLBLB, 2004). For details of current projects, see: http://flblb.com/auteur/nicole-augereau/ [accessed 30 June 2016].
51. Augereau, *Tap Tap Haïti*, 77.

on Augereau's graphic style, suggesting that other modes of external representation of the country are possible.

COMICS POST-EARTHQUAKE

One of the striking aspects of Augereau's *Tap Tap Haïti* is the way in which it captures, in the form of the *carnet de voyage*, street scenes and architectural detail now lost in the wake of the January 2010 earthquake. The question of drawing Port-au-Prince *post*-disaster is raised starkly by Fabory Mara in "A town nonetheless," his project of creating a *carnet de voyage* of contemporary Haiti: he asks "how do we draw it without making a disaster into a show?"[52] Mara's aim is to "sketch those broken-up urban spaces and those ruptured lines," using the formal resources of his chosen genre to capture processes of destruction and reconstruction, seeking at the same time to avoid an exclusively external gaze by drawing "through the eys of its inhabitants."[53] His sketches are accompanied by a self-reflexive account of his practice, in which he foregrounds collaboration with local artists, including those associated with *atis rezistans*, the collective based in Grand Rue, Port-au-Prince. Although Mara's conclusion relates to the inability of the *carnet de voyage* to capture the disaster and its aftermath, his creative intervention nevertheless reflects the increasing visibility of comics, *bande dessinée*, and cognate genres in debates about contemporary Haiti. *Bédéistes* were among those who sought collectively to raise funds for and awareness about the country in the aftermath of the 2010 earthquake,[54] while cartoons in publications such as *El listin diario* also provided a site in which the persistent racism toward Haitians evident in the Dominican Republic manifested itself.[55] The form has also functioned strongly as a means of education in post-earthquake Haiti, used notably by agencies such

52. Fabory Mara, "Une ville tout de meme," *Bouts du monde: Carnets de voyage* 25 (2016), 126–33 (127).

53. Mara, "Une ville tout de meme,"128. There are echoes between Mara's approach and the work of Yanick Lahens in the immediate period following the earthquake, who adopts in a text such as *Failles* (Paris: S. Wespieser, 2010) an aesthetics of literary fragmentation that seeks to capture the cityscapes of Port-au-Prince without reducing any impression of their brokenness.

54. See, e.g., *100 Dessins pour Haïti* (Brussels: Casterman, 2010).

55. See Daly Guilamo, "Dominican Funnies, Not So Funny: The Representation of Haitians in Dominican Newspaper Comic Strips, after the 2010 earthquake," *Journal of Pan African Studies* 5/9 (2013), 63–82.

as UNESCO who adopted a comic strip recounting the character Ti Joel as a contribution to the fight against cholera (an outbreak subsequently proved to have been caused by UN peacekeeping troops from Nepal who carried local strains of the disease with them).[56] Another United Nations body, the UNDP, produced the comic *Bon Kalite sove lavi* to communicate the benefits of respect of building regulations.[57] Much of this activity, while providing much-needed forums for the dissemination of work by contemporary Haitian artists such as Chevelin Pierre, serves a primarily pedagogical purpose. *Tents beyond Tents*, a project led by the Dutch-based activists of the Cartoon Movement in which again Chevelin was involved, suggests different approaches, with April Shemak detecting in this work "an alternative cartography" that challenges the dehumanizing tendencies of much contemporary digital mapping and reinscribes the struggles of everyday life into spaces often left blank.[58] Produced for an international audience, *Tents beyond Tents* constitutes a form of "comics-mapping," representing refuge spaces in graphic form via testimonies and portrayals of the inhumanity of everyday living conditions.[59]

Despite the involvement of an educated Haitian artist and scénariste, *Tents beyond Tents* remains aware of its own limitations and in particular its own relative privilege. Shemak focuses on the work's concluding *case*, an image of an unnamed and silent woman staring at the reader:

56. "Haiti: UNESCO publishes comic book to help fight cholera and to promote hand washing," http://www.unesco.org/new/en/no_cache/unesco/themes/pcpd/dynamic-content-single-view/news/french_only_haiti_unesco_publishes_comic_book_to_help_fight_cholera_and_to_promote_hand_washing/#.V13dxY-cHIU [accessed 30 June 2016]. A special issue of the creolophone comic strip *Chimen Lakay*, produced by the International Organization for Migration, was also devoted to the issue of cholera: https://issuu.com/iomhaiti/docs/chimen-lakay-3_14nov_ [accessed 30 June 2016].

57. "*Bon Kalite Sove Lavi*: Première bande dessinée sur la construction en Haïti," http://www.ht.undp.org/content/haiti/fr/home/presscenter/articles/2012/09/10/-bon-kalite-sove-lavi-premi-re-bande-dessin-e-sur-la-construction-en-ha-ti.html [accessed 30 June 2016].

58. See April Shemak, "The Cartographic Dimensions of Humanitarianism: Mapping Refugee Spaces in Post-Earthquake Haiti," *Cultural Dynamics* 26/3 (2014), 251–75. Several *planches* of *Tents beyond Tents*, the title of which alludes to the Haitian proverb "beyond mountains there are more mountains," are included in *New Internationalist*, January–February 2012, 20–25. The full work is available here: http://www.cartoonmovement.com/comic/29 [accessed 17 June 2016].

59. Shemak, "The Cartographic Dimensions of Humanitarianism," 263.

It is a gaze that challenges the comfortable vantage point of the reader/viewer/voyeur to consider the implications of what we are seeing, which is that there is no solution in sight for displaced Haitians. At the same time, this image is in tension with the role of reportage in the comics since this woman does not speak, which reveals the limits of comics as a space of testimony. She represents those voices that remain silenced.[60]

This issue of silencing relates back to the dynamics of representation addressed at the opening of the article. Although these NGO-funded graphic interventions often involve local artists, their control remains international, and another important development post-earthquake is the visible emergence of a more independent Haitian comics industry. Central to the preceding study has been an illustration of and reflection on the representational asymmetries evident in the area of Haiti and comic art, according to which it is evident that Haiti has—now for over a century and half—been more subject to external graphic representation rather than serving as a source of representations in its own right. The corpus of comics, *bandes dessinées*, and cognate forms devoted to the country is remarkably eclectic, but tends to be characterized by a conscription of Haiti to serve purposes and speak to audiences elsewhere. The story of comics *in* Haiti itself is yet to be written, and although there are traces of the genre at various moments in recent history, the absence of an established and home-grown comics industry is increasingly apparent. Haiti itself does not, unlike other parts of the Francosphere, have a well-established BD tradition, but it is possible nevertheless to construct the outline of the form's emergence in this national context.[61]

The artist often identified as the country's first *bédéiste* was André Le Blanc, born in Port-au-Prince in 1921, but active for many years as a cartoonist in the USA (where he worked as an assistant to Will Eisner) and also in the 1950s in Brazil. Le Blanc is remembered in the history of comics not for his Haitian origins, but as the illustrator of *La Bible en bandes dessinées* (1963; published in English as the *Picture Bible*). Another pioneer of Haitian origin, Victor Emman-

---

60. Ibid., 270–71.

61. For a discussion of *bande dessinée* in the French Caribbean, see Christophe Cassiau-Haurie, "La bande dessinée en Guadeloupe, Martinique et Guyane : lorsque la belle endormie se réveille. . .," available at: http://takamtikou.bnf.fr/dossiers/dossier-2011-la-bande-dessinee/la-bande-dessinee-en-guadeloupe-martinique-et-guyane-lorsque [accessed 26 May 2016].

uel Roberto Wilson (born 1928), was active as an artist elsewhere, in his case in Quebec, although he had been involved in a comic called *Zobopes* (meaning "ghosts" in Creole) before leaving the country in the early 1950s. The number of *bandes dessinées* published in Haiti itself has, however, historically been low. Georges Anglade describes a school friend Lionel, "disappeared" under the Duvaliers, who had shown great talent for producing comics, and whose disappearance deprived Haiti of an important artist in the area:

> Just like that one Sunday afternoon at the airport they took away twelve of the Mafalda albums by Quino, deleted the Tintin collection by Hergé, expelled Asterix and took Achille Talon away from his own daddy. . . because those were indeed his equals and the potential for his creations.[62]

A key figure among the artists who managed to live in exile under the Duvaliers, Hervé Télémaque, included cartoon aesthetics among the multiple influences in his work in the *nouveau réalisme* movement and beyond, to the extent that his art has been described as "akin to comics themselves."[63] The satirical power of BD gave way nevertheless to Duvalierist propagandist purposes in the aftermath of their dictatorship. In the turmoil following the ousting of Jean-Bertrand Aristide in 1991, a comic entitled *Il était une fois François Duvalier* began to circulate, vaunting the achievements of the previous regime and harnessing the popularity of the genre to erase the democratization that had followed Jean-Claude's departure in the 1986 earthquake. Such developments suggest that previous Haitian aversion to *bande dessinée* was rapidly being eroded.[64]

These fragments of a history of the genre are increasingly eclipsed by rapid developments in the past decade, accelerated by attempts at cultural reconstruction following the 2010 earthquake. Contempo-

62. Georges Anglade, *Rire haïtien: Les lodyans de Georges Anglade; Haitian laughter: a mosaic of ninety miniatures in French and English*, trans. Anne Pease McConnell (Coconut Creek, FL: Educa Vision, 2006), 167.

63. See Peter Black and Laurence Grove, *Comics & Culture* (Glasgow: BHP Comics, 2016), 54. Work by Télémaque appeared in the exhibitions "Vraoum! Trésors de la bande dessinée et art contemporain" at the Maison rouge in Paris in 2009, and *Comic Invention* in Glasgow, 2016.

64. See Garry Pierre-Pierre, "Return To Evil Duvalierism Is Rearing Its Head In Haiti Once More Under Its Military Leaders," *Sun Sentinel*, 24 May 1992, http:// articles.sun-sentinel.com/1992–05–24/news/9202100092_1_jean-bertrand-aristide -duvalier-regime-haitians [accessed 30 June 2016].

rary diasporic artists such as Guy Michel have been active for some years in the French comics industry (as a collaborator on popular series such as *Les contes du Korrigan*), but without evidence of their origins apparent in their art. Work in the genre is also now being developed in the country itself by contemporary Haitian artists such as Chevelin Pierre (who has also drawn for the NGO-published *Chimen Lakay* mentioned above), as well as by others in his atelier, including Kendy Joseph, who seek to assert a national tradition that challenges previous external representations while endeavoring to present Haitian culture and society to a wider external audience.[65] One of Chevelin's most prominent works is *Bizango*, a series of albums focused on supernatural forces present in Haiti since the time of the Revolution; Kendy's *Zafè Lakay* addresses similar issues, but through the adventures of a group of young Haitians that fits into a comic tradition evident since the emergence of the genre; and also produced from the same studios are two albums by Karl Heins Desroches about Amwari, a Dessalinean superhero dressed in the colors of the Haitian flag, who discovers his powers during a visit to Citadelle Laferrière and channels the force of the Revolution into the present. *Le nouvelliste* finds in these developments evidence of a "boom in Haitian comics," and not only are comics prominent in the annual "Livres en folies" festival, but an organization to promote their visibility, the Fondation de bande dessinée haïtienne, was founded in 2006. The stated aim of FOBDHA is to develop the profile of comics as a legitimate element of contemporary Haitian artist production, and to support a professionalized BD culture that would not only contribute to the creative economy but also challenge stereotypes produced and perpetuated in the genre elsewhere.[66]

Contemporary BD production in Haiti is gaining visibility and achieving recognition at international comics fairs. Digital dissemination is part of this success, for it allows artists to avoid the challenges of physical production and circulation endemic in Haitian publishing, subverting the Eurocentrism of the industry.[67] It is possible

65. For a 2015 interview with the artist, see "Chevelin Pierre: Une vie bien dessinée," http://www.maghaiti.net/chevelin-pierre-une-vie-bien-dessinee/ [accessed 30 June 2016].

66. "FOBDHA pose la première pierre," http://lenouvelliste.com/lenouvelliste/article/62455/FOBDHA-pose-la-premiere-pierre [accessed 30 June 2016].

67. Another highly active and visible contemporary *bédéiste*, Alain Possible (Teddy Keser Mombrun), has commented on his influences in a way that undermines

that—in the terms of a 2011 article in *Le nouvelliste*—these developments will have a significant impact, and begin in a Haitian context to "snap comics out of its lethargy" to redress at last the asymmetries of a representational imbalance that has lasted, as I have argued, for over 150 years. In contemporary Haiti, comics are already increasingly evident as a medium for the exploration of issues previously addressed elsewhere: in this article, written in the aftermath of the 2010 earthquake, it was noted: "the duty of historians of historic memory lies not only with historians but also with creators of comics."[68]

In an important and widely cited collection of essays, *Haiti Needs New Narratives*, Gina Ulysse has outlined the ways in which, after the earthquake of January 2010, those studying the country need to contribute to challenging long-standing stereotypes and often archaic representations of Haiti and Haitians. *Bande dessinée* is increasingly contributing to such a maneuver.[69] The publisher's publicity for the volume claims that, for Ulysse, the "Haiti of the public sphere is a rhetorically and graphically incarcerated."[70] Although the meaning of the "graphically" does not explicitly refer to comics, it is clear that the capacious and flexible genre of the *bande dessinée* has the emancipatory potential in contemporary Haiti to provide a space for the exploration and recounting of new national narratives. These are narratives—disseminated in new forms and to new audiences—that will challenge misrepresentations of the past while allowing the imagination of possible futures.

---

any francophone assumptions of a Haitian debt to the *école franco-belge*: "I am more interested in modern comics. *Asterix* and *Blake and Mortimer* are very much classics, indeed academic works. They cannot be imitated. My comics are more laid back. I'd be tempted to believe that they are more like Kid Paddle, The Simpsons, or Spirou." See "Alain Possible et ses coups de coeur BD," available at: http://lenouvelliste.com/ lenouvelliste/article/71843/Alain-Possible-et-ses-coups-de-coeur-BD (accessed 17 June 2016).

68. "Sortir la bande dessinée de sa léthargie," available at: http://lenouvelliste .com/lenouvelliste/article/94888/Sortir-la-bande-dessinee-de-sa-lethargie [accessed 17 June 2016]. There is also evidence of interest among diasporic artists: for instance, when asked in a 2012 interview about current projects, Edwidge Danticat replied, in the context of comments on new directions her work was taking mid-life: "I would love, and I mean LOVE, to do a graphic novel à la Marjane Satrapi, whose work I absolutely adore. I have a graphic novel script, but if anyone is interested in collaborating, please call." See http://www.wildriverreview.com/Literature/Interview/Edwidge-Danticat/Create-Dangerously/Nagy/McConnell/January-2012 [accessed 30 June 2016].

69. Gina Athena Ulysee, *Why Haiti Needs New Narratives: A Post-Quake Chronicle* (Middletown, CONN: Wesleyan University Press, 2015).

70. Available at http://www.upne.com/0819575449.html [accessed 30 June 2016].

V. Tintin and the Academy

MICHEL SERRES

Light

Hergé did not want a name, I suppose, since he signed with the initials of his first and last names, Remi and Georges. This acronym at once shows and hides the fact that he was only just beginning to be or to exist, like a child. Such modesty isolates his essence and occludes it. Tintin has no name either, not even a nickname, just an onomatopoeia. We wish merely to intimate these two shadows, without giving them a name.

So who was this person who enchanted our childhoods, and how could we enumerate his traits? Georges was a luminous, diaphanous, dazzling but calm whiteness. The master or inventor of the clear line in his work, he lived in a house of soft hues and inhabited a limpid and pure body. I remember him as a kind of transparent being, whose intelligence floated on air, and from the first time we talked together I knew I was conversing with an angel. He is like Tintin, but of all his characters most resembles Blessed Lightning. In the high mountains of Tibet all the keys to his secret are to be found: white snow, a monk in a state of rapture, a lost friend, and a good abominable snowman. No villains are sacrificed or punished, our atrocious world of victories and defeats is finally leveled out, a great conversion that is the exact opposite of the one he was brought up with. The clear lines of his art reveal him in his full incandescence.

Georges, then, or Hergé, who signed with a colorless name, fell in love with a colorist.

According to Chinese wisdom, thirty spokes converge on the hub of a wheel, but the small empty space at the center gives it its force, coherence, and function. Like a dawn light, more than twenty albums radiate out from Hergé's life. But how do we name this crystalline,

YFS 131/132, Bande Dessinée: *Thinking Outside the Boxes,* ed. Laurence Grove and Michael Syrotinski, © 2017 by Yale University.

transparent, white light, which when refracted—through what prism?
—gave us all those images in which millions of children and adults
have for so long recognized themselves? What can we possibly call it?
Is it genius? Certainly, of all of the worthies and venerable personages
that I have met in my life, I think I can say that Georges stands out as
the only true genius. Genius is defined not only in terms of its ever-
growing reputation, but above all by its secret relationship with the
two most positive manifestations of life: the comic and childhood.
Young nieces and white-haired uncles alike laugh together at Molière
and Aristophanes, whose force and vigor have never been surpassed.
The greatest moments in a culture begin with these intense explo-
sions of youthful gaiety: creativity is born out of laughter. Hergé loses
any lingering negative values in the snows of the Himalayas, and as a
result his work becomes the expression of one, immense "yes," that
is unique or at least rare in a century that, in its art and its acts, loved
destruction and ruin, and celebrated sterility. What does this "yes"
tell us children from seven to seventy-seven as we contemplate our
own work yet to be created, a "yes" that is naive, native, trusting, living, vital, cheerful and new? In what way is it transparent, or candid?

The blank domino is equivalent to all the colors, potentially,
depending on where it is placed: here it is worth one, there two or
three. It owes this performance to its blankness: it is both zero and
the combination of all the colors, it contains and erases them, all
and nothing. White light is refracted into the spectrum of the rain-
bow and absorbs it, just as the peacock's tail folds back into itself
after it has fanned out. If you want to become everything, accept that
you are nothing. Yes. A transparent void. A supreme abstraction that
is both detachment and polyvalence. Turn white and you will understand everything: now you can become, at will, a fish, a plant, a
flower, an archangel, or a visionary. Hergé, signing with the initials
of two first names (although Remi was indeed his family name but is
very familiar as a first name when it is written Rémi), thus without
a family name and as such with a vague identity, began by drawing
an almost anonymous black and white character, whose name was
an onomatopoeia, and whose head was as round as the moon, with
barely any features, knowing everything and able to do anything, ca-
pable of everything possible, and gathering around him a fish (Haddock), flora (*Tournesol*, or Sunflower [Professor Calculus], Castafiore),
Jolyon Wagg. . . The blank domino produces and includes the series of
all dominoes. The creative center, whether Tintin's head or Georges'

genius, gives off an incandescent light, like the snow or glaciers of Tibet. Thirty spokes or rays, the whole world, Asia, America, the islands of Oceania, Incas, Indians, and Congolese, all converge on the hub where the empty, transparent circle of the middle alone gives the entire wheel its cohesion and fullness, its existence and perfection, the candid center, Tintin's head, Georges' angelic soul, the air underneath the feet of Blessed Lightning, an ice floe, childhood, everything that says yes.

Circumstances, encounters, waiting, traveling, fortune and misfortune, work, hard labor even, overwhelming, heavy, intense work, invading every day and waking hour, filling the nights, giving body and soul over to the ravages of time, all these details of a life devoted to his work, converge together at the center on a man, my friend, whose face, I can publicly testify, when transfigured by his work, was radiant like the sun, shining white. How can one sketch his portrait, in the middle of the rose window, since the light that emanated from him produced all of his drawings, all of the portraits exploding on the periphery of the window, countless vignettes that have fascinated us since our bleak childhood? And that still fascinate us because this white blob, Tintin's inoffensive and almost inexpressive, childlike, indeterminate head pierces the page, turning the frame into one of those fairground windows through which someone who wants to have their photograph taken as a hero, film star, or king, can put their head or torso, and reappear on the other side within a stage set of a virgin forest, a palace, or an opera. But they could equally find their neck and shoulders stuck in a bull's muzzle, and go staggering off into the props.

All readers thus project their own body into the channel left by this blank absence and say as they call him to mind: I am Tintin. For the same reason, adventurers, whatever their names, in turn identify with and are part of a thousand other different individuals from every class, ethnicity, culture, or geographical location. Going upstream from this crowd to its animator or creator, one reaches this clear and calm, almost absent light, whose multiple transparencies produce obscure reflections.

Who has not traveled across Shanghai, Tibet, Scotland, or the Middle East without saying to themselves: I recognize this landscape, which looks strangely like the ones I saw in my childhood through the eyes of Chang or of the Emir's son. How is it possible, when I was stuck in a valley in the Garonne region during the war, that I could have already traveled so much? Enchantment turns things around: the world mimics those memorable frames, its models reflect its images, life begins to follow art's magic spells.

I even know some people who would never bother to look at a flower in a field unless they had first seen a poppy in one of Renoir's paintings, or never contemplate the Île de France before they had seen a Corot. This banal experience, which tells us much about experience in general, has its source in the author himself who obeys this strange law that inverts the order and arrangement of things: he yields to this law, and is its commander.

The man of letters sinks without trace, his blood, sweat, and tears immersed in a work that by itself begins to produce life as it goes on, and the world as it reveals itself, and this man in particular who one day put his hand to work.

A magic circle in which each feeds off the other, the man and the work, a spiral that only stops at the moment of death: we will never know if the frame remains blank because the cartoonist died, or if he died because Tintin this time will not find a way out; a never-ending inventiveness, as if Marlinspike/Moulinsart were a cornucopia from which these boundless stories flowed, proof that countless people and things are hidden there, in the suits of armor and the outhouses. Keep a close eye on whoever gets out of these, or leaves behind any clues: there lies the treasure.

Diamonds, rubies, necklaces, whose value expands exponentially along the path opened out by this invading helix, all the way to the stars, but which returns to earth to be inspired by diametrically opposing locations, in a castle, in a fetish, in a cave, in a statue, in the body of the author itself, who is thus both the product and the producer.

Georges radiated the white light of a diamond from this treasure. He always seemed to be stepping out from his castle, which haunted him, or which he inhabited. The circle rises from some unknown source and ascends like an opulent spiral that goes to the farthest corners of the world, and casts its spell on them, but it always returns to the vertical axis of the self: Mozart composes bars that emerge naturally from the music itself, whose bars produce Mozart's music, and ultimately Mozart himself, who composes bars.

Georges was endlessly stepping in and out of that windmill [*moulin*]. So the portrait of the man can be reduced to the eye of his work, as one says the eye of a storm, a calm and sunny space, the place where the treasure was hidden, and where Georges shone, tranquil and diaphanous. In the many happy hours when he would wait for us on the steps of his house, his arms wide open, his eyes and face lit up with his smile and his goodness, I never walked along the path at Dieweg[1] without being overcome by an emotion that was more than just gratitude toward the person who had filled my childhood with joy, but I sensed, through my tears, that he was a kind of magician.

Bombing raids, deportations, wars, and mass crimes devastated our childhoods, which were filled with despair and pain and shame toward our fellow men, except for the single enchantment offered to us by the Amazon and China shining behind the clear-line drawings, and the astonishing forgiveness of the abominable snowman, misunderstood by everyone and who up close became merciful and good, a conversion in the middle of the immaculate desert. The only light in the heart of darkness. What is the point of living if no one ever makes the world an enchanted place? How and where is one to live if there are no enchanted places in the midst of all the destruction?

Indeed, what if we had only survived, in those unbearable times and places, thanks to such utopias? Once again, the eye of the storm, the only place where a frail boat is out of danger, the blank silence in the midst of all the screaming. Does the world not need to cover itself over in order to protect itself from us and our discoveries?

Enchanted things and enchanted bodies appear as if they are submerged in clear water, shining under it like diamonds or pearls, transfigured by the sheen of a lacquer, a light or dawn from the East, whose nature and origin is hidden from us; their halo both dazzles us and protects them.

In order to make them radiate in this way, we are most often content to immerse them, with occasional success, within the transparency of language, or the resplendence of a style: we see them shine behind lucid words, or stiffen and set behind their rigor, when they are not cowering beneath their ugliness or the impoverishment of their terms.

"Trees and plants," La Fontaine the fabulist said, "have for me become creatures endowed with speech. Who would not take this as a magic spell?"

Here a sunflower [*Tournesol*] and a chaste flower [*Castafiore*], both plants, are likewise able to speak, but also a fish [*Haddock*], and a

---

1. [TN: Dieweg is the name of the cemetery where Georges Rémi is buried.]

dog, an animal that ordinarily barks. To complete the miracle, one can in turn put words and languages under the spell of a ritual chant, which is where the word enchantment comes from. Things are submerged in words, and words are immersed in music: a double transfiguration of the world through the work of poetry, enter Wagner the pianist whose rising and falling scales fill the space in Marlinspike/Moulinsart. The comics artist does not hear it this way with his broken ear. Enchantment for him needs no chant or song: the ridiculous diva murders the tune about the jewels, and loses her own, which everyone believes have been stolen, whereas they are shining calmly, nesting in the frame.

Comics open up an original path, different to that of language, rhythm, or sound, and allows living beings and things to shine within their own forms, and in their own very singular medium: the mute poetry of clear lines. Panels replace rhymes and metrical feet with this classical storyteller, who created a hundred different acts, and whose stage is the universe. This is where I find his name, or the image of his medium, brilliant and calm as water.

In the past, portrait artists would encircle the heads of saints, martyrs, virgins, or archangels with a halo, whose light was a sign of their transfiguration. But we should laugh at those who make fun of this: most cultures, modern or ancient, have a particular word to denote the glory of certain bodies that sometimes erupt into an explosion of energy or of love: goodness, ecstasy, or fervent concentration. We recognize this as the sign that someone is thinking: an idea escapes or emanates from his body in a golden glow.

Social prestige is merely a pale imitation of this true halo that surrounds the face. The great painters, endowed with razor sharp vision, can see this. Or rather, they project, in their painted work, their divine experience or attention when they reproduce the things in the world, just as they are at the very moment they are born out of the hands of their creator: infant, initial, first-named, beginning.

I am not sure which to choose: does the halo describe the light that emanates from the model or the comics artist, or rather is it the source of light that illuminates both of them, or indeed should we see it as the eye that truly sees?

Instead of recounting and describing the circumstances of his life, like a wheel with spokes around its hub, I have chosen instead to sketch the portrait of my friend, as the subject and object of this life.

There he is, in the middle of the radiant circle, a white brilliance, the light of a dawn, a bright halo, the eye of the painter and of the storm, sparkling and calm, just as I knew him, and as I loved him, in his exquisite reserve.

—Translated from the French by Michael Syrotinski

JEAN-LUC MARION

Terrifying, Wondrous Tintin

For Charles and Jean

"How very odd. . . Did I say something wrong? [*J'ai donc l'air si ter-rible?*; literally, Do I look so terrifying?]" (*The Black Island*, 61, 13).[1] Tintin has just climbed on to the quayside out of a boat, in which he crossed the sea to the Black Island (death, in other words) near Kiltoch, which is part of the British Isles. To get to this island, he had to go from the continent across the Channel, on either side of which lay two mortal dangers: a gunshot (1), and a leap from the top of a cliff (8–9). The sea here, as in the Bible, signifies death; the islands upon islands, also as in the Bible, signify the end of the world. Tintin, or the person who is always in mortal danger at the end of the world, and the end of the world often begins at 26, rue de Labrador (the bomb attack in *King Ottokar's Sceptre*, 11, 15), or at Marlinspike Hall (the gunshots in *The Seven Crystal Balls*, 42, 14 ff.). Yes, Tintin is *terrible*, because his adventures (not for nothing do the Latin translations call them *pericula*) constantly place him in danger, they terrify us, and they terrify Tintin, the one whose very being is, *par excellence*, always at stake, the one who lives his life existentially. But this is not the case at the moment he climbs on to the quayside: for once, the adventure is over, the danger has passed, and the final "punchline" is only intended to make us smile. So why does Tintin ask himself (and us) if he looks so terrifying [*terrible*]? The obvious answer is that he is not the one who occasions or provokes terror, but it is the "Beast," who has for Tintin alone become "the poor beast" (61, 7) – just as later on the yeti is transformed from an abominable snowman into "The Poor Snowman" (*Tintin in*

---

1. All references to the Tintin albums are from the Archives Hergé [Tournai, Belgium: 1973], vol. 1. Where two numbers separated by a comma appear after the name of the album, the first one refers to the page number, and the second to the frame number.

YFS 131/132, Bande Dessinée: *Thinking Outside the Boxes*, ed. Laurence Grove and Michael Syrotinski, © 2017 by Yale University.

222

Tibet, 60, 6). As always with Hergé, the waiting press reporters are crowded together in an identical, tired-looking huddle, and are still afraid of the "beast," precisely because they are unaware of the transformation that has taken place. The *Morning News* still refers to him as "the animal" (*The Black Island*, 62, 1, photograph 3); what is terrifying for the press occludes what is really terrifying, Tintin himself. If Tintin simply conformed to what the press sees as terrifying, he would remain a banal adventurer, a simple Indiana Jones without the animation of cinematography. But there is another sense, precisely, in which he appears as terrifying, or to have *"l'air si terrible."* In what sense?

I hope I may be excused for referring here to Sophocles, despite the supposedly incommensurable registers or forms of writing: "At many things—wonders , terrors (*deinâ*)—we feel awe, but nothing more terrifying (*deinôteron*) than man!"[2] The connection is perhaps strange, but becomes clearer when we understand that the Greek *deinôn* can equally mean "wondrous" and "admirable" as well as "terrifying," and that these three aspects combine to give an excellent definition of Tintin. The proof comes from Captain Haddock, who is a fine judge of character ("Beasts! Swine! Cowards!" he says in *The Crab with the Golden Claws*, 22, 1) and who quickly gets the measure of Tintin: "He's done it! . . . What a boy!"[3] (Ibid., 24, 2). He is indeed a boy, but there is something terrifying and wondrous about him, like a devil. A good little devil, but a devil nonetheless. Tintin is thus a "terror," a disturbing "devil." Only Thompson and Thomson have not noticed, even though from the very first albums he constantly has them make fools of themselves: they are the only ones who believe what the press keep repeating, namely that he is a member of the press: "It's Mr Tintin, the reporter from *Le Petit Vingtième*. He's leaving for the Congo." (1, 1). As we all know, though, the press is only interested in itself. So then! Tintin is not a reporter, but the most terrifying devil of all the world's inhabitants (as the many devils who constantly surround him know all too well).

Tintin's talent of being in the world consists entirely of opening up a world for us, which as it turns out is our own world. Indeed,

2. Sophocles, *Antigone*, verse 333.
3. We see this already in *Tintin in the Land of the Soviets*: "It isn't human . . . it's a demon . . . Nothing we can do against it!" (115, 5) and it rebounds, of course, on Snowy: "That Snowy . . . Some dog!" (*Tintin in the Congo*, 62) two other dogs agree. But how could a dog be "some dog" (even in the sense of being "doglike"), if he did not reflect Tintin's own glory?

if the Adventures of Tintin and Snowy have spread out across the world, slowly at first (until World War II), and then spectacularly, to the point where they have been translated not only into every living language, then into Latin and Ancient Greek, but also into minor or threatened dialects, which might otherwise have disappeared[4]; if the target age of the readership "from 7 to 77" (which is a rather boldly Biblical formulation) has extended beyond both upper and lower limits, and has passed from one generation to the next, to the point where it would be almost as impossible to count the readers of Tintin as to count the grains of sand in *The Crab with the Golden Claws*, or in *Land of Black Gold*; and finally, if tintinophilia now takes the form almost of a *strenge Wissenschaft*, mobilizing all the resources of archive studies, publishing, philology, literary criticism, philosophy (analytical, dialectical, hermeneutic, phenomenological, and so on), psychoanalysis, sociology, geography and ethnology, political and ideological, and even economic history, theology and religious science, such that we might fear the imminent constitution of a sort of World Society of Tintinophilia Studies, which would frame and no doubt curb the progress of this research, and the (sometimes carcinogenic) growth of hermeneutic analysis—the reason for all of this seems obvious to me. Tintin opens up a world, our world, of which we would have no or little knowledge without him. Or rather, although it is intimately our own world, it does not overlay our little individual world, nor the world we visit and travel in as tourists and lovers of fine things; for Tintin does not go to Paris (Thompson and Thomson do, by mistake, in *The Temple of the Sun*, 53, 6), nor London, Rome, Madrid, Venice, Cairo, L.A. or Rio de Janeiro; and it is only in the first few albums that he goes through Berlin, Moscow, New York, and Chicago, before he *knows* the world. Tintin opens up and travels around a world in an entirely different sense, which its (discreet) exoticism masks rather than defines. That sense is as follows (and my personal experience no doubt holds good for many readers). The first album that I got to open, only because of a long and providential illness (my family was quite serious, and had no time for cartoons like Mickey Mouse, which diverted you from "real" books, without pic-

---

4. It was the same translator who was responsible for standardizing the German dialect spoken in Luxemburg both in the vernacular texts of the Catholic liturgy, in accordance with Vatican II, as well as in *L'Affaire Dichten*, that is, the translation of *L'Affaire Tournesol* [*The Calculus Affair*].

tures), was *The Crab with the Golden Claws*. As a ten-year-old, I discovered within its pages things that I had no real direct experience of (and to this day still have not had) many things that still today largely define our world: counterfeit money (3, and then again in *The Black Island*), opium (14), whisky (15), under-qualified crews flying the flag of convenience (12–18), the Touaregs who served as auxiliaries in the French army (32 ff.) and the Berber rebellion (36), smugglers changing the identity of their boats (36), physical torture (53), and even the global reach of the Yokohama police force (61). This is the real world: I had read it before knowing it was real, but just laughed at it without understanding it, and now that I understand today, it frightens me. The second book I read was *King Ottokar's Sceptre*. In it I discovered sigillography ("Do you mean you've never heard of it? [. . .] It's extremely interesting"—the academic expression *par excellence*, 2), miniature cameras (3) and their misuse (41, 44, and 46), Central European cuisine (4–6), close protection (11) and its limits, the importance of a good anti-lock braking system (14) which had not yet been invented, a study on the Bosnian question which is just as relevant today (19–21), my first encounter with the Cyrillic alphabet (25, 4 and 28,1), what safety glass is (28, 5), opera in general and "Gounid"[5] in particular (29, 13), and then the Iron Guard and the complicities that benefitted Nazi expansionism. This was how I learned about my world, as well as the counterfeiters in *The Black Island* and the drug traffickers in *The Cigars of the Pharaoh*, *The Blue Lotus*, and *The Crab with the Golden Claws*, the Gran Chaco war in *The Broken Ear*, the oil wars in *Land of Black Gold*, the scientific wars in *Destination Moon* and *Explorers on the Moon* (as well as nuclear fission), espionage and Stalinism in *The Calculus Affair*, the arms and slave trade in *The Red Sea Sharks*, military regimes in *The Broken Ear* and *Tintin and the Picaros*, the omnipresence of the press and televisual illusion in *The Castafiore Emerald*, and finally of course colonialism, in its naive form (in *Tintin in the Congo*), and its more detailed and tragic form (in *The Blue Lotus* and *The Red Sea Sharks*). The world that Tintin opens up is thus not his world (he has no intimate world of his own), nor my world (he is not telling my story, nor that of anyone close to me), but our world, *the* world—the one I did not yet know about when I read the albums, never suspecting that it would

5. ". . . by Rossini, Puccini, Verdi, Gounid . . . sorry! By Gounod" (*The Castafiore Emerald*, 33, 10).

become my world, and everyone's world. So for me, the meaning, the names and figures of this world preceded the experience, always and fortunately always a partial one, that I would subsequently have of the world (as was the case for every reader). Tintin could thus be seen as a kind of *"Bildungsroman,"* since our reading begins, and indeed forever remains, childlike: we become ourselves as we read, or at least become incomplete adults (which is the very definition of an adult) by knowing in advance what we will go on to experience later (or not). Just as Greek children would learn their mythology, that is, the entire gamut of all the symbolic meanings of their real world, the words for their passions, the concepts for their future speeches, actions, and decisions by learning Homer by heart, and just as others have perhaps done by reading Virgil, Dante, the Song of Roland, Shakespeare, Balzac, or Proust, we have done likewise by diving with Hergé into the wondrous and terrifying world of Tintin (there are others, of course, but they surely include Tintin). Tintin *le terrible*, indeed, since "No good ever comes of getting mixed up in other people's business" (*King Ottokar's Sceptre*, 1, 7), and since he gets mixed up in the business of other people's worlds. Tintin only gets into trouble because he cares to open up another world to us, his travelling companions, but a world that is our world. Tintin, wondrous and terrifying with every adventure, risks making us exiles from our own world.

How, then, does he manage to draw us into a world that is more essential for us than the one we had previously believed to be our own? How does he get us to pass from a world that appears narrow and impoverished, and which we assumed to be "real," to another, supposedly imaginary world, but one that is in fact saturated with information and facts until then unknown to us and that actually constitutes our ultimate reality? The answer to this paradox, however difficult it may be, is nonetheless found explicitly in the very first frame of the first page of the first album of Tintin's adventures, *Tintin in the Land of the Soviets*:

> At *Le Petit Vingtième* we are always eager to satisfy our readers and to keep them up to date on foreign affairs. We have therefore sent Tintin, one of our top reporters, to Soviet Russia. Each week we shall be bringing you news of his many adventures. N.B. The editor of *Le Petit Vingtième* guarantees that all photographs are absolutely authentic, taken by Tintin himself, aided by his faithful dog Snowy![6]

6. Archives Hergé [vol. 1], op. cit., 42, 1.

This apparently whimsical text in fact performs what philosophy terms a phenomenological reduction. Let us see how this works. In what Husserl calls a natural attitude, "readers" of course know that the possible truth about Soviet Russia is not to be found in *Le petit vingtième* (a comic supplement for children) but, if it is to be found anywhere, it is in *Le vingtième* for grown-ups.[7] They also know that Tintin does not exist, and that the photos are not "authentic" since there are no photos whatsoever, only drawings. And yet the adventures only begin when this evident truth is inverted: the person who goes abroad (and the foreign country *par excellence* for a Catholic Belgian in 1929 is called the Soviet Union) is the actual witness since he is one of their "top reporters," namely Tintin; it is not because his photos are alleged to be authentic that he is their "best reporter": if they are authentic, it is because they are . . ."taken by Tintin himself." So Tintin makes no claims to authenticity, but he stimulates an interest in the authentic. Another world thus opens up through Tintin, one in which the criterion of truth is not a question of what "we" know, read, or surmise, but of what Tintin sees, risks, and thus lives through. The truth of the world—of the world of adventures, in other words of Tintin's experiences, of the world according to this other radically different and new point of view, defined solely by what Tintin sees—is thrown radically off balance. The same world that was characterized by what "people" thought (the press, "public opinion," the world of adults, and so on) is taken apart, and then redefined from the perspective of another center, that is, Tintin (the reporter who writes no reports, the brother of Quicke and Flupke, the eternal adolescent, etc.). This process of reversal transfers certainty ("The editor of *Le Petit Vingtième* guarantees . . .") from a natural attitude to an attitude of adventure, as a *reduced* world, since in an adventure the world is experienced or lived by the hero—Tintin as the transcendental subject—in the absolutely certain knowledge of an immanent event. This unquestioned immanence comes from the risk involved in each adventure, which makes it something indisputably experienced, or lived. Danger, whereby Tintin and Tintin alone is always risking his life ("Tintin, you've done it now," "Fire! Bang!," "This time I'm well and truly done for!"), itself operates this transcendental

<hr />

7. *Le petit vingtième*, in which Hergé first published Tintin's serialized adventures, was the children's supplement to the Belgian daily *Le vingtième siècle*.

reduction.[8] *Adventure as such thus performs this reduction*: the only thing that appears to me with certainty is what I experience, in the manner of something that at each moment befalls me, and thus affects me immediately. And as far as this experience is concerned, this world that is certain because it is authenticated by Tintin and by him alone, the "real" world (that of the grownups who read *Le grand vingtième*) becomes in effect a fable (from the point of view of *Le petit vingtième*, that is the *reduced Vingtième*). This explains how this reversal could account for (even require), at least for the first few albums, the reappearance of Tintin in flesh and blood at the end of each adventure. The actor who played Tintin in front of an "enormous crowd" at the Gare du Nord in Brussels[9] would have been an imposter if he had laid claim to any kind of natural attitude, but he became an unwitting phenomenological spectator by incarnating the subject of this reduction.

One might object, however, and ask what "aid" Snowy could bring to such a reduction. Surely his powerlessness in this regard disqualifies our interpretation? Yet we only need to follow the thread of Tintin's second adventure to understand his role: *Tintin in the Congo* only inverts the world of natural attitude (in which Tintin remains, it appears, ". . . a young reporter," 1, 1) into the world of adventure through Snowy's stubborn interference, which determines the entire plot through a series of confrontations he has with other animals: a spider (1), a parrot (2–5), an electric ray (6), a shark (7–8), mosquitoes (10), crocodiles (12–14, 33, 48), monkeys (15–16), antelopes (16), a lion (22–24), a leopard (36–37), an elephant (38–42), and a rhinoceros (56). As it turns out, Tintin can only enter into the adventure set in motion in an animal register by disguising himself as an animal, for example by becoming a giraffe (55) or a monkey (17–18). What is more, he is also saved by a monkey (41–42), by a hippopotamus (48), and finally by a buffalo (57–60), who causes him to jump involuntarily into a plane bound for America. It makes perfect sense, then, that he should fight adversaries who are themselves disguised as animals, the leopard-men (31–32). Snowy, indeed, also disguises himself as a snake, laterally, as it were, within the animal kingdom (34). The adventure thus unfolds from the point of view of animals, who transfer the certainty of the so-called "natural" world of men to the infinitely more

8. Op. cit., 88, 1 (see also 142, 2; 123, 4; and 163, 4.
9. Op. cit., 8.

natural world, because it is lived by animals, and according to a model of animality. In this respect, within an African authenticity (and this supposedly "paternalistic" album would take on an entirely different dimension), Snowy performs the phenomenological reduction instead of Tintin, who follows him. This is why, moreover, the final image places the effigy of Snowy on a pedestal alongside the statue of Tintin. Better yet, in this still very early album Snowy, crowned and seated on his throne, can say at least once to Tintin: "Approach, my loyal subject..." (50, 6). The "friendly pooch" has truly become a subject, but he has earned it, since he shares the transcendental status of his master:[10] inverting the world, transferring the certainty of natural attitude on to the experience of adventure. In short, Snowy confirms that Tintin's role is to bring about a reduction of the everyday world to the certainty of lived experience through adventure.

We can now understand Tintin's strangest character trait: he has none; and also his strangest facial feature; he has none. Indeed, his face is hardly worth describing: a circle, barely punctuated by a minuscule nose, a mouth that simply alternates between a dot and a small circle indicating astonishment, no vivid facial expression (hardly any anger or determination), and his language always correct and measured. In short, he is the opposite of the clearly defined characters such as Captain Haddock, Professor Calculus and the Thom(p)sons, Bianca Castafiore, or Jolyon Wagg, who stand out a mile, and who are enlivened by their own personal quasi-dialects. Tintin alone speaks like ordinary people, and is comfortable everywhere, whether he is in a Tibetan lamasery or in a temple, at a reception, in a salon, at the opera, or in an army barracks, in a tent, or in a rocket. He is a boy for all occasions, and goes unnoticed, almost invisibly—to the point where, when the Syldavian schemers want to photograph (*identify*) him, not only is his face precisely outside the frame (*King Ottokar's Sceptre*, 3, 13), but at the end of the story Tintin recognizes himself in this non-face ("But look! That's me!" [*C'est moi, cela*] (60, 11–12). He identifies with his non-face, which he describes perfectly using a neutral pronoun, "that" [*cela*], a neutrality that any other face would precisely

10. Snowy addresses Tintin almost derisively as a "subject," transcendental of course, at the only moment in all of their adventures when he precisely does not completely merit this status. There are other instances when Snowy essentially determines what happens in place of Tintin: for example, the fate of Syldavia (*King Ottokar's Sceptre*, 58, 1–7), or the fate of the whole expedition (*Tintin in Tibet*, 45, 8 - 47, 4).

aim to transcend to become an irreducible individuality. Tintin has no face, which is why of all Hergé's characters he was the only one allowed to have a suitable human double. One could go so far as to say that Tintin cannot be represented—he is nowhere in the world, but the world appears in him. To see Tintin would be to destroy his transcendental function.[11]

If Tintin is faceless, he also has no history (no parents or memories, no psychological scars or character flaws, no long-term plans, nor any particular culture, belief, or faith). Nor does he even have a place of his own: he quickly leaves his apartment on the rue du Labrador to go and stay with a friend, in an oversized castle (that is constantly being invaded by strangers from every walk of life), which is apparently in the Brabant, but in fact an imitation of a castle in France. He of course annihilates any sexual difference within himself since, although unambiguously male, he never feels limited by this paralysis, nor attempts to do anything to overcome it. It is not Hergé who is misogynistic in only offering caricatures of women (Mrs Finch, Mrs Snowball, Bianca Castafiore, Mrs Wagg, Peggy Alcazar, etc.), but rather Tintin, who simply does not *see* women as women, even when he is looking at them (the spirited actress in *The Cigars of the Pharaoh* [6, 11]: "That's a woman's voice. . ."). Faceless and characterless, timeless and placeless, sexless and with no sexual desire, Tintin appears not as a hero, but on the contrary as an anti-hero, or so as not to compete with Haddock for this title, as a non-hero, in short, the degree zero of a hero.

Yet in the final adventure, on the last page, even in the last frame, does Hergé not use his final *word* (his ultimate literary act) to give him the name of "Caesar" (*Tintin and Alph-Art*, 42, 4), which spontaneously signifies, for Tintin himself, the hero *par excellence*: "Have you heard of Caesar? – Eh?. . . Caesar. . . Julius?" (39, 11). Tintin was thus to die a hero, just as he had lived, but just as he *was not*. How can we understand this paradox? Here again, only a philosophical ref-

---

11. To my knowledge, the first time Tintin poses for a photograph is in *The Blue Lotus*, which is precisely at the moment of an attempt on his life (48, 12 – 49, 13); and the first actual photo published of Tintin illustrates the Japanese poster that puts a price on his head (25, 16). As for the photographic reports that later mark the end of his adventures, they indicate precisely this end. It is a return from the reduced and certain world of what Tintin has lived through to the unreliable and supposedly real world of current affairs, the false and public world of which *The Castafiore Emerald* offers such an unsurpassable description. Tintin remains *de facto* and *de jure* invisible.

erence can help explain: if Tintin reduces the world down to what presents itself to him in order to constitute its meaning, he does not belong to it, since he opens it up. So he has to see the world, receive it and see it without being part of it —"Veni, vidi, vici." He has to act as a transcendental spectator, outside of the world, without any of the characteristics of those who populate it, a realm of consciousness confronting the realm of the world, a being for whom what is at stake is being itself, confronting intra-wordly beings. He has to thus repeat the neutrality of the transcendental *I*, even that of *Dasein*, or the neutrality of the one who reduces and constitutes the world.

How can we characterize the world that has thus become our world, because it is reduced to the immanence of Tintin's lived experience as a transcendental subject? Let us return to the best known element of Hergé's aesthetic, *la ligne claire* (the clear line): it surrounds each figure with a clean and uniform contour, eliminates any shadows that might distort the silhouettes (a kind of anti-Caravagism), foregoes any subjective deformation, and so on. Each phenomenon in the world is consequently extracted and transposed, as it were, as if onto a stained glass window, both simplified and preserved, reduced to its essential features. This reduction is of course evident if we compare the swarming lines of the pencil sketches (where the rough lead strokes overlap, correct each other, and burst out of the frame), to the final version, where the India ink excludes all the other lines except for the last, definitive one: the phenomenon acquires a certainty through this literal reduction. The clear line indicates, in terms of the technical skill of drawing, what it is of the world that Hergé retains (that is, what he eliminates and chooses) when Tintin reduces it. The most surprising thing, suddenly, is not that Georges Remi was influenced by the ideologies of his time (how could he alone have escaped them?), as some petty BD police officers would have us believe, but that he was able to filter them so intelligently: his anti-Sovietism ultimately conforms quite closely to the reality we know today; his anti-capitalism is quite close to the economic realities of the modern world (*The Broken Ear*, *Land of Black Gold*, etc.); his colonialism was of course paternalistic to begin with, but then inverted into a militant anti-colonialism (from *Tintin in America* and *The Blue Lotus* onwards, not to mention in *The Red Sea Sharks*); he was fortunately anti-racist, but this was always underpinned by personal and real intersubjective relationships (with Chang in *The Blue Lotus* and *Tintin in Tibet*); his fascination with technology always took the form of a journey of the mind (*The Shooting Star, Destination Moon* and *Explorers on the Moon*), and so on. Ideological confrontations, then (the non-reality of the transcendent world as it appears to the conscious mind, the world of *Le vingtième*), are always reworked from the perspective of an immanent lived experience, in essence defined ethically and no longer ontically, since this becomes irrelevant: Basil Bazarov sells the same weapons to Las Dopicos as he does to Sanfacion, and there is no just war (*The Broken Ear*, 34); the supporters of General Alcazar terrorize the same favelas as the supporters of General Tapioca, and there is no war of liberation (*Tintin and the Picaros*, 11, 9 and 62, 10); there is no real difference between the secret agents of Syldavia and of Borduria: "But how can we tell friends from enemies?/ Go for the ugliest. That won't be difficult – you'll see./ Now which has the ugliest mug? It looks about fifty-fifty." (*The Calculus Affair*, 30, 2–3). In short, then, the clear line reduces the world to the immanence of lived experience; it performatively enacts the end of ideologies by questioning them from an essentially ethical perspective. Nothing could be more wrong-headed or unjust, therefore, than to accuse Hergé of having an ideology, since everything about his reduction (both in his narrative style and in his drawing) disqualifies all ideologies from a more essential point of view.

The best example of this transposed reworking of the world that reduces it to actual lived experience is provided by the progressive apprehension with respect to religion we find in the *Adventures*: indeed, we gradually see the ethical point of view win out over all other points of view.[12] At first (a period that most commentators always privilege, and in bad faith, since it really only concerns one album, *Tintin in the Congo*), religion comes down to institutionalized Christianity, not so much in the Catholic church (which is never mentioned or represented) as in the Christian missions, churches within the Church (could one call these "reductions" in Africa?). In other words, it is a "Constantinian" phase. Very soon afterwards, however, a second phase appears, which is one of violent critique of any form of Revelation, in which the *Aufklärung* (Enlightenment) does not hold back from blasphemy. So the Thom(p)sons desecrate mosques (*The Crab with the Golden Claws*, 50, 1–4, and *Land of Black Gold*, 34, 5)

---

12. I had explained at length the following analysis to Hergé during an interview in the fall of 1975, in his Studios on avenue Louise. Although he was a little surprised at first, he did not challenge it, admitting finally that he has "learned a lot about himself."

and boot the behinds of praying Muslims (22, 8). And Tintin, in order to calm down a madman who clearly epitomizes the ridiculous
paradigm of prophecy ("I am Philippulus [a diminutive in Latin!]
the prophet! I proclaim the day of terror!. . . The end of the world is
nigh!," in *The Shooting Star*, 7, 12), does not hesitate for a moment
to use the Name of the Father: "Hello, hello, Philippulus the prophet!
This is your guardian angel, speaking from heaven [*Ici Dieu le Père*].
I order you to return to earth" (20, 4). Finally, when Captain Haddock
wants to turn water into whisky and fails, Tintin protests, as anyone
with any sense would know: "How in the world could water turn itself into whisky?. . . It's impossible." All Captain Haddock can think
of in reply is: "Impossible? Impossible? No, blistering barnacles, it's
not impossible!. . . He manages it every time." To which Tintin asks
in surprise: "Who's *he*?"[13] We cannot help but think of Christ, either
at Cana, or at the Last Supper, as Hergé himself surely would have
done, because of his strong Catholic upbringing. So what does Captain Haddock answer? Christ? No, not Christ, but: "Bruno the master
magician!" (*The Seven Crystal Balls*, 7, 1–4). Clearly, the miracles of
Christ (the Son) are nothing but magic tricks, just as the Name of the
Father is a fraud. And to cap it all, the very first religion of revelation
gets its comeuppance: Bruno will indeed perform his magic trick, but
in front of a yellow star of David, which is half-hidden by a bat, and
is thus eerily prescient (16, 4). The suggestion could not be clearer:
prayer, the sacraments and divine election, Islam, Christianity, and
Judaism, all evaporate in the light of reason as so many ridiculous
and harmful illusions. Or, at best, this might be a question either of a
theology of the death of God (D. Bonhoeffer), or of a "demythologiza-
tion" (R. Bultmann).[14]

13. My emphasis.
14. Another example, which is this time directed toward natural religion: Tintin
discovers by chance, albeit scientifically, the date of an eclipse (*Prisoners of the Sun*,
52, 11–13). He lets this date be known in the form of a wish to be granted by the Great
Inca (53, 8–11), and plays the role of the person who arrests the motion of the sun, a
false Joshua and a true imposter, in the name of a science that he dissimulates like
an evil priest. Lying in this way through what one might call an "efficient cause," he
terrorizes a people who are kept in the dark because of his hidden knowledge (58, 6–
59, 11): the *Aufklärung* or Enlightenment turned back against itself! This is, without
doubt, Tintin's most painful behavior, given how much he lies, cheats, and abuses
knowledge which is, moreover, not even his knowledge (he learns it from a newspaper, from the transcendent, non-reduced world: "What an extraordinary coincidence!"
[52,11]). By contrast, we admire the joy and generosity of the Great Inca and his final

The third phase is thus even more interesting, since the last albums mark a stubborn recovery, at the level of the pure immanence of lived experience, of an ethical reality as the most fundamental reality (how could one not think of Levinas?). *Tintin in Tibet* describes a journey that is not only geographical but, in crossing the desert of death (snow, ice, mountains), a spiritual conversion to the three great theological virtues. Tintin is praised by the Grand Abbot, an authority who is all the more credible because he is non-Christian, for his charity: "Blessings upon you, Great Heart, for the strength of your friendship"; and Captain Haddock is praised for his faith: "You too, rumbling thunder—Blessings upon you, for in spite of all, you have the faith that moves mountains" (61, 4–5); as for Snowy, who quite rightly complains that he is being forgotten ("What about me? Don't I get a word?," 61, 6), he deserved to be praised for his hope, not only because he tracked down the Yeti by following its scent (53, 8 ff.), but also because he risked martyrdom by warning the monastery at whatever cost: "To the monastery, double quick! Message or no message, I'll make them follow me" (46, 8 and 17). This is all clearly a reference to and repetition of the 1 Corinthians 13:13.

Flight 714, one of the most challenging works by Hergé, still remains to be interpreted, and I will confine myself to the least contested points. It is in many ways a meditation on the end of time (inverting the caricature of Philippulus): the flames of the volcano will separate the bad from the good, who will be saved by an intermediary who communicates with the beyond. The chosen few will climb a ladder to their salvation (58, 3), which is a reference to Jacob's ladder. There is nothing natural about this event, not only because there is never the slightest indication confirming that they are extraterrestrials, but because those who are rescued remain trapped within the amnesiac "dream," one of the characteristics of biblical interventions of God. This is not, however, the essential point, since there is more. In the bunker (a confining hell), two villains argue about which of them is "the devil incarnate!" (31, 4) because both of them have

---

victory: he forces Tintin to keep quiet, and thus to admit a kind of revelation: ". . . I have your promise of silence (*j'ai votre parole de ne rien révéler*)" (61, 10). What is this revelation? It is of a alternative society (a quite natural one, of course) that is entirely different from and much more just than Western industrial society, like that of the Indians, the Chinese, the Arumbayas, the Tibetans, the Gypsies (*contra* Husserl!), even the "Sondonesian nationalists" (*Flight 714*, 31, 8). So Tintin was wrong, and the Great Inca right.

taken a truth serum. So what we have, then, is the Last Judgment in which, according to the logic of John's gospel, no outside judgment intervenes, but each person condemns himself by acknowledging his truth (John 17). Now, when Carreidas confesses his first crime as the theft of a pear ("Outside that shop, among the fruit and vegetables, on the twelfth of September 1910, I stole for the first time. A pear. I was four years old. It's as clear as if it were yesterday" [24, 12]), it is hard not to think of the theft of a fruit from a pear tree that Saint Augustine confesses as his first real sin (*Arbor erat pirus . . .*).[15] As a confession in due form, Carreidas' confession is a sin, and one that is not pardoned, since he brags about it as a success (while Saint Augustine repents as if it were a failing): "Six months later, I stole a ring of my mother's. And I allowed her to blame the maid, Elena./ Poor Elena! But how she protested her innocence. But they threw her into the street . . . And I nearly died of laughing! Even then I was the devil incarnate!" (24, 15 – 25, 1). It is also hard not to think of Rousseau here, who allows poor Marion to be accused instead of him for the ribbon he himself had stolen.[16] From a series of confessions to Rousseau's *Confessions*, it seems that the whole album sets out to describe (and thus also to acknowledge) the irreducible reality of radical evil, even to the point of invoking hell: the bad guys commit suicide trying to kill the good guys (51, 12), thereby confirming Rastapopoulos's pitiful complaint: "Boo-hoo-hoo. Nobody loves me!" (32, 8).

Tintin and the Picaros goes one final step further. In spite of the aporetic nature of this album too, it can be read as a plot constructed around lies, each one continually generating others. Professor Calculus lies to everyone by surreptitiously rendering the finest whisky undrinkable (1–2, 34–35, 49–50); Tapioca by falsely accusing Bianca Castafiore (5 and 8); the journalists by accepting the possible guilt of Captain Haddock and Tintin (6 and 10); Nestor by drinking in secret (7) and listening at the door (11); Alvarez by presenting a prison as a private residence (14); Sponsz by filling such an apartment with microphones and cameras (15–16, 22); Pablo by pretending to be a traitor to his bosses, and thus betraying to the second degree (23–26); Alcazar

15. *The Confessions of Saint Augustine*, II, 4.

16. *The Confessions of Jean-Jacques Rousseau*, translated and with an introduction by J.M. Cohen (London: Penguin Classic, 1953). Book 2. And when Carreidas replies by recalling his great-aunt, who died of sadness and shame because of him (31, 5), we are certainly reminded of Perceval who, setting off on his adventures, also caused his mother to die of sorrow.

and Tintin by stealing the bus from the Picaros (52–55), then putting on their costumes to surprise Tapioca (55–56). Then, out of this disastrous tangle of lies in which nobody can trust anyone else, one promise that is kept emerges, and remains true right to the end despite everything: Alcazar promised Tintin no blood would be shed when he came to power (45), and he keeps his promise, despite his victim himself wanting this (57, 3–7). The mimetic war between Tapioca and Alcazar finally ends, because Alcazar has suspended vengeance and thus brought about peace without bloodshed: but he was only able to do this because he had to keep his word. Ethics becomes the only serious form of politics. Jolyon Wagg understands this all too well, when he exclaims: "Good old Alcazar! . . . Give him a big hurrah!" (62, 7).[17] Montaigne, for whom non-lying was the foundation of politics, would have saluted him in the same way: "Our intelligence being by no other way communicable to one another but by a particular word, he who falsifies that betrays public society."[18]

This move from the ontological to the ethical could thus define an essential characteristic of Tintin's adventures: the world, once it has been reduced to what is experienced by the transcendental *I* in the pure immanence of risk, becomes a constant interplay between truth and lies, loyalty and betrayal, friendship and enmity, good and evil. And the rest, in the final analysis, disappears into insignificance. This is the truth that Tintin, the terrifying and wondrous Tintin, produces, and we are thus once again able to speak and read. This is the alphabet of that language.[19]

—Translated from the French
by Michael Syrotinski

17. The reader might recognize the echo of a much earlier exclamation by Tintin: "Long live General Alcazar! Bless his cotton socks!" (*Tintin and the Broken Ear*, 21, 16).

18. Montaigne, *Essays*, II, 19, trans. Charles Cotton, revised by William Hazlett (New York: Edwin C. Hill, 1910). Public virtue moreover goes hand in hand with private virtue: "As for you, my dove . . . I promised you a palace. Bueno, I keep my word. This is all yours from now on." (62, 8). Alcazar, or the man who from now on keeps his word.

19. [Jean-Luc Marion's original French text served as a preface to a longer study of Tintin, organized thematically and alphabetically, which explains the title of the collaborative volume, also a direct reference to Hergé's final album, *Tintin and Alph-Art*: Alain Bonfand/Jean-Luc Marion, *Hergé: Tintin le Terrible, ou l'alphabet des richesses* (Paris: Hachette, 1996). TN]

Contributors

JAN BAETENS is Professor of Literary and Cultural Studies at the University of Leuven (Belgium). He has a special interest in word and image studies, particularly in so-called minor genres such as novelization, comics, and the photonovel, on which he has published widely. With Hugo Frey, he co-authored *The Graphic Novel: An Introduction* (Cambridge UP, 2014). He is also a published poet (in French) and has written various essays on contemporary poetry, among which *Pour en finir avec la poésie dite minimaliste* (Les impressions nouvelles, 2014) and *A voix haute: Poésie et lecture publique* (Les impressions nouvelles, 2016).

JEAN-YVES FERRI works as both artist and scriptwriter, providing deft observation of everyday life and historical events. With Manu Larcenet he created the five-volume *Le retour à la terre* (2002 onwards), and from 2007 drew and scripted *De Gaulle à la plage*. Following Albert Uderzo's retirement, Jean-Yves Ferri (script) and Didier Conrart (artwork) have been responsible for the continuation of the *Astérix* series, producing the top-selling *Asterix and the Picts* (2013) and *Asterix and the Missing Scroll* (2015).

CHARLES FORSDICK is James Barrow Professor of French at the University of Liverpool, and has been since 2012 Arts and Humanities Research Council Theme Leadership Fellow for "Translating Cultures." He has published on travel writing, colonial history, postcolonial literature, and the cultures of slavery. He is also a specialist on Haiti and the Haitian Revolution, and has written widely about representations of Toussaint Louverture. His publications include *Victor Segalen and the Aesthetics of Diversity* (Oxford University Press, 2000) and *Travel in Twentieth-Century French*

YFS 131/132, Bande Dessinée: *Thinking Outside the Boxes*, ed. Laurence Grove and Michael Syrotinski, © 2017 by Yale University.

and Francophone Cultures (Oxford University Press, 2005). With Laurence Grove and Elizabeth McQuillan, he co-edited *The Francophone Bande Dessinée* (Rodopi, 2005), and continues whenever possible to include comics in his teaching and research.

THIERRY GROENSTEEN, born in Brussels in 1957, curated the Comics Museum in Angoulême from 1993 to 2001. He has also been the chief-editor of two leading journals: *Les cahiers de la bande dessinée* and *Neuvième art*. The latter has become the online journal *NeuviemeArt2.0*. Groensteen is the founder of the publishing company L'An 2, now part of the group Actes Sud. He has taught for many years at the École européenne supérieure de l'image, in Angoulême, and curated many exhibitions. An occasional scriptwriter and novelist, he is the author of numerous books about the history, the semiotics, and the aesthetics of comics, including *Un objet culturel non identifié* (2006), *La bande dessinée, son histoire et ses maîtres* (2009) and *Mr Töpffer invente la bande dessinée* (2014). The University Press of Mississippi has already published his authoritative essays *The System of Comics* and *Comics and Narration*.

LAURENCE GROVE is Professor of French and Text/Image Studies and Director of the Stirling Maxwell Centre for the Study of Text/Image Cultures at the University of Glasgow, having previously studied and taught at the University of Pittsburgh, the Newberry Library, Chicago, and Middlebury College. His research focuses on historical aspects of text/image forms, and in particular *bande dessinée*. He is President of the International Bande Dessinée Society (www.arts.gla.ac.uk/ibds). As well as serving on the consultative committees of a number of journals, he is co-editor of *European Comic Art*. Laurence (also known as Billy) has authored (in full, jointly or as editor) ten books, including *Comics in French* (Berghahn, 2010 and 2013) and approximately fifty chapters or articles. He has recently co-curated the *Comic Invention* exhibition at The Hunterian, Glasgow (2016), and has long terms hopes of seeing a National Centre for Comics.

DOMINIC HARDY is Professor of Québec and Canadian Art History and Associate Dean, Faculty of Arts at the Université du Québec à Montréal, where he founded the Caricature et satire graphique à Montréal research team in 2009 and the Équipe de recherche en histoire de l'art au Québec in 2012. In the years 2013–2015, he co-organized with students and colleagues in Canada and France a series of conferences on the relationships between caricature, visual satire, and art history (Quebec, 2013; Montreal, 2015; Paris, 2015). The author of chapters and articles that have appeared in Canadian, American, British, and French publications, he has also co-edited, with Annie Gérin and Jean-Philippe Uzel, the special issue of the Canadian art history journal *RACAR* devoted to *Humour in Visual Arts and Culture* (2012) and, with Micheline Cambron, the first collection of studies of the work of Quebec caricaturist Albéric Bourgeois (*Quand la caricature sort du journal: Baptiste Ladébauche 1878–1957*).

CATHERINE LABIO is Associate Professor of English at the University of Colorado Boulder. She specializes in comparative approaches to the study of modern and contemporary literature, economics, and the visual arts. She has authored *Origins and the Enlightenment: Aesthetic Epistemology from Descartes to Kant* (Cornell UP, 2004), edited *Belgian Memories* (*Yale French Studies* 102, 2002), and co-edited *The Great Mirror of Folly: Finance, Culture, and the Crash of 1720* (Yale UP, 2013). She has published essays on a wide range of topics, including articles on comics in *Critical Inquiry* and *Cinema Journal* and served as Review Editor of *European Comic Art* from 2009 to 2016. She is currently working on two monographs tentatively titled *The Year of Wonder and Despair: France and the Mississippi Bubble of 1719–1720* and *The House of Comics*.

JEAN-LUC MARION is one of France's foremost contemporary phenomenologists and historians of modern philosophy. He held the Chair of Metaphysics at Paris-Sorbonne from 1995–2012, has been a member of the Académie française since 2008, and has held visiting professorships around the world, including currently at the University of Chicago. He has published widely on Descartes' ontology, rational theology, and metaphysics (*On Descartes' Metaphysical Prism, Cartesian Questions*, and *Further Cartesian Questions*). He is pursuing a long-term inquiry into the question of God (*The Idol and Distance* and *God Without Being*). His most recent work has explored the phenomenology of givenness, in *Reduction and Givenness and Being Given: An Essay on the Phenomenology of Givenness*, and *In Excess: Studies on Saturated Phenomena*.

BILL MARSHALL is Professor of Comparative Literary and Cultural Studies at the University of Stirling, Scotland, having previously held posts at the Universities of Southampton and Glasgow, and served as the Director of the Institute of Modern Languages Research in the School of Advanced Study, University of London. He is the author of: *Victor Serge: The Uses of Dissent* (1992), *Guy Hocquenghem: Beyond Gay Identity* (1997), *Quebec National Cinema* (2001), *André Téchiné* (2007), and *The French Atlantic: Travels in Culture and History* (2009). He has also edited books on *Musicals – Hollywood and Beyond* (2000), *Montreal-Glasgow* (2005), and a three-volume Encyclopedia on *France and the Americas* (2005). His current project is on the "Uses of Prehistory" in modern and contemporary French culture.

MARK McKINNEY is Professor of French at Miami University (Ohio). With Alec G. Hargreaves, he edited *Post-Colonial Cultures in France* (Routledge, 1997). He also edited *History and Politics in French-Language Comics and Graphic Novels* (University Press of Mississippi, 2008). He authored *The Colonial Heritage of French Comics* (Liverpool University Press, 2011) and *Redrawing French Empire in Comics* (Ohio State University Press, 2013). With Laurence Grove and Ann Miller, he was a founding editor of *European Comic Art* (2008–2016). He has published numerous other essays on postcolonialism in comics and prose fiction.

ANN MILLER is a University Fellow at the University of Leicester, where she was formerly Senior Lecturer and Director of Studies for French (after an earlier career as a teacher and teacher trainer). She is the author of *Reading Bande Dessinée: Critical Approaches to French-Language Comic Strip* (Intellect, 2007), and co-editor of *Textual and Visual Selves* (U of Nebraska Press, 2011). She was co-editor of *The French Comics Theory Reader* (U of Leuven Press, 2014), and has translated numerous other books and articles on comics. She is joint editor of *European Comic Art*.

KEITH READER was Professor of French successively at the Universities of Kingston, Newcastle, and Glasgow, and is currently Visiting Emeritus Professor at the University of London Institute in Paris. He has published extensively in the fields of French cultural and political history, critical theory, and film. Relevant monographs include *Robert Bresson* (MUP, 2000) and Jean Renoir's *La règle du jeu* (Tauris, 2010). He is the author of numerous articles and reviews and has served on the Editorial Boards of *French Studies*, *Modern and Contemporary France*, *French Cultural Studies*, and *Studies in French Cinema*.

MICHEL SERRES served as a marine officer for the French national maritime service before doing doctoral research in philosophy, on Leibniz. During the 1960s he taught with Michel Foucault at the Universities of Clermont-Ferrand and Vincennes and was later appointed to a chair in the history of science at the Sorbonne, where he still teaches. Serres has also been a full professor at Stanford University since 1984, and he was elected to the Académie française in 1990. Through his explorations of the parallel developments of scientific, philosophical, and literary trends, Michel Serres has built a reputation as one of modern France's most gifted and original thinkers.

MICHAEL SYROTINSKI (PhD Yale 1988 in French and Comparative Literature) is Marshall Professor of French at Glasgow University, and currently Head of the School of Modern Languages and Cultures there. He taught previously at the University of Aberdeen, where he held the Carnegie Chair of French, and at Illinois State University. He has published widely on French philosophy, critical theory, and contemporary 20th- and 21st-century French literature (particularly Jean Paulhan), and on Francophone African literature and philosophy, within a postcolonial frame of reference. Among his best-known publications are *Singular Performances: Reinscribing the Subject in Contemporary Francophone African Writing* (Virginia UP), and *Deconstruction and the Postcolonial* (Liverpool UP). He is also one of the main translators of the recent Anglophone edition of Barbara Cassin's *Dictionary of Untranslatables* (Princeton UP). He is currently general editor of the critical theory journal, *Paragraph* (EUP).

NIKOLA WITKO, having grown up in Mauberge and studied in Tournai, created the Sierra Nueva group in Brussels before going on to participate in numerous alternative *bande dessinée* journals, including *Feraille, Lapin*, and *Psikopat*. His work as part of the Requins Marteaux team, including for the spoof *supermarché Feraille*, encapsulates Witko's iconoclastic dark lampooning of consumer society. He is author of numerous albums, for which he both scripts and provides artwork.

Yale French Studies is the oldest English-language journal in the United States devoted to French and Francophone literature and culture. Each volume is conceived and organized by a guest editor or editors around a particular theme or author. Interdisciplinary approaches are particularly welcome, as are contributions from scholars and writers from around the world. Recent volumes have been devoted to a wide variety of subjects, among them: Levinas; Perec; Paulhan; Haiti; Belgium; Crime Fiction; Surrealism; Material Culture in Medieval and Renaissance France; and French Education.

Yale French Studies is published twice yearly by Yale University Press (yalebooks.com) and may be accessed on JSTOR (jstor.org).

For information on how to submit a proposal for a volume of *Yale French Studies*, visit yale.edu/french and click "Yale French Studies."